ABOUT MANNING MARABLE

Manning Marable is Professor of History and Political Science and Director of the Institute for Research in African-American Studies at Columbia University. Born in 1950 in Dayton, Ohio, he is the author of *How Capitalism Underdeveloped Black America* and numerous other books. Dr. Marable's public affairs commentary series, "Along the Color Line," upon which this essay collection is based, is published in over 280 newspapers and journals.

BLACK LIBERATION IN CONSERVATIVE AMERICA

BLACK LIBERATION IN CONSERVATIVE AMERICA

MANNING MARABLE

SOUTH END PRESS

BOSTON

Library of Congress Cataloging-in-Publication Data

Marable, Manning, 1950-

Black liberation in conservative America / Manning Marable.

p.   cm.

ISBN 0-89608-560-0 (cloth : alk. paper). — ISBN 0-89608-559-7 (paper : alk. paper)

1. Afro-Americans — Politics and government. 2. Conservatism-United States — History — 20th century. 3. Afro-American — Social conditions — 1975-   I. Title.

E185.615.M2784   1997

973'.0496073—dc21   96-48679
                                                                         CIP

South End Press, 116 Saint Botolph Street, Boston, MA 02115

02 01 00 99 98 97   1 2 3 4 5 6

ACKNOWLEDGMENTS

This work represents the contributions and assistance of many people. My mother, June Morehead Marable, encouraged me to write a newspaper column as a teenager growing up in Dayton, Ohio. Both my mother and father, James Palmer Marable, Sr., still read my commentaries in Dayton's local African-American newspaper, and always have something to say about them.

My children—Malaika, Sojourner, and Joshua—have all grown up with "Along the Color Line." Many times we sat at the dining room table, folding the photocopied articles and sealing envelopes. Increasingly, the experiences and activities of my children have been incorporated in my popular writings. These articles always receive the warmest response from readers.

Most of the essays here were written since my appointment as Director of the Institute for Research in African-American Studies at Columbia University in 1993. Daria Oliver, my Executive Assistant, is largely responsible for managing the Institute's flow of activities, meetings, and correspondence. Without her constant help and advice, this book never would have been completed. Cheri McLeod-Pearcey, the Institute's secretary, typed the entire manuscript and its various revisions, and on several occasions offered important suggestions in the text. For several years one of the Institute's graduate assistants, Monique Williams, was responsible for coordinating the column, regularly updating the addresses of our newspapers, contacting editors and publishers, and maintaining a comprehensive clipping file on events and issues in black American politics and society. Monique's dedication to black people, as well as her energy and intellect, inspired everyone around her. Three other graduate students at the Institute—Johanna Fernandez, Devin Fergus, and Timothy McCarthy—were helpful in collecting data and doing background research for important essays.

I usually write 30 to 40 "Along the Color Line" commentaries each year. Collecting and organizing the columns thematically was only the first stage in developing the final draft. A longtime friend and former Managing Editor of the *Progressive*, Linda Rocawich, generously agreed to help edit and revise each article. Her ideas for reorganizing the text and merging different columns into longer, more fully developed essays were invaluable. My relationship with South End Press extends back to 1980, with the publication of my first collection of essays, *From the Grassroots*. Once again the South End Press collective, and especially my editors, Dionne Brooks and Loie Hayes, were always helpful.

Finally, special thanks are due to my wife and intellectual collaborator, Leith Mullings. This book is only one product of a very rich and creative political and personal relationship. I hope that some of Leith's politics and passion for the liberation of black folk is adequately expressed in my own words.

—Manning Marable
November 6, 1996

INTRODUCTION

RETHINKING BLACK LIBERATION:
PAST, PRESENT, AND FUTURE

Black Liberation in Conservative America is largely a collection of political commentaries written during the period 1991-1996 and published in my series "Along the Color Line." These commentaries currently appear in more than 280 newspapers throughout the world, more than half of which are black American weekly newspapers, such as the Chicago *Defender*, the Baltimore-Washington *Afro-American*, and the San Francisco *Sun-Reporter*. In many respects, "Along the Color Line" has largely defined my public and political life since it was started two decades ago.

The political realities of 20 years ago now seem a world removed from today. The Soviet Union—still a global superpower in the mid-'70s when I started writing "Along the Color Line"—no longer exists. Communism throughout Eastern Europe has collapsed. Communist China today has arguably the most aggressively capitalist economy on earth. With some notable exceptions, political parties that espoused liberal to left policies in Europe and North America have been defeated. "Globalization" and the information revolution have rapidly transformed the nature of work and the character of production. As traditional industries disappeared, and as agricultural production globally moved from labor-intensive to capital-intensive methods, millions of working people were displaced. Hundreds of millions of Third World people migrated from rural areas to cities, and from their own countries into Western Europe and North America, in the struggle for survival. Third World countries with socialist and labor parties had few options except to adopt neo-liberal, capitalist policies.

These massive transformations in the structure of the global economy and labor force have generated a sharp increase in income inequality and greater class stratification. The real wages of working-class people have steadily declined, and job insecurity now increasingly affects middle-class households as well. In our central cities, millions of jobs that once could sustain families have been destroyed. In communities like Central Harlem today, there are 14 applicants for every available job in the fast-food industry. Members of families confined to the poorest neighborhoods for several generations have never had the experience of a job in their lives. When large numbers of people cannot obtain employment, the quality of life for the entire community suffers: grocery stores and retail establishments close down, social institutions like churches and schools are weakened, the quality of housing deteriorates, and the level of violence connected with crime inevitably increases. Conversely, the same global economic forces have concentrated vast wealth in the hands of a small, privileged elite, which is also increasingly multinational in character.

In the United States, these economic trends created the political space for the triumph of an extreme version of conservatism. In the early 1980s, this reaction was symbolized by the administration of Ronald Reagan. Reaganism was, in many ways, the mirror opposite of the New Deal: government was the problem, not the solution. Federal programs were abolished; industries were deregulated; affirmative action and environmental laws were not enforced; the capital gains tax was significantly reduced; and taxes on corporate profits virtually disappeared. Key elements within the Democratic Party at first tried to attack and reverse the politics of the Right. The 1983 mayoral victory of Harold Washington in Chicago, and the Rainbow Coalition's presidential campaigns for Jesse Jackson in 1984 and 1988, illustrated the potential power of a progressive, multiclass, and multiracial opposition.

But liberals, labor, and the Left in the United States failed to consolidate an alternative formation or movement to challenge conservatism. As a result, by the 1990s the political terrain shifted even further to the right. Although a Democrat was elected to the presidency in 1992, the Clinton administration pursued policies that only 20 years before would have been described as "Liberal Republicanism." The "mainstream" of the Democratic Party equivocated or retreated on minority economic set-asides, minority scholarships, affirmative action, majority-people-of-color legislative districts, employment legislation, universal health care, and urban development. Clinton embraced the death penalty, passed a repressive crime bill that seriously threatened civil liberties, and signed a Republican welfare bill that will devastate the households of millions of poor women and children.

One might have predicted that these reactionary economic and political trends, nationally and globally, would have revived the organizations and movements closest to the masses: civil rights groups, labor unions, feminists, poor people's advocates, community activists. Certainly there were numerous examples of resistance across the United States in the 1990s, but a strong, coherent opposition to the Right has not coalesced. Reaganism and the corporations had delivered a devastating blow to organized labor, greatly demoralizing and reducing its ranks. By the early 1990s, the AFL-CIO was losing 300,000 members every year. The growth of nonunion jobs in high technology, service, and other expanding sectors of the economy reduced labor's influence. Politically, when President Clinton signed the 1993 North American Free Trade Agreement (NAFTA) over the vigorous objections of the AFL-CIO, he sent an anti-union message nearly as devastating as Reagan's 1981 crushing of the air traffic controllers' strike.

Similarly, the civil rights community failed to mount a significant challenge against the Right. Economic stratification and, ironically, the successful implementation of reforms like affirmative action greatly expanded the social base of the black middle class. By the mid-1990s, one in six black households earned incomes exceeding $50,000 annually. A small but very class-conscious elite of African-Americans, Asian-Americans, and Latinos was increasingly represented in corporate management, government bureaucracies, the criminal justice system, and the armed services. The emergence of three powerful and influential African-Americans—General Colin Powell, Commerce Secretary Ronald Brown, and Supreme Court Associate Justice Clarence Thomas—symbolized the drift toward conservative accommodation within the leadership of minority communities.

The most critical mistake in black politics was the tendency to emphasize electoralism at the expense of activism. For 30 years, since the end of the Civil Rights Movement, African-American leadership increasingly came from elective offices. The vast majority of these officials were Democrats tied to a political party that had begun to distance itself from black interests and issues. The pressure to break with the Democrats briefly intensified with the successes of the Jackson presidential campaigns, as it became apparent that a left-of-center bloc of racial ethnic minorities, women, labor, and others could be effectively mobilized. But Jackson himself had no desire to renounce the Democratic Party's hierarchy and, in effect, demobilized his own coalition. Most African-Americans in Congress were elected from black-majority districts and, as long as they played the political game by the establishment's rules, they could usually win reelection without difficulty. Gradually, the political independence and liberal agenda of the Congressional Black Caucus deteriorated, as many newly elected members pursued their own narrow interests or cut deals undermining a black united front. On major legislative issues, such as NAFTA and Clinton's 1994 crime bill, a significant number of blacks in Congress broke ranks to embrace the Right.

The conservative trend was represented within the Republican Party by black neo-conservative theorists such as Thomas Sowell, and by a small number of black elected officials such as Congressmen Gary Franks of Connecticut and J.C. Watts of Oklahoma. Far more pervasive was the growing pragmatism of African-American leaders in the Democratic Party who espoused a type of "postblack" or "deracialized" politics. African-American elected officials like former Virginia Governor Doug Wilder or Cleveland, Ohio, Mayor Michael White increasingly advocated agendas that were "color blind"; in other words, that black officials had no further special responsibility or obligation to their African-American constituents than they had to the white electorate. A series of African-American politicians were elected as mayors of major cities—David Dinkins in

New York, Thomas Bradley in Los Angeles, Wilson Goode in Philadelphia—but the quality of urban life for most African-Americans continued to decline. Venerable black institutions like the NAACP and the National Urban League seemed disoriented or in disarray. The chaos surrounding the dismissal of Benjamin Chavis as Executive Secretary of the NAACP in 1994, followed by the 1995 conflict ousting NAACP President William Gibson, reinforced the popular mood that the Civil Rights Movement was dead.

Into the leadership vacuum of black America stepped Louis Farrakhan. To many black working- and middle-class families, Farrakhan's philosophy of conservative black nationalism, economic self-help, and racial pride made sense. As white political parties repudiated affirmative action and dismantled the social reforms of the Second Reconstruction, Farrakhan pointed to the necessity for black solidarity in the face of racism. To blacks in neighborhoods plagued by crime, Farrakhan's vigorous opposition to black-on-black violence and drugs was widely praised. The overall economic strategy of the Nation of Islam, however, was taken directly from conservative black educator Booker T. Washington. Entrepreneurship and black small businesses may indeed create thousands of new jobs, but at a time when millions of African-Americans, Latinos, and other poor people are desperately seeking work at living wages, black capitalism is no solution. Farrakhan's homophobic, anti-Semitic, sexist rhetoric alienated many potential allies for the Black Freedom Movement. Nevertheless, the levels of desperation and alienation had become so profound within the black community that when Farrakhan called for a "Million Man March" on Washington, DC, the popular response was overwhelming. A massive crowd of as many as one million African-American males came to the Washington Mall on October 16, 1995, by far the largest public demonstration by black people in U.S. history.

The enthusiasm and emotion generated by the Million Man March had less to do with Farrakhan's reactionary ideology than with the deep desire among African-American people to move their communities forward. The movement had somehow lost its way, and the masses desperately endeavored to reclaim their own spirit and history. In a time of white conservatism and corporate exploitation from the ghetto to the globe, how could the struggle advance?

*   *   *

Leaders are not "born," they are "made." Social movements are not only the products of unpredictable historical forces, but also carefully planned, collective actions. By finding their own voice, by defining their own needs and objective circumstances, oppressed people truly can make their own history. The basic social, economic, and political problem confronting black Americans for nearly a century was Jim Crow segregation. Women and men of uncommon courage built institutions that permitted our people to sustain themselves and to survive. They crafted a complex strategy of resistance, focusing at first on legal challenges against white supremacy. The struggle in the courtroom gave way to the crusade for justice in the streets, employing the tactics of nonviolent direct action. The leaders of this movement recognized the necessity of speaking simultaneously to their own constituency and to the larger world. The struggle for black freedom and equality was based not on narrowly parochial needs or racial self-interest, but on appeals to a just and more democratic society that was universal. As our strategy and political language gradually captured the imaginations of oppressed people across the globe, our movement acquired the legitimacy and power to overturn the structures of legal racism.

We are again at a decisive moment in black history, where a new paradigm must be developed to advance the boundaries of our politics. We cannot simply duplicate the strategies and tactics of the Civil Rights Movement of the 1960s, because the issues that confront us are fundamentally different. The internal class composition of the black community has been radically altered; it is now characterized by an affluent professional and managerial elite, a black working class with declining incomes, and a black ghetto class of the unemployed and single-parent households that is experiencing a social holocaust. The conservative black nationalism approach suggested by Farrakhan cannot provide the basis for advancing the movement. Building strong black institutions to provide the goods and services black people need is certainly important. But petty capitalist enterprises will not generate the jobs we need to effectively reduce mass unemployment. Racial separatism does not bring together people from different ethnic and racial backgrounds who nevertheless share common material and social interests. Patriarchy and homophobia divide the black community, as well as the progressive community as a whole. Our political power is reduced when our organizing is based on chauvinism of any kind.

The place to begin the reconstruction of the black liberation movement—as well as the larger progressive, left-of-center movements in the United States—is at the nexus of three crucial sites of struggle: community, class, and gender.

By "community" I mean the socioeconomic and environmental context of daily life for most families and households. Nearly all of us live in communities of one kind or another, with their own cultural and geographical dimensions, patterns of social interaction and exchange, and even languages and traditions. It is from the site of community that many of us wage struggles in the living space around the reality of day-to-day existence: access to decent and affordable housing, public health services, crime and personal safety, the quality of the environment, public transportation, the education of our children. These basic human concerns transcend narrowly defined racial interests: an effective program for health care in a community, for example, cannot address only African-Americans. It is where people live that usually defines how they become most active in the civic arena. And if one surveys the actual racial and ethnic composition of most U.S. urban communities, it becomes apparent that neighborhoods are almost never strictly defined by race. Harlem, black America's most famous community, is today more than 40 percent Latino. The largest city of the English-speaking Caribbean is arguably Brooklyn. In the next decade, Latinos will outnumber African-Americans as the largest group of people of color in the United States. We must build partnerships across racial identities to serve the broader collective interests of people who live side by side, ride the same buses and subways, send their children to the same substandard schools, and wait for health services in the same over-crowded hospitals and emergency clinics.

By "class" I mean more than the stratification of incomes or the social status derived from various levels of wealth. Class—the divisions based on the relations and forces of production, and the social consequences of the unequal al-location of property and power—always prefigures the range of social possibilities and life chances, beyond the so-cial realities of gender, race, and community. This is not to suggest that either gender or race can be understood as by-products of rigid economic categories, or that they exist as secondary factors in the class struggle. Race and gender function both independently and interdependently with economics. But what history does show is that the way things are produced and distributed within society, the patterns of ownership and divisions of property, sets into motion certain consequences, which in turn influence everything else.

During the period of American capitalist hegemony across the globe, especially from 1945 to the late 1970s, part of the surplus was allocated to U.S. workers, who saw their real incomes dramatically improve. Class as a social category almost ceased to be used in mainstream political discourse. In the 1990s, the situation regarding class in American life has dramatically changed. *Black Liberation in Conservative America* documents in some detail the disas-trous decline in real incomes for millions of Americans. For example, families in the upper 5 percent tax bracket have increased their incomes by 25 percent since 1979, adjust-ing for inflation. But for middle-income households, real in-comes during the same period declined 1 percent; for low-income households, real wages have declined 13 per-cent. The income decline was even greater for black and Latino families, and for households headed by young adults or single parents. The destruction of jobs and lower wages are a direct result of new technologies and the glo-balization of capital, in which businesses relocate overseas in pursuit of low-wage, nonunion labor. Even for those workers who have jobs, the pressure of corporate downsizing has created an environment of fear and insecurity. Black and progressive politics needs to focus specifically on the issues of employment and a living wage, initiating a public conversation about the importance of work for all people. For example, the Association of Community Organizations for Reform Now (ACORN) ran a Jobs and Living Wage Campaign in 1995 in Chicago, an excellent model of practical class politics. The use of local and statewide initiatives to increase the minimum wage provides an important vehicle for mobilizing both the unemployed and low-wage workers. These struggles over jobs and income can also be merged into community-based initiatives around economic development and urban renewal. A new class-centered activism, combined with the potential revitalization of the AFL-CIO, could generate an increase in effective multiracial protest.

The basis of the politics of "gender" in the black community is partially the fact that the primary victims and scapegoats of the Right are women of color and their children. The demonization of poor and low-income black women is a central theme in the ideological and policy assault against the entire black community. When we talk about mobilizing African-American neighborhoods around community concerns, we must recognize that the majority of our households are single-parent families. The majority of neighborhood activists who focus on improving the quality of public schools, on access to decent health care facilities, and on the issue of community safety are overwhelmingly black women. Struggles for the empowerment of African-American women must be at the very center of how progressive politics is defined. This includes deepening the struggle against sexism within black institutions and political organizations, the advancement of black women as leaders and theoreticians in the overall movement, and greater emphasis on programmatic demands and initiatives speaking to the real issues affecting African-American women and girls. As long as African-American males define the assertion of "manhood" as a central goal of their politics, and deny the voices and insights of their sisters, the black movement will continue to be fragmented and pulled toward the patriarchy of the Right.

Many might suggest that "race" still remains the central terrain for black struggle. Of course, "race" as a social category directly manifests itself in community, class, and gender contexts. Where we live, how we work, and our experience of gender are all profoundly affected by the inequality of race. Black women's lives and struggles are not mirrored in the perspectives and interests of white middle-class women. Working people who are black not coincidentally have unemployment rates twice that of white workers. Race matters, but race is most real as a social force when it manifests itself in the consequences and conditions of inequality and discrimination.

Practical steps to improve the quality of life within communities, such as organizing against police brutality and harassment in our neighborhoods, or taking measures to reduce the level of gang violence, or mobilizing parents to improve the curriculum of public schools, all contribute to the empowerment of racial ethnic minorities and other oppressed people. Sometimes activism can be effectively channeled through electoral politics, as in voter registration and education campaigns. But more frequently, it is through the institutions of civil society—within extended kinship and friendship networks, in our cultural and social organizations, and among co-workers on the job—that practical political activism is expressed. All constructive forms of resistance and collective mobilization by black people directly or indirectly challenge and undermine institutional racism. When people recognize that through their collective actions they can change the way things are, they truly feel empowered. Liberation begins by winning small battles, day by day, creating greater confidence among the oppressed, ultimately building toward a democratic vision that can successfully change the very foundations of this system.

Nearly a century ago, W.E.B. Du Bois predicted that the central problem of the 20th century would be "the problem of the color line." What was clear to Du Bois was that African-Americans would effectively challenge racism only when they understood the dynamics of inequality and oppression on a global scale, and when the politics of racial justice was closely connected with a larger critique of capital and class. So I remain optimistic, despite the recent reactionary victories of the conservative Republicans and the neo-liberal accommodationism of the majority of the Democrats. The vast contradictions of race, class, and gender increasingly polarize this nation as the political space for a progressive alternative becomes more than a possibility.

Radical democratic change within society is a question not just of politics, but of vision. Can we rethink what we mean by black and/or progressive politics and craft a new, more effective paradigm for activism? Can we construct a theory and practice that challenges racism while also addressing the contradictions and inequalities of gender, class, and community? Can we redefine the category of "blackness" itself, away from its racial and biological concepts and identity-based politics and toward a progressive politics and common language that bring together oppressed people with very distinct ethnicities, cultures, and traditions? To paraphrase Malcolm X, the decisive struggle is not between black and white, but between the world's haves and have nots. The future of black liberation is inextricably linked to how successfully we answer these questions, while speaking to the vast majority of humanity.

*   *   *

As in every collection of previously published essays, there are certain limitations imposed by their composition and the historical moment in which they were written. "Along the Color Line" articles are designed for a mass audience, rather than an academic elite. Nearly all essays in their original form were less than 1,000 words. The journalistic style and approach emphasizes getting to the heart of an issue quickly, exploring conflicts and contradictions, and succinctly presenting possible solutions. The limitations of this genre are found in its lack of subtlety and nuance. Most political issues don't present themselves in simplistic, black-versus-white terms. What this style of writing yields, however, is an intimacy with important events that define a moment in time. When something significant occurs, the political essayist is forced to analyze personalities and issues quickly, based only on what is known at that moment. A collection of such political writings spanning several years reveals something of the character of that period, as well as the audience for whom the texts were written.

The column has also served as a venue for presenting new theoretical concepts to a black audience. Some of these articles, initially published as newspaper columns, were later substantially expanded and revised into essays appearing in journals and anthologies. I often use material from my columns as the basis for public lectures and political workshops. Consequently, many of the central arguments and even some of the language in the essays from my recent books *Beyond Black and White* and *Speaking Truth to Power* are also presented here. In preparing this volume, I eliminated many of the articles that paralleled or repeated too closely the topics and themes in other works. Some repetition in the content of this book and previously published work was inevitable. Nevertheless, reading the columns as they were written retains a special value, in that they are immediate responses and commentaries on the dynamics of racial politics as they occurred in the period 1991-1996. Taken as a whole, the "Along the Color Line" columns presented a perspective that pointed toward the construction of a new paradigm for black and progressive politics.

The immediate social background that helped to create this project of political journalism and social analysis was the 1970s. At the beginning of the decade, there was a series of domestic and global confrontations against the corporations and western capitalist democracies: Vietnam, Latin American and African liberation movements, Black Power, Attica, the emergence of feminist and gay and lesbian movements, the Wounded Knee confrontation and the American Indian movement. With the moral and political collapse of the Nixon administration over the Watergate scandal, it seemed that the Republican Party would be discredited certainly for many years to come. Many liberal Democrats were elected in the congressional races of 1974. Within the African-American community, there had been a series of stunning political victories. The number of black elected officials increased from barely 100 in 1964 to almost 2,000 in one decade. Jim Crow segregation had been outlawed across the South, and blacks were elected to positions of power in many cities and towns for the first time since Reconstruction. For most progressive activists, this was a tremendously optimistic period of social struggle. The oppressed on a global scale, whether defined by the struggles of race, class, gender, sexual orientation, nationality, or ethnicity, appeared to be gaining ground. The logic of history itself was on our side.

My approach to politics at this time reflected most of these assumptions. I had become active in the National Black Political Assembly, a black nationalist formation seeking to build an independent political force within black America. I became involved in the Institute of the Black World in Atlanta, a progressive, Pan-African research center founded by Vincent Harding. I was interested in grounding myself more closely in the newly emerging struggles across the black South, relating these issues to the global struggles against colonialism and inequality.

In the summer of 1976, I accepted a teaching position as Chairperson of the Political Science Department at Tuskegee Institute, in the heart of Alabama's Black Belt. I was no stranger to this community. Many summers as a boy I traveled with my father to visit his extended family in this small southern town. Nearly a century earlier, the Alabama State Legislature had allocated several thousand dollars for the establishment of an all-Negro vocational and normal school in the surrounding Macon County. Booker T. Washington, barely 25 years old and a recent graduate of Hampton Institute, was chosen to head the new enterprise. Within two decades, Tuskegee Institute had become the largest educational institution for black people at that time in the world.

I was familiar with Tuskegee's rich history, as well as its political contradictions. In the Civil Rights Movement, the town became the focus of a powerful struggle against racial gerrymandering and the denial of blacks' voting rights. Yet the town was largely divided between two distinct and divergent black neighborhoods: the affluent, well-educated elite on the west side, attached professionally to the college and the Veterans Administration Hospital, and the working-class laborers, rural farmers, and entrepreneurs who lived on the other side of town. My father's family was part of this latter group, closely connected with an emerging black political and small-business leadership that came into being after desegregation.

The local newspaper, the *Tuskegee News*, still reflected the racial divisions that were deeply rooted in Macon County's history. Most of the articles focused on the small and rapidly disappearing white business and planter elite, which had prospered under Jim Crow but was now losing its power and privileges. The newspaper's editor, a conservative white Democrat, wanted to broaden the general appeal of the publication to reach the growing black middle- and working-class community.

Within weeks after arriving in Tuskegee before the beginning of the fall semester, I visited the office of the *Tuskegee News*. I introduced myself and offered to write an occasional article on politics and public policy issues for the newspaper. I did not request any payment for the articles selected for publication. My primary goal was to speak to important political and social issues affecting black Americans, both locally and nationally. I hoped that the series would provoke discussion and debate, contributing in some small way to the Black Freedom Movement. The white editor of the *Tuskegee News* did not share any of these political perspectives or interests, but he did want to sell more newspapers to local black residents. In August 1976, my regular commentary series began. In its early years the series was called "From the Grassroots," after the theme of a famous 1963 speech by Malcolm X. In the early 1980s the series was renamed "Along the Color Line."

In the two decades since its inception, "Along the Color Line" has served several distinct purposes. The columns are almost always "conjunctural"—that is, they comment on and about what is happening politically at a given moment. When major events occur, there is a need to analyze what's happened and to frame issues within a broader social context. Historians have the luxury of pondering over archival materials, carefully weighing the evidence and reflecting critically on the motivations and interests of all personalities and parties in conflict. Time is the ally of scholarly detachment and reflection. I was trained as an historian, and part of my intellectual orientation is to push back from the site of the here-and-now to view the past through a distant mirror.

The weakness of the historical method is its inherent tendency to make us neutral observers, rather than actors in the making of history. The chimera of scholarly objectivity can lead intellectuals away from an engagement with the real issues people care passionately about. Scholarship must inform and educate, but for oppressed people it must do more than this. Social analysis should empower people to acquire a better understanding of their world and how it actually works—who benefits from the existing structure of power and who doesn't. A critique of social reality is always strengthened by the perspective of history, because patterns from the past can powerfully influence what happens in the future. But the primary purpose of social analysis should not be merely to interpret reality, but to transform it.

From the beginning, "Along the Color Line" also analyzed internal debates and issues within the African-American community. There is a belief, especially within white America, that black people are somehow monolithic as a social and political group. African-Americans know better. The entire political history of black America has been essentially a series of debates: Frederick Douglass versus Martin Delany in the 1850s; Booker T. Washington versus W.E.B. Du Bois in the early 20th century; Paul Robeson versus Walter White in the 1940s; the competition and conflicts within the Civil Rights Movement of the 1960s involving the NAACP, National Urban League, Congress of Racial Equality, Southern Christian Leadership Conference, and the Student Nonviolent Coordinating Committee; Black Power versus integration in the late 1960s; black nationalism versus revolutionary marxism in the 1970s; the ideological development of black neo-conservativism in the 1980s by the likes of Thomas Sowell, Tony Brown, Glen Loury, Robert Woodson, and Shelby Steele; and the controversies involving the "black public intellectuals" in the 1990s, including Cornel West, Henry Louis Gates, bell hooks, Patricia Williams, Michael Eric Dyson, and Gerald Early.

Frequently, there have been leaders within the black community who have utilized the myth of the monolithic black community to stifle internal voices of dissent: "If we're all black, and if we all experience racism in common, there must be a unified response and leadership to address our problems." But movements of any oppressed people cannot advance unless there is a healthy degree of internal criticism and discussion. The columns often spoke critically of the contradictions among black leaders, but never made *ad hominem* attacks on an individual's character or personal motives. For example, one can certainly criticize Jesse Jackson for all sorts of reasons, but he merits our respect for his important contributions to our movement. I disagree vigorously with the political perspectives of both Colin Powell and Louis Farrakhan, but our profound differences should not keep us from engaging in a serious dialogue with those who share their views within the black community.

I have never believed that scholarship takes place outside the boundaries of society. We live and work in a real world, where triumphs and tragedies occur daily across the divisions of race, class, and gender. We are witness to the struggles all around us. The task of the radical intellectual is to illuminate the contours of social reality, to challenge those who benefit from the unequal division of resources. "Along the Color Line" has allowed me to interpret contemporary events as a passionate advocate for the interests of my people. Although the essays provide information that can be used by a widely diverse audience, my primary purpose has always been to reach African-Americans. Through this political discourse I make certain assumptions that many in polite academic circles might not approve; they may find comfort in the mainstream, isolated from the political and economic turbulence of today's social landscape. But it is only when we stand against the current, confronting the powerful forces of prejudice and inequality, that the tools of scholarship become meaningful.

INEQUALITY
AND PUBLIC POLICY

RESTATING THE PROBLEM:
RACE AND INEQUALITY

The poet Langston Hughes suggested years ago that the black American's search for democracy in the United States was "a dream deferred." Perhaps we should now add that this dream has been so long delayed, corrupted, and compromised that many black folk now question the viability of the entire political project called American democracy.

Any understanding of American society and history must begin with the study of the black American experience. This is because the status and existence of black people, the quality of our lives and the range of possibilities which we can realistically achieve through our own endeavors, is the essential litmus test for the viability of American democracy. It is the distance between America's rhetoric versus its reality, between what America says about itself versus what it actually is.

African-Americans are at the center of the definition about what it has meant to be "an American." The reality of "blackness" has all too often been the criterion for determining a series of questions about the relationship between the people, the state, and civil society. Who is a citizen, and who is not? Who has voting rights, and who has not? Who rides in the Jim Crow section of the bus, and who does not? Who lives in the ghetto, and who does not? Who is the first person to get a job, and who is the last?

The basic paradox one must confront in any consideration of the role of race in American life is the simultaneity of the "marginalization" and "inclusion" of people of color. African-American culture has been central to the construction of the cultural and the aesthetic contours of America. Likewise, the issue of race has been absolutely central to the major political conflicts in the American experience, from the Civil War to the Civil Rights Movement. Economically, black labor was essential in the construction of this nation, from the unpaid exploitation of slavery to the underpaid labor of African-Americans in central cities in the 1990s. Yet despite our centrality, we continue to be marginalized by the mainstream of the dominant social order. We are unequal members of the household, but never members of the national family. In the language of "hip-hop" culture, we are "dissed" in the very house we have helped to construct.

From the vantage point of African-American history, from the depths of our sorrow and anger, we ask ourselves: why do we continue to be marginalized? Who benefits from this marginalization? Who is responsible for maintaining the structure of power and privilege which makes this marginalization an enduring fact of American life?

African-Americans understand that race is not a valid biological concept; that it has no genetic validity. Stripped of the rhetoric of superiority and inferiority, the science of race is nothing but a fraud, grounded in power, privilege, and violence against those who are oppressed. Yet our lives are defined and circumscribed by the brutal reality of racism, a system that denies the humanity of millions of people, limiting their education, employment, health, housing, and future.

This is why all the recent talk about "reverse racism" is sheer nonsense. When African-Americans control all of the banks and financial institutions in our neighborhoods, all of the real estate and commercial enterprises, we might begin to talk about discrimination against whites. When our government truly reflects the real percentages of African-Americans, Latinos, and other racial minorities within the general population; when the corporations that exploit black, brown, and poor consumer markets are actually controlled democratically by those who produce the wealth, then we might seriously discuss the possibility of "reverse racism." Whiteness in a racist, corporate-controlled society is like having the image of an American Express card or Diners Club card stamped on one's face: immediately you are "universally accepted."

Let's restate the problem of black liberation in a white, conservative, and capitalist society: to end racism, we must end inequality. Our goal cannot be simply the assimilation or integration of black elites into the white cultural and corporate mainstream. Nor can we combat inequality by going it alone, divorced from real and potential allies. The problem of the 21st century is the challenge of multicultural democracy—whether American political institutions and society can and will be restructured to incorporate the genius and energy, the labor power and social struggles of millions of people who have been denied full equality—Latinos, Asian-Americans, American Indians, Arab-Americans, African-Americans, women, working people, the unemployed, the poor, and many others.

CLASS POLARIZATION
AND THE NATIONAL INSURANCE SCANDAL

Blacks face an unprecedented crisis within the U.S. political and economic system. Politically, both the Democratic and Republican parties have largely repudiated the legacy of legal reforms created by the Civil Rights Movement and the social welfare expenditures of the Great Society of the 1960s. White politicians campaign aggressively against affirmative action, minority economic set-aside programs, and majority-black legislative districts. Within the deep structure of the political economy and legal apparatus, a disproportionate number of black people are caught within a vise of unemployment, social inequality, and imprisonment. Indeed, the single most important material reality of U.S. society in the 1990s, for all races, is the vast polarization of classes—the unprecedented rise in personal incomes and profits for a small minority of U.S. house-holds, and the expansion of social misery, falling incomes, and inequality for the majority of the nation's population.

We can measure rising inequality by comparing family incomes. From 1980 to 1992, families with incomes averaging in the bottom 25 percent in the United States saw their share of the total national income fall from 7.6 percent to 6.5 percent. Real average annual incomes for the bottom 25 percent, adjusted for inflation, fell sharply from $12,359 in 1980 to $11,530 12 years later. At the same time, by contrast, the upper 25 percent of U.S. families saw their share of the national income rise from 48.2 percent to 51.3 percent. Their real average family incomes increased from $78,844 to $91,368.

But these figures actually underestimate income inequality in the United States. One recent study by economist Lynn A. Karoly found that those with incomes in the top 10 percent earned over five and a half times as much per hour in 1992 as did workers in the bottom 10 percent. And when we measure total net wealth rather than salaries or wages, an even sharper class division becomes clear. As of 1993, the top 1 percent of all income earners in the United States shared a greater net wealth than the bottom 95 percent combined. In short, a small number of individuals—two to three million at most—control the overwhelming majority of the resources.

This massive inequality can also be measured in our cities. Professor Larry C. Ledebur of Wayne State University conducted a survey of the 85 largest metropolitan areas in the United States, and found that the average income of all wage earners living in these cities fell by 16 percent between 1973 and 1989. In 1990 in the New York borough of Manhattan, where I live, the poorest one-fifth of the population earned an average annual income of $5,237. The richest one-fifth earned an average annual income of $110,199. In neighborhoods less than three miles apart, the vast income gap between affluence and poverty can only be described as *obscene*. In West Harlem, for example, a predominantly African-American and Dominican community, the average annual family income was $6,019. The average incomes for families in one district of Manhattan's Upper East Side was $301,209 a year. In other words, for every dollar the wealthiest households have, the poorest have two cents.

An identical profile of income inequality can be found in every U.S. city. In Los Angeles in 1990, the median annual incomes of the poorest fifth and the wealthiest fifth were $6,821 versus $123,098, respectively. In Chicago, the median annual incomes were $4,743 versus $86,632; in Detroit, they were $3,109 versus $63,625; and in Orleans Parish, in the city of New Orleans, the rich made 30 times as much as the poor, $83,389 compared with $2,793. Millions of median-income households are forced to have three or more wage earners just to stay even. Millions more have been pushed into unemployment and poverty. For America's privileged and powerful elite, though, things have never been better.

The greatest and most painful measure of inequality separating African-Americans from the white middle and upper classes is health care. The average life expectancy in the United States as of 1992 was a bit more than 75, an all-time high. The average white woman now lives to be nearly 80 years old. Yet the typical black man dies just shy of his 65th birthday—even before he can collect Social Security.

African-American health statistics are a national scandal. Blacks are twice as likely as whites to die before their first birthday; they have the highest cancer rate of any group in the United States and double the rate for hypertension. The death rate for HIV- and AIDS-related illnesses is three times higher for black men than for white men, and nine times greater for black women than for white women. More than one in five blacks have no health insurance, and nearly half don't visit a dentist regularly.

Even the basic health care delivery systems inside the black community are in crisis. Seven decades ago, more than 200 segregated hospitals served the black community. These included Provident Hospital in Chicago, founded in

1891; Howard University Hospital in Washington, DC, established in 1866; Meharry/Hubbard Hospital in Nashville, Tennessee; Richmond Community Hospital, Norfolk Community Hospital, and Newport News General Hospital in Virginia; and Southeast Specialty Hospital in Greensboro, North Carolina. These wonderful institutions were designed to provide health services for all African-Americans, regardless of their ability to pay. Millions of African-Americans—especially the elderly, the poor, children, and working people—were provided for.

After desegregation, as African-Americans were finally permitted to enter the front doors of formerly all-white hospitals, the black hospitals continued to provide valuable training to thousands of African-American doctors, nurses, and other health care professionals. They also developed special units and programs that concentrated on the specific health care problems of the inner-city, such as drug addiction.

But now many of these hospitals are on the critical list. Provident Hospital closed its doors in September 1987. Meharry/Hubbard was forced into merger negotiations with a largely white hospital. Howard University Hospital lost $38 million in the past three years, and was forced to fire more than 200 employees in 1991, according to the *New York Times*. While many white hospitals turn away poor people and those without health insurance, black hospitals—which serve those most in need—are unable to survive in these desperate times.

It is in this context of crisis that the debate over health care policies must be analyzed. Since the 1992 presidential campaign, much talk and many promises have resulted in no action to address the fact that 37 million Americans have absolutely no health insurance, and millions more die prematurely because of inadequate health care. Like the right to vote, health care should be considered—but isn't—a fundamental human right.

Some aspects of inequality are strictly economic and might seem more amenable to creative solutions. Most urban Americans, for example, are ripped off when they buy automobile insurance. City drivers with safe driving records frequently pay two or three times the rates of suburban drivers—an inequality disproportionately borne by African-Americans because they are disproportionately city, rather than suburban, drivers.

Several years ago, Susan P. Baker, a researcher at Johns Hopkins University, reviewed the records of fatal automobile accidents in more than 3,000 cities. Baker discovered that the greatest percentage of auto fatalities occurred on rural roads, where fewer drivers use seat belts. Based on fatal accidents per member of the population, Manhattan, the central borough of New York City, is actually the safest place to drive. Yet Manhattan has some of the highest auto insurance rates in the country.

During a visit to Baltimore, I learned that the city's residents pay two times the auto insurance premiums charged suburbanites who live just beyond the city limits. Baltimore citizens pay as much as four times what residents of rural Maryland pay for the same coverage.

It's instructive to examine what occurred when the city dwellers of Baltimore proposed a workable, concrete solution to this inequality. Community leaders and activists from many groups—African-American, working-class, low-income, and religious—recognized that the outrageously high auto insurance rates in Baltimore were blatantly discriminatory and unfair. Millions of dollars that left the city every month in auto insurance premiums could be put to more productive uses. So, in 1989, they created the "City-wide Insurance Coalition," with the goal of bringing the city's auto policy rates down from the stratosphere.

In November 1989, the Coalition asked Mayor Kurt Schmoke, an African-American, to finance a $52,000 feasibility study for the creation of a publicly owned, nonprofit insurance cooperative. Schmoke ignored the request until the city's Interdenominational and Baptist Ministerial Alliance applied pressure. In January 1991, Schmoke reluctantly released $26,000 for the study and, in August 1991, it was completed. The results showed that if city residents initiated a self-insurance program, they would receive at least a 21 percent drop in premium costs in the first year alone, approximately $250 per vehicle in the city. The savings would be even greater in the second and subsequent years. The cost to set up the insurance cooperative would be more than $100,000, but residents would save millions and millions of dollars on their 250,000 vehicles.

Support for this proposal began to build rapidly. The largest community coalition in Baltimore's history came together, with 164 organizations joining by the summer of 1992. Members of the city council praised the idea of a nonprofit insurance cooperative and voted their unanimous approval. A task force established by the mayor studied the plan and gave it a favorable review.

Despite all this activism, enthusiasm, and grassroots effort, the local media gave very little publicity to the Coalition. And Kurt Schmoke, a mayor widely noted for his advocacy of "community empowerment," was at best highly reluctant to embrace and support a popular proposal that would save his constituents millions of dollars. Was the relative absence of media coverage and Schmoke's curious behavior a result of behind-the-scenes leverage by the powerful, private insurance companies?

In the fall of 1992, Schmoke released $50,000 to begin a final study to design a business plan and determine the exact rates to be used. The overall study, plus other indirect costs, would come to $160,000. Unfortunately, Coalition leaders were told they must raise $60,000 before the mayor would kick in the remaining $50,000. It could be that Schmoke hoped the Coalition's energy and resources would collapse in the face of this latest delaying tactic.

A successful urban-based, nonprofit insurance cooperative would not only have lowered premium payments, it would also have presented a model for public activism that could create economic and social bridges across race and class boundaries. Further, publicly owned cooperatives could provide other services and goods to the general population. The Citywide Insurance Coalition led the fight to empower Baltimore's working-class and low-income people of all races with the motto, "The Self Assured Can Self Insure."

The conservative political agenda of the 1980s and 1990s, from Reaganism to Newt Gingrich's "Contract with America," rests fundamentally on this core reality of escalating and expanding inequality. The ruling elites have to hide these statistics, or at minimum, blame the hardships of white working-class people on the behavior of blacks, Latinos, and other people of color. "Race" is deliberately manipulated to obscure class inequality and its decisive manifestations: poverty, unemployment, and social unrest.

ECONOMIC ANXIETY AND SELF-RELIANCE

Millions of Americans share a pervasive uncertainty about economic issues every day. The 1990-1991 recession ended, only to be followed by a never-ending series of dips and spurts in the stock market. An increasing number of working people feel a deep sense of permanent insecurity.

After World War II, corporate America and the labor union movement reached a tacit agreement: so long as radicals were thrown out of trade unions and labor rarely went on strike, the corporations promised job security and steady increases in wages. With the growth of competition from Europe and Japan by the late 1970s, the historic agreement between corporate America and the labor movement went sour and then disintegrated under the attacks of Reaganism. Today, for all workers in the bottom half of the labor force, job security is a thing of the past.

Millions of Americans have been thrown out of work, pressured from high-paying, skilled manufacturing positions into low-skilled, low-paying jobs as cashiers, food preparation workers, janitors, and office clerks. The loss of jobs is particularly striking in factories. As late as 1979, there were 21 million factory jobs across the United States, representing 23 percent of the entire labor force. By 1994, factory employment had declined to only 18 million jobs, or about 16 percent of the total workforce. The number of manufacturing jobs nationwide dropped 8.3 percent from the beginning of 1989 through February 1994.

Technology eliminates tens of thousands of jobs each month. In the field of telecommunications, for example, automation has wiped out jobs for telephone repair workers and switchboard operators. In 1993 alone, 60,000 telecommunications employees lost their jobs. In the three years following the 1990-1991 recession, businesses throughout the country hired about three million new employees. That's less than half the number of workers hired during the three-year period that followed the 1981-1982 recession. And many of these newly created jobs barely pay above minimum wage and/or have relatively few benefits.

A 1994 *New York Times* poll documented just how widespread the anxiety about jobs was three years after the recession. Of workers in households earning less than $30,000 annually, 44 percent of those polled were worried either "a lot" or "some" that during the next two years they might be laid off, required to work reduced hours, or forced to take pay cuts. Among blue-collar workers, the level of anxiety was most severe, with 48 percent stating they were "nervous about layoffs, reduced hours, or wage cuts." African-American workers were also among those most worried, with 40 percent saying they feared for their jobs.

One significant feature the poll revealed was the degree of job anxiety among better-off Americans. Of those polled, 36 percent of white-collar managers and professional employees said they, too, were nervous about layoffs and salary reductions, as were 34 percent of those living in households earning more than $50,000 annually. During the two years preceding the poll, about one of every four American workers personally experienced either a reduction in the number of hours worked, a layoff, or a reduction in take-home pay.

The impact of economic anxiety, lower wages, and layoffs is often translated into the growth of what economists and urban anthropologists call the "informal economy." In the cities, there is an increase in all kinds of illegal activity, from prostitution to drugs, just to survive. More generally, there is an increase in cash exchanges for labor, in which people sell their time and energy for a wage that is never taxed or recorded. The types of activities include baby-sitting, furniture making, auto repair, home construction and repair, housekeeping, and food preparation. In the United States today, there is an informal market worth an estimated $600 billion, not including such illegal activities as drugs, gambling, and prostitution. About $3.5 billion per year is taken in by sidewalk street vendors; another $10 billion is earned off-the-books by food sellers; $8 billion is earned by housekeepers.

The growth of the underground economy is also due to the collapse of the formal jobs sector, especially in the inner-cities. Because of racism—in New York City, for example, yellow cabs frequently refuse to take passengers to predominantly black or Latino neighborhoods after dark and sometimes refuse to pick up black passengers at all—a gypsy-cab industry has developed to provide services to black and Latino customers. But in the last analysis, self-help measures, barter, and illegal work will not address the economic crisis that millions of Americans experience. Unless we reorder national fiscal priorities, cutting the military budget and making full employment at good wages our primary priority, the economic crisis may spiral out of control.

FIGHTING FOR A LIVING WAGE

My first real job, in the summer of 1968, was working in a large warehouse, unloading boxcars and cleaning toilets. I earned the minimum wage, which was $1.60 an hour at the time. In today's wages, that would equal $6.45. By working all summer, I earned enough to cover most of my first year's college tuition.

Today, millions of Americans work more than 40 hours each week and never take home enough money to feed and clothe their families. In early 1996, minimum-wage workers made $4.25 an hour, or approximately $170 for a 40-hour week. Almost 60 percent of such workers were women. Nearly two-thirds were adults trying to support their families.

In 1995, President Clinton proposed a modest increase of 90 cents an hour, but it was rejected by the Republican-controlled Congress. As columnist Bob Herbert observed at the time in the *New York Times*, it had been "nearly seven years since the minimum wage was increased." If this modest increase had been granted, Herbert noted, "The $525 in additional [annual] wages could have provided food for three months, or 10 months' worth of electric bills, or new clothing for several children."

Conservatives argued that increasing the minimum wage would discourage businesses from hiring workers with limited educational backgrounds and skills. But Labor Secretary Robert Reich cited a series of studies to prove that increasing the minimum wage does not have that effect. More to the point, Reich stated, "It is fundamentally immoral to expect people to work full-time for $8,600 a year." The Republican Congress finally gave in and passed a bill granting a 90-cent increase in the minimum wage but spreading the raise over a two-year period. President Clinton signed the bill in August 1996, but it isn't enough.

One national organization leading the fight for decent wages is ACORN. In 1995, ACORN mobilized the Chicago Jobs and Living Wage Campaign, a coalition of more than 40 community groups, labor unions, and religious leaders. The Campaign called for a city ordinance requiring businesses that receive subsidies or hold city contracts to pay their workers at least $7.60 an hour. The majority of Chicago's city council supports the living wage ordinance, but it has been continually opposed by Mayor Richard Daley.

In Missouri, ACORN was organizing support for a state-wide initiative to raise the minimum wage to $6.25 in 1997. A petition drive sought a place for the measure on the state's ballot in November 1996. In St. Louis, ACORN started a petition campaign to require all companies in the city to employ local residents through community-based hiring halls and to require all subsidy recipients and city contractors to pay employees fair wages. And in Houston, Texas, ACORN and a local of the Service Employees International Union (SEIU) obtained 12,000 signatures to place an initiative increasing the minimum wage for the city on the ballot.

The effort to achieve decent wages for working people, however, will not be won without a struggle. In St. Paul, Minnesota, in 1995, voters defeated a local initiative that would have required any company receiving more than $25,000 in public subsidies to pay their employees at least $7.21 an hour. Activists from ACORN, the New Party, and religious and labor groups were viciously attacked by politicians and the press. A sophisticated campaign was orchestrated by one of St. Paul's largest public relations firms to mobilize opposition. Advocates for a living wage were smeared as "Stalinesque" and "job killers." Despite this setback, the fight for decent wages in St. Paul continues.

ACORN has initiated other protest actions on the principle that everyone has a human right to a job and/or an adequate income. In 1994, ACORN launched a national campaign against the accounting firm of Price Waterhouse. Because the firm has federal housing contracts worth nearly $9 million, it is required by law to make efforts to hire low-income residents from local communities. When Price Waterhouse made no effort to comply with the law, ACORN eventually forced it to initiate a "first source" hiring program committing the company to employment of low-income residents. ACORN's successes prove that grassroots mobilization among low- and moderate-income people, building from the bottom up, can achieve real victories.

Labor unions and civil rights organizations must continue to lead a national campaign for a further hike in the minimum wage, as well as for full-employment legislation. We cannot wait for Congress or the president to "do the right thing." Only through public protests and mobilization can we win a living wage for all.

LAW AND LIBERATION—
HAYWOOD BURNS AND SHANARA GILBERT

On April 3, 1996, W. Haywood Burns, one of the nation's leading civil rights attorneys and the former Dean of the City University of New York (CUNY) Law School, was killed in a car crash in Cape Town, South Africa. Also killed in the crash was Professor Shanara Gilbert of CUNY Law School.

The loss of Burns and Gilbert represents a genuine tragedy for the black liberation movement. Burns was a founder of the National Conference of Black Lawyers and was best known for representing prison inmates following the 1971 Attica uprising. He was a general counsel to Martin Luther King, Jr., and an attorney for activist Angela Davis. From 1987 to 1994, Burns directed the CUNY Law School, making that institution a leader in public interest law. Gilbert was a founder and Co-Director of the CUNY Law School's Defender Clinic, and a member of the board of directors of the National Conference of Black Lawyers.

I was asked to give the commencement address to the CUNY Law School a month after their deaths, to honor the lives and political legacies of Burns and Gilbert. I told the graduating class of young lawyers that America today represents two conflicting realities, two divided images of what we can become as a society and as a people. There is an elitist version of America, where there are no fundamental social problems, where the best government is one that does absolutely nothing, where everyone who is arrested is presumed to be guilty, and where the legal system punishes only those who have committed crimes.

There is an America of Clarence Thomas, where affirmative action is only "reverse discrimination," where sexism doesn't exist, and where poverty is the fault of those who are poor. There is an America where the people of Colorado can vote, as they did, for a referendum denying lesbians and gay men their constitutional rights, and Supreme Court Associate Justice Antonin Scalia can declare, as he did, that such discrimination is "eminently reasonable." This is an America where inequality is an accepted fact of life, where undocumented immigrants are viewed as threats to national security. This is an America where instances of political inertia or police corruption are never related to the problems of minorities and poor people.

But there is another ideal of what our country can be. That ideal rests on the assumption that all human beings, regardless of their differences—of income, language, culture, religious faith, gender, or sexual orientation—might find genuine opportunity through their own hard work and with help from others, including government. And that ideal rests on the assumption that they might achieve a decent and productive life for themselves and their children.

Gilbert and Burns had a passionate commitment to the concept that the law should be used as a catalyst, to empower those whose voices are often unheard. When the law is used as a means to define the greater public interest, when legal services can be extended to indigent people, or where the law fights for women who are the victims of abuse, the concept of justice becomes real.

One of the greatest legacies of Haywood Burns and Shanara Gilbert is that they understood that justice is not an abstraction from the lives and problems of everyday people. The law can become a powerful force for addressing the contradictions of America's political and economic system—poverty and homelessness, homophobia and anti-Semitism, sexism and racism. When the widest range of people have access to the highest-quality legal education, the democratic ideal comes alive. Burns and Gilbert inspire us to remember that the purpose of the law is not simply order, but justice.

LESBIANS, GAY MEN, AND INEQUALITY

The battle for human equality and social justice knows no color boundaries. Black Americans and Latinos, Asian- and Native-Americans, are all too familiar with the stinging darts of prejudice and bigotry. Yet across this country, the historic opponents of racial and ethnic equality have been sharpening their rhetorical knives against another minority group—lesbians, gay men, and bisexuals.

For decades, homosexuals in the United States have experienced deeply entrenched patterns and policies of discrimination, including expulsion from the armed services, firings from places of employment because of sexual orientation, denial of full legal rights for gay couples, rejection from public accommodations, being denied rental of apartments and other dwellings, as well as less systematic instances of violence and bigotry. Many states have passed so-called anti-sodomy laws targeting homosexuals. The rights guaranteed to all Americans under the Constitution are all too frequently denied to gays and lesbians.

Beginning in the 1950s, lesbian and gay liberation groups arose to call for greater civil rights and political empowerment. In cities such as San Francisco and New York, gays created political associations and quickly became a growing influence inside the liberal wing of the Democratic Party. During the past two decades, seven states and more than a hundred communities throughout the United States passed anti-discrimination laws designed to reinforce and protect gay peoples' rights. These laws never created "special rights" or a uniquely protected status for homosexuals; they only guaranteed them the same basic legal rights all Americans take for granted.

The Reagan administration created a more repressive environment for lesbian and gay rights across the country by encouraging an aggressively homophobic rhetoric at the highest levels of government. Under the Bush administration, this government attitude was augmented as right-wing think tanks like the Heritage Foundation began to take direct aim at the rights of homosexuals. In 1992, a statewide ballot measure in Oregon proposed an amendment to the state's constitution reclassifying homosexuality as "abnormal, wrong, unnatural, and perverse." The measure would have forced all levels of state government to actively discourage homosexuality. This proposal was so controversial and extreme that few believed at first that it could pass. Nevertheless, 43 percent of Oregon's voters backed this hate-filled measure.

In Colorado the same year, conservatives pursued a more clever strategy of hate. An amendment placed on that state's ballot prohibited the passage, by any community or city in the state, of local ordinances to protect gays' and lesbians' civil rights. Advocates claimed they were not trying to suppress the rights of homosexuals, but only wanted to prohibit the definition of lesbians and gays as a protected class or minority group with "special rights." The language of the ballot measure seemed "reasonable" compared to the Oregon initiative. An intense, grassroots mobilization by the Right appealed to Christian groups by declaring that the Bible condemns homosexuality as a sin. Despite overwhelming opposition to the measure from liberal cities such as Denver, Aspen, and Boulder, the amendment passed with 53 percent of the popular vote. Many gay and liberal groups responded by calling for a nationwide boycott of Colorado, a proposal adopted by many city councils and professional associations that had scheduled conventions and activities in the state.

The successful homophobic language of Colorado's amendment was adapted for use in new statewide measures targeting gays and lesbians in at least 10 other states. Conservatives persuaded thousands of voters that they were only voting against "special rights" for lesbians and gays, that they were not really making a statement favoring discrimination against them. This duplicitous tactic continued to be employed until a 1996 Supreme Court ruling overturned the Colorado amendment.

Gays and lesbians were targeted first—because homosexuals were perceived as most vulnerable politically. But what progressives should argue—in Colorado and elsewhere—is that the far Right is trying to destroy the basis for *all* civil rights legislation, not just against gays and lesbians, but against *all* women, people of color, people with physical disabilities, and others. The argument that a "majority" of voters should have the right to take away a minority group's rights is not only false, it is dangerous. We must have the courage to state clearly to the public that *sometimes the majority is wrong.* A majority of white southerners in the 1950s undoubtedly favored Jim Crow segregation laws, and they were wrong. The battle for full human rights for all is not just an issue for lesbians, gay men, Latinos, African-Americans, and other minorities. It is an issue for everyone. If the rights of any single person in our society are in jeopardy, it is only a matter of time before our own rights are destroyed.

Homophobia is a much broader problem, however, than the fear, hatred, and prejudice expressed at the ballot box. It also includes the patterns of violence, oppression, and discrimination used to perpetuate the unequal status of lesbians, gays, and bisexuals within society.

Homophobes excuse their prejudice with many "justifications." Among the most common is the assertion that homosexuality is a "lifestyle choice" or merely a "perverse" form of sexual behavior—an assertion that precludes viewing gays and lesbians as an oppressed minority. In this interpretation, homosexuality is something like having a tan: sometimes you have it, like on vacation or in the summer, and sometimes you don't.

Although homosexuality as a form of human behavior is as old as humankind, orthodox science has perceived lesbians and gay men with the same prejudices as the larger society. Until two decades ago, the American Psychiatric

Association listed "homosexuality" as a type of disease or mental disorder. It was only several years ago that serious scholarship focused on the possible biological and genetic differences that separate heterosexuals and homosexuals.

One critical study was produced in 1993 by J. Michael Bailey, a psychologist at Northwestern University, and Richard Pillard of Boston University School of Medicine. Pillard interviewed 147 lesbians, 115 of whom had twin sisters and 32 of whom had adoptive sisters. Each of the 147 pairs of sisters were raised in the same households. Bailey and Pillard then subdivided the women into three sets: identical twins, fraternal twins, and genetically unrelated sisters. The identical twins, of course, had identical genetic compositions, whereas the fraternal twins had the same genetic relationship as ordinary siblings. Bailey and Pillard discovered that 48 percent of the lesbian or bisexual identical twin subjects had a gay twin; 16 percent of the fraternal twin subjects had a gay twin; but only 6 percent of the lesbian and bisexual subjects had adoptive sisters who were also lesbians. Only 5 percent of the women's brothers were gay.

This study strongly implies that homosexuality is partially a matter of biology and genetic inheritance, as well as, to some extent, the product of environment, cultural identity, and socialization. Results of a similar study by Bailey and Pillard among gay men in 1991 were strikingly similar. Instances in which both brothers were homosexuals were 52 percent for identical twins, 22 percent for fraternal twins, and 10 percent for adoptive brothers.

Bailey and Pillard's studies have immediate and profound implications for the debate over gays and lesbians in the U.S. military, as well as for anti-gay legislation like that approved in Colorado and considered in Oregon. If being lesbian or gay is at least partially due to involuntary inheritance—like the color of a person's skin—then much of the rationale for the conservatives' and evangelical Christians' attacks on homosexuals is undermined. To discriminate against a person for having characteristics over which she or he has no control is irrational and illogical. Part of the liberal justification for the modern Civil Rights Movement of a generation ago was based on this argument: it was both unfair and anti-democratic to stigmatize people of African descent for being born black.

The problem with the liberal thesis is the danger that it seriously underestimates the factors of hatred and violence fueling the reaction against homosexuals. Creating fixed biological castes of "homosexuals" and "heterosexuals" can be translated into permanent political hierarchies of "oppressed" and "oppressors." In a conservative political environment, a reactionary government might even try launching a scientific campaign to isolate the genetic differences between gays and straights, in order to find "a cure for homosexuality."

All of us pay the price for homophobia. Consider the federal government's relative inactivity in combating the AIDS epidemic, which conservatives still characterize as a "gay plague." From the end of 1989 to September 1992, the number of AIDS cases increased by 100 percent, yet the federal budget for AIDS/HIV-related research over the same period grew by only a third. Dr. Anthony S. Fauci, coordinator of AIDS research for the National Institutes of Health, estimates that "fewer than a third" of all "worthy" scientific projects combating AIDS are currently funded. In fiscal year 1992, the U.S. government spent more than three times the amount of money on "Star Wars" military research ($4.2 billion) and more than five times the amount on farm subsidies ($6.9 billion)—payments to farmers for not growing crops—than on all AIDS research ($1.2 billion). The real price for homophobia is hundreds of thousands of newly diagnosed people with AIDS every year.

There has never been any form of prejudice without violence. Institutions of all kinds—from churches and schools, to prisons and financial establishments—perpetuate the reactionary beliefs and policies that deny the fundamental human rights of lesbians, gay men, and bisexuals. Institutional discrimination is both fueled by and tends to exaggerate interpersonal bigotry and harassment. This hatred, while spread throughout our society, has been particularly well studied in educational and military institutions.

According to a 1992 survey of more than 200,000 college freshmen nationwide, conducted by the Higher Education Research Institute at the University of California, Los Angeles, as many as "38 percent of all students surveyed, and 49 percent of the men, said they believed there should be laws prohibiting homosexuality." A similar 1991 poll of male college seniors stated that a third of this group also favored outlawing homosexuality.

On college campuses, conservative college students have organized to oppose or block the adoption of courses on homosexual history and culture as well as efforts to create special residential units for gays and lesbians. Gay student groups seeking official recognition and funding for their organized activities at many colleges often run into difficulties or are banned completely.

Not surprisingly, this climate of hostility and hatred leads directly to harassment, intimidation, and violence. Lesbian and gay students frequently experience harassing telephone calls and notes from straight students. *The Chronicle of Higher Education* recently reported a detailed example of the systematic harassment of one Stanford University student who was merely "thought to be gay." On several occasions, the student's belongings, books, and research materials "were thrown from a third-story balcony of his men-only dormitory." Thousands of lesbian and gay students each year are verbally assaulted and intimidated, and many are even physically attacked. Thousands of gays on many campuses still remain "in the closet" out of fear and peer intimidation. Relatively few colleges have created special programs designed to address the harassment and violence directed against their lesbian and gay students.

Until 1942, no specific rule or regulation barred homosexuals from serving in the American military. The homophobic ban against gays paralleled the Jim Crow segregation experienced by African-American troops, who weren't allowed to integrate units until 1948. Over the ensuing years, a fiercely repressive environment within the military targeting homosexuals affected gays and heterosexuals alike. Thousands of lesbians and gay men were "uncovered" and purged from the ranks with dishonorable discharges. Anyone could sabotage anyone else's career by making allegations concerning his or her sexual orientation. Women in the service who rejected male sexual advances could be threatened with the dangerous accusation of "lesbianism."

Homophobia has become so pervasive in the U.S. military that thousands of gay and lesbian enlisted personnel and officers routinely deny their real sexual orientation. Many preserve their place in the armed forces by resorting to "sham" or "convenience marriages" with people of the opposite sex. A recent *New York Times* article documented the reality of hundreds of such convenience marriages at bases across the country. By marrying, gay soldiers can take advantage of the substantial housing allowance allocated to married personnel. Lesbians and gay men who marry acquire an essential "cover" of heterosexuality, permitting them to survive. President Clinton's "compromise" decision on the military's ban against homosexuals does little to end this pattern of discrimination, covert behavior, and intolerance.

The homophobia of our schools and military is also reflected within our laws and judicial system. As of 1993, 24 states still retained anti-sodomy laws. In 1986, in the notorious *Bowers v. Hardwick* decision, the U.S. Supreme Court upheld Georgia's anti-sodomy law.

An inextricable connection brings all oppressed people together around a fundamental, collective interest. That connection is the pursuit of justice—equal treatment, compassion, and simple human fairness. This does not mean that the grievances of various oppressed people are identical or interchangeable. But the path to African-American liberation has numerous intersections with other movements, especially the struggle for gays' and lesbians' equal rights. Heterosexual black leaders who imply that gay rights are "irrelevant" to black folk must be criticized. We must remind them that gay black men and women are our brothers and sisters, our sons and daughters, our neighbors and co-workers, our lovers and friends. Fighting for equality means equality for *all* human beings.

PRISONS, PROFITS, AND INEQUALITY

The primary response of the U.S. government, elected officials, and the corporate elite to the growing crisis of inequality has been the massive expansion of public and private security forces, and the incarceration of literally millions of black, Hispanic, and poor people. Between 1980 and 1990, the number of police in the United States doubled. As of 1995, 554,000 officers were employed by local and state police forces and legislation signed since then promises 100,000 more. Beyond this, an additional 1.5 million private security officers are currently employed to guard office buildings, stores, affluent neighborhoods, and corporate headquarters all over the country. Private patrol cars now cruise entire communities of middle- to upper-class Americans, whose streets are closed off to outside traffic. Much of the new suburban housing being built today in "planned communities" is surrounded by walls and gates, wired for electronic surveillance, and guarded 24 hours a day by private security personnel.

Even more striking has been the massive expansion in recent years of the U.S. prison system. In 1983, in *How Capitalism Underdeveloped Black America*, I exposed the brutal realities of our criminal justice system and its racist impact upon African-Americans. At that time, more than 650,000 Americans were imprisoned in federal, state, and local facilities. The U.S. incarceration rate was the world's second highest, exceeded only by that of the apartheid regime of South Africa.

By 1996, the U.S. prison population had increased to 1.6 million. In the state of California alone, between 1977 and 1992, the prison population soared from less than 20,000 to more than 110,000. To appreciate this massive scale, one should consider this: the California state prison system—not including the rest of the United States—is the second largest in the world after China's. As of 1992, 344 of every 100,000 residents of the United States were in prison and another 174 were in jail. Every seven years, the number of incarcerated U.S. citizens doubles.

Meanwhile, the prison industry has become one of America's biggest and most profitable businesses. Between 1979 and 1990, prison construction nationwide increased by 612 percent, and annual expenditures for corrections topped $14 billion. More Americans work full-time for the prison industry than for any Fortune 500 corporation, except General Motors. In New York, Governor George Pataki is demanding three new maximum-security prisons by the year 2000, at a cost of nearly $500 million.

According to the Buffalo-based Office of Urban Initiatives, prisons provide tens of thousands of new jobs. In California, prison labor generates $1.3 million in profits each year. Most prisoners are paid subminimum wages, usually $2 or less per hour. In Oregon, inmates are marketed through state-sponsored tours of prisons. Research by Professor Henry Louis Taylor of the State University of New York at Buffalo indicates that 10 percent of Arizona's prison inmates work for private companies at subminimum wages.

The racial oppression that defines U.S. society as a whole is most dramatically apparent within the criminal justice system and the prisons. Today, about one-half of all inmates in prisons and jails—or more than three-quarters of a million people—are African-American. In 1992, of every 100,000 black American males, 2,678 were prisoners. Black men from age 30 to 34 were imprisoned at a rate of 6,299 per 100,000; for younger black men aged 24 to 29, the rate was 7,210 per 100,000.

A recent study focusing on one state by the Center on Juvenile and Criminal Justice in San Francisco, directed by Vincent Schiraldi, offers a devastating perspective on the race and class realities of incarceration. In California in 1995, almost 40 percent of black men in their 20s were imprisoned or on probation or parole on any given day. By contrast, only 5 percent of white males and 11 percent of Latino males in the same age group were enmeshed in California's criminal justice system. Blacks comprised only 7 percent of California's population, but they accounted for 18 percent of those arrested in the state, and over 30 percent of its prison population.

Schiraldi explains that the higher numbers of black men in prison are due to unequal sentencing rates and discriminatory arrest patterns. Other factors include harsh new sentencing laws, the prison construction boom, the absence of decent jobs, and the poor quality of urban education. Many young men who are imprisoned never learn marketable skills that would permit them to enter the labor force. Nationwide, about a third of all African-American males in their 20s are today either in prison or jail, on probation or parole, or awaiting trial.

What does this mean in terms of the typical daily experience of an average black male in the United States? Author Adam Walinsky cites a recent study of African-American men aged 18 to 35 in Washington, DC:

> On any given day in 1991, 15 percent of the men were in prison, 21 percent were on probation or parole, and 6 percent were being sought by the police or were on bond awaiting trial. Thus, the total involved with the criminal justice system was 42 percent. The study estimated that 70 percent of black men in the District of Columbia would be arrested before the age of 35, and that 85 percent would be arrested at some point in their lives.

Washington's racist pattern of arrest is not unusual. In nearby Baltimore on any given day in 1991, 56 percent of the city's African-American males were in jail or prison, on probation or parole, awaiting trial or sentencing, or had warrants issued for their arrest.

These statistical profiles of racial oppression should *not* obscure the class dimensions of who is arrested and imprisoned in the United States. In 1989, more than 14 million Americans were arrested. Today about 2 percent of the total male labor force is in prison. According to a 1991 survey by the U.S. Department of Justice, about a third of all prisoners were unemployed at the time of their arrests. Only 55 percent held full-time jobs. About two-thirds of all prisoners have less than a high school level of education and few marketable skills that would permit them to be competitive in the labor market.

The only solution to the crisis of imprisonment is to honestly address the deeper socioeconomic and political factors that create crime. With few exceptions, people who have full-time jobs at wages that can support families, who own their own homes, and who have access to a decent quality of life do not commit violent crimes. This is not to say that everyone in prison today is a product of an unjust and disruptive social environment. Yet, building more prisons and incarcerating more young people will never end the spiraling rate of crime.

The prisons of the United States are vast warehouses for the poor and unemployed, for low-wage workers and the poorly educated, and most especially for Latino and African-American males. Wealthy and powerful white-collar criminals—management-level embezzlers, stock market cheats, and shady bank directors like those who raked in millions of dollars in the S&L scam—almost never go to prison for the crimes they commit. For the most oppressed, however, prison is ironically an improvement in their life's circumstances, offering at least a low modicum of health care, meals, shelter, and occasionally some modest training programs. Today, there are hundreds of thousands more black men in prison or stuck in the criminal justice system than are enrolled in colleges or universities. A young black man has, statistically, a greater likelihood of being jailed or arrested than he has of obtaining a job that can adequately support himself, a partner, and family.

This draconian reality is what gives Nation of Islam leader Louis Farrakhan such legitimacy and authority among millions of African-Americans today. Many blacks are convinced there is a political and economic conspiracy blocking black advancement within the social order. Most politicians have repudiated affirmative action and the enforcement of civil rights. The young black men of an entire generation have become the central targets of the criminal justice system, and no one within the white establishment seems to give a damn.

CLASS WARFARE IN AMERICA

The most striking event of the 1996 presidential primaries was the emergence of right-wing demagogue Patrick Buchanan as a major candidate for the Republican nomination. Though his threat faded fast, Buchanan's primary and caucus victories in Alaska, Louisiana, and New Hampshire shocked and outraged the Republican establishment.

His eclectic program covers a wide range of themes: trade protectionism, restrictions on legal and illegal immigration, the outlawing of abortion and reproductive rights, opposition to affirmative action, and anti-corporate rhetoric. To some extent, in his right-wing populism, Buchanan is reminiscent of George Wallace, the arch-segregationist governor of Alabama who ran as an independent presidential candidate in 1968. But the key to Buchanan's movement is the growing reality of class warfare within the United States and, especially, the deteriorating status of white workers.

Several interrelated factors have contributed to the sense of crisis among millions of whites. The first factor is the steady decline of real incomes for the majority of working people. In the 1980s, millions of new jobs were created in the U.S. economy, but relatively few were at wage levels that could support families. Low-paying or part-time service work accounted for 85 percent of all new jobs. Nearly 20 percent of all workers had absolutely no health insurance, and two out of five had no pension coverage. Economist Lester Thurow observes that "median household incomes have fallen more than 7 percent after correcting for inflation and family size, to $31,241 in 1993, from $33,585."

The most significant thing about this decline in incomes was that, during these years, the country's per-capita gross domestic product was rising. Moreover, the share of wealth held by the top 1 percent of the U.S. population doubled from what it was only 20 years ago. As Thurow states: "In effect, we are conducting an enormous social and political experiment—something like putting a pressure cooker on the stove over a full flame and waiting to see how long it takes to explode."

Not only have American workers witnessed a decline in their standards of living, but they also face an increasingly insecure and uncertain future. In 1995, a study of employment trends in the metropolitan Chicago area was completed as part of the MacArthur Foundation's Working Poor Project. The study indicated that during the next 10 years, about 140,000 new jobs will be created in Chicago. About half of these jobs will be available to workers with a high school education—but none will pay more than an annual wage of $23,000, which is hardly enough to maintain a family. And the competition for skilled blue-collar jobs will be greater than ever before.

Another factor is the racial dimension of the class struggle. In unprecedented numbers, millions of white people are confronting what many African-Americans and Latinos have known for years—unemployment, poverty, and hunger. A recent study by Isaac Shapiro of the Center on Budget and Policy Priorities documents the growing crisis of non-Hispanic whites. Half of all Americans living in poverty, nearly 18 million people, are white. For white female-headed households, more than one in three are poor. From 1979 to 1991, the poverty rate nearly doubled for white families headed by an individual aged 25 to 34. Whites comprise nearly half of all Americans on AFDC and are the majority of those who receive food stamps. In 1991, 12.6 million whites received Medicaid.

For millions of white Americans, "whiteness" used to mean a relatively privileged lifestyle, a standard of living superior to that of most racial minorities. Now as they lose ground, they are desperately trying to understand why their whiteness no longer protects them. It is in this uncertain economic environment that Buchanan appeals to alienated, angry white workers. To many of them, the American Dream has become a nightmare. Buchanan offers them easy scapegoats—immigrants, blacks, Latinos, welfare recipients, the homeless, feminist and gay/lesbian activists—to explain their misery. But the empty rhetoric of Buchanan won't reverse the class warfare that is destroying millions of U.S. households, including those of whites.

A half-century ago, at the end of World War II, American unions and capital made a bargain. In return for union docility, the corporations agreed to share profits in the form of higher wages and benefits. By the early 1970s, U.S. workers enjoyed the highest living standard in the world. As AFL-CIO President George Meany declared, "We believe in the American profit system."

But as global competition increased, capitalists cut costs, lowering wages and firing workers. Millions of jobs were shipped abroad to exploit low-wage, nonunionized labor. In many factories, occupational safety standards deteriorated, and employees lost many of their health benefits and pensions. But most unions had collaborated with the bosses for so long, they were unable to mount a counteroffensive against the corporations.

When President Reagan smashed the air traffic controllers' union during its 1981 strike, he sent a clear message to the corporations that union-busting was on the immediate agenda. By 1987, nearly three-fourths of all contracts covering 1,000 or more workers included wage concessions. Approximately 200,000 workers abandoned their unions through decertification elections in the 1980s. By the end of the decade, union membership had declined to

16 percent of the American labor force. Workers lacked an effective, progressive labor movement that could fight for higher living standards.

But perhaps the major reason millions of American workers feel betrayed is the widespread wave of corporate layoffs. In the 1990s, as Wall Street stocks reached all-time highs and corporate profits soared, millions of workers were thrown out of work. In December 1991, General Motors announced that it was firing 74,000 workers. Barely one year later, Sears fired 50,000 employees. Soon other corporations began to fire thousands of workers to improve their profitability. In 1993, Boeing dismissed 28,000 workers, Philip Morris cut 14,000, and IBM slashed 60,000 jobs. The next year, Delta Air Lines announced 15,000 layoffs, NYNEX cut 16,800 jobs, and Scott Paper fired over a third of its total workforce, more than 11,000 people. In January 1996, AT&T Chief Executive Officer Robert Allen, whose annual salary was $3.3 million, announced that his corporation was firing 40,000 employees.

Who can expect American workers to feel any loyalty to companies that are concerned only with profits and not people? Corporate executives pay themselves millions of dollars in salaries, fringe benefits, bonuses, and stock options, while millions of people are losing their jobs. In 1975, the average chief executive officer of a corporation received about 40 times the salary of an average worker. Today that ratio has jumped to *190 times as much.* The typical CEO of America's 100 largest corporations receives about $900,000 in annual salary and $3.5 million in overall compensation.

We need governmental policies that create jobs and promote income growth for working people. One essential step toward that goal is the reallocation of government expenditures from wasteful military spending to the social and economic infrastructure that makes productivity possible. We urgently need to make massive public investments in housing, streets, highways, railroads, bridges, hospitals and clinics, and public schools and universities to create new jobs. The noted scholar Seymour Melman, Chairperson of the National Commission for Economic Conversion and Disarmament, observes that 750,000 additional jobs would be created "if $165 billion were transferred from the military to education, transportation, environment, housing, etc. If an additional annual $80 billion, raised by restoring 1980 tax levels on the super-rich, were spent on conversion, an additional 2.5 million jobs could be created."

It is time that we placed the welfare of working people and their families ahead of the corporations, the powerful, and the privileged.

STRONG BLACK WOMEN

VIOLENCE AGAINST AFRICAN-AMERICAN WOMEN

A specter of violence threatens African-American women at every level of our society. Black women can experience violence individually at work, on the street, and in the home. They also can experience violence collectively through large institutions and social systems, such as the criminal justice system and prisons, social organizations, and within the economy. In either case, what creates a context for the violence is the deafening silence that meets our sisters when they are abused, violated, and murdered. Crimes against black women are not taken seriously within our society, and we black men have not done enough to check our own behavior and to challenge sexism within our communities, to end the pattern of violence.

The most under-reported violent crime committed against women of color is rape. For the National Women's Study, funded by the National Institute on Drug Abuse, more than 4,000 adult women were interviewed about rape in 1990 and 1991. The researchers found the number of rapes in the United States to be more than five times larger than the National Crime Survey had estimated and reported. Police statistics seriously underestimate instances of rape and other violent crimes against women. The National Women's Study estimated that more than 12 million women have been rape victims at least once. Almost 62 percent of them were attacked when they were minors. About 29 percent were attacked when they were younger than 11 years old.

Most of us do not want to admit how widespread violence is within our communities. About half of all women in the United States will be victims of domestic violence at some point in their lives. In 1990, for example, there were almost 45,000 cases of domestic violence in New York City alone and more than 88,000 cases of family violence throughout New York state.

Women are also subject to violence at their places of employment. Murder is the leading cause of death for women at work, according to a study completed by the National Institute for Occupational Safety and Health in 1991. The risk of being killed by accident on the job is much greater for males than for females, but the risk of being murdered on the job is much greater for females. Forty percent of the women who die on the job are victims of murder. That's a significantly higher proportion than the comparable figure for men, which is only 10 percent.

The pattern of violence against women must be seen in the broader political context of the federal government's assault on the poor. The Republican-controlled Congress has targeted poor women by fighting proposals to increase the minimum wage. The political assault on welfare has been framed in the public discourse in starkly racial terms, as if virtually all women receiving public assistance are black and Latina and live an "affluent lifestyle." But, according to economist Julianne Malveaux, nearly half of all women on public assistance also do some kind of paid work, usually at less than $5 an hour. The actual AFDC payments can vary dramatically, from $613 a month for a woman and two children in California to only $121 a month for that same family in Mississippi. And in racial terms, the largest single group of welfare recipients, as of 1992, was not black or Latina, but white.

Perhaps the most pervasive form of institutionalized violence committed against women is represented by the criminal justice system. A comprehensive statistical overview of the status of women in prison has been compiled by the Justice Works Community, a Brooklyn-based, nonprofit project that serves women prisoners, former prisoners, and their families. The project's research shows women to be the fastest-growing population in U.S. prisons and jails. As of 1994, approximately 90,000 women were incarcerated throughout the United States. From 1980 to 1990 the number of women in prison increased by 300 percent.

The vast majority of black women who are in prison are the mothers of dependent children. About 40 percent of all women prisoners were either sexually or physically abused prior to their incarceration. While 75 percent of women prisoners are serving sentences for nonviolent offenses, the remaining women, those convicted of violent crimes, were usually charged with offenses against a spouse, relative, or acquaintance. Many of these women, especially black and Latina women, were only defending themselves against an abusive partner.

What is the cost of this massive incarceration of women in the criminal justice system? In a New York state prison for one year it is $30,000; in a New York City jail, the cost is $59,000 per prisoner. Hundreds of millions of dollars nationally are spent to warehouse women prisoners, a massive waste of both human and financial resources.

We need to look at alternatives to incarceration and prosecution, such as community service, employment assistance, job training, alcohol and drug treatment, health care, and mental health services. In effect, for black and Latina women, prisons and jails are the first responses by the state and by those in authority to social problems like family violence, poverty, and addiction.

But even more important, we need to break the African-American community's silence about violence against women—the devaluing of black womanhood in our homes and neighborhoods, at the workplace, in our courtrooms, in social service agencies, in the political arena, and at virtually every level of society. As the Institute on Violence has stated, "Violence is part of a larger system of power, control, and domination that devalues all of humanity." Sexism, racism, class exploitation, and other forms of inequality and domination reinforce each other, shoring up a structure of oppression that is subtle as often as it is overt. We need to recognize the ways in which violence against black and Latina women is a manifestation of inequalities based on gender, race, and class.

We cannot create a movement that frees or liberates black people on the basis of race if we acquiesce in the violence and patterns of oppression experienced by black women, which are rooted in gender inequality. Inevitably and inextricably, such patterns of domination reinforce each other. Our vision must be one of a society in which social relations are not coercive or exploitative, where our children are freed from the shackles of hunger, fear, and poverty, and where our sisters are not victimized by the dynamics of rape, domestic assault, and homicide.

BLACK WOMEN IN POLITICS

Election year 1992 was widely described by political observers as the "Year of the Woman." Thousands of women—of all races and ethnicities—ran for elective office for the first time. The number of women in the U.S. House of Representatives increased from 29 to 47, and in the U.S. Senate from two to six. Women gave Clinton 46 percent of their votes, providing a major share of his electoral victory. The "gender gap" also existed within the black electorate. According to exit polling data, 86 percent of all African-American female voters chose Bill Clinton, compared to only 77 percent of black male voters.

A new influx of African-American women entered Congress, including Eddie Bernice Johnson of Texas, 56 years old, a businesswoman with prior political experience in the state house and state senate; Cynthia McKinney of Georgia, a 37-year-old college instructor who had served in the Georgia State Legislature; educator Corrine Brown of Florida, 45 years old, who had served in the state house; and businesswoman Eva Clayton of North Carolina, 58 years old, with prior political service as a county commissioner. But the year's biggest story was the victory of 45-year-old attorney Carol Moseley-Braun, an Illinois Democrat elected to the U.S. Senate. Moseley-Braun became the first African-American elected to the Senate in nearly two decades and the first black woman to serve in the Senate in U.S. history.

This increase in women's political power encountered strong resistance and criticism from the media and other quarters. Women's groups were harshly criticized as "bean counters" by President-elect Bill Clinton when, during the transition period, they demanded a greater share of his administrative appointments, especially at the upper levels. More serious was the barrage of criticism aimed at Carol Moseley-Braun.

The criticisms ranged from her personal behavior to her political decisionmaking. Critics noted that Moseley-Braun had sold her "modest" South Side home in Chicago, moving into a $3,300-a-month penthouse apartment, while members of her campaign staff had not yet received paychecks. She vacationed with Campaign Manager and "boyfriend" Kgosie Matthews, who had been paid $15,000 per month during the campaign, and who was accused of sexual harassment by several women working for Moseley-Braun. While key staff positions had gone unfilled throughout December, her remaining staff, according to press reports, was "busy planning lavish parties for her swearing in." The *Chicago Sun-Times* editorialized: "Where is Carol Moseley-Braun? Moseley-Braun's conspicuous absence during a vital transition period—her unavailability to answer questions or to detail plans—raises questions among her most ardent supporters about her dedication to the job." Although Moseley-Braun campaigned for high office attacking the Senate Judiciary Committee's handling of Anita Hill's allegations during Clarence Thomas's confirmation hearings, she curiously expressed no interest in serving on this vital Senate committee.

Another prominent African-American woman under press attack following the election was Johnnetta B. Cole, President of Spelman College, who had served as head of the Clinton transition team on education, labor, and the arts and humanities. Dr. Cole is perhaps black America's most prominent and successful leader in the field of higher education. But when Dr. Cole was rumored to be under consideration as a candidate for secretary of education, she came under furious assault and McCarthyist criticism from several quarters. The Jewish publication *Forward* attacked Dr. Cole for being favorable to Fidel Castro for her work years ago as a member of the national committee of the Venceremos Brigades, a group sponsoring friendship trips to Cuba. Dr. Cole was also accused of being pro-Palestinian. Within days, CNN, the *New York Times*, the *Washington Post*, and other publications were running similar stories. The assault was so distorted and vicious that even black moderate journalist Carl Rowan, a strong anti-communist himself, came to her defense.

What the attacks on Dr. Cole and Senator Moseley-Braun had in common was that they were directed at prominent, dedicated, and articulate African-American women who were climbing into positions of power. Moseley-Braun's errors of judgment are indeed minor compared to the sad and sorry public and private records of many white male senators. Moseley-Braun and Cole were attacked primarily for racial and gender reasons, make no mistake about it. And the real tragedy is that the majority of African-American public leaders, politicians, and educators stood by silently while these gifted, hard-working women were being vilified by the white media and white officials. We need to understand that the empowerment of *all* African-American people requires the support and defense of strong black women.

THE LYNCHING OF LANI GUINIER

Lani Guinier is one of the most talented, intelligent, and capable scholars of civil rights law in America. As a professor at the University of Pennsylvania Law School, she tried to bridge the racial divisions among students. As a civil rights litigator, she stands firmly in the tradition of Charles Hamilton Houston and Thurgood Marshall, as a champion for equal rights. Without question, she would have been the ideal choice for Assistant Attorney General for Civil Rights, the post to which President Bill Clinton appointed her in the spring of 1993. Yet Lani Guinier was the victim of a carefully orchestrated campaign of character assassination by the extreme Right and, in the moment of truth, was betrayed by the administration she had sought to serve.

What were the basic charges leveled against Guinier? In brief, conservatives initiated their attacks by terming Guinier the "Quota Queen." Clint Bolick, protégé of William Bradford Reynolds, the Reagan administration's assistant attorney general for civil rights, claimed in the *Wall Street Journal* that Guinier favored racial quotas and wanted to impose what he described as a "racial spoils system" that would "further polarize an already divided nation." Nothing was further from the truth. Guinier sharply opposed strict racial quotas.

Others condemned Guinier as an enemy of democracy and majority rule because she had endorsed so-called radical reforms in the political process. What radical reforms? Guinier has endorsed proportional representation, or cumulative voting, in certain instances in which minorities are unable to receive equal access to representation within the current political process. Cumulative voting is, in fact, far more democratic than the current one-person, one-vote system used throughout the United States. For example, in a city with seven city council districts, each voter now has one vote in one district; with a cumulative voting system, each voter would instead have seven ballots, which could be cast in any combination for any individual candidate or group of candidates. Such a procedure would encourage multiracial coalition-building across neighborhood lines and break down the racial gerrymandering by electoral districts that often occurs.

Then conservatives charged that Guinier was "radical" because she had argued that majority runoff requirements in primaries may violate the 1965 Voting Rights Act. The conservatives who criticize Guinier on this point fail to observe that John Dunne, the Bush administration's Assistant Attorney General for Civil Rights, agreed with Guinier's interpretation, asserting that runoff elections in primaries are like "electoral steroids for white candidates."

William T. Coleman, Jr., a prominent black Republican and civil rights lawyer, has observed that "much of the criticism of Ms. Guinier is nothing more than a disagreement with current law" on civil rights. Many of the suggestions in Guinier's writings that were dismissed and smeared as "radical," Coleman notes, were "adopted by the Department of Justice in the Reagan and Bush administrations." Far from being outside the mainstream, it was Lani Guinier's critics and attackers who were at the fringes of political and intellectual legitimacy.

At the moment of truth, however, President Clinton, Guinier's friend of two decades, betrayed that friendship and his own political principles by pulling her nomination from the Senate Judiciary Committee. Clinton's behavior was nothing less than weak-kneed and spineless. At first, he proudly crowed about her nomination to black constituents. Then, as the right-wing assault and mountain of lies spread, the president became increasingly cautious, hiding once again behind Attorney General Janet Reno. Finally, when "neo-liberal" publications such as *The New Republic* came out against Guinier, the pressure became just too much for the white southerner to handle.

Even reactionary and racist commentators such as Patrick Buchanan understood that Clinton's failure to support Guinier's nomination was political stupidity. By abandoning Guinier and by not permitting her to defend herself before the Senate subcommittee, Clinton alienated his core political base and showed a failure of political courage. An articulate explication of her ideas could have persuaded a majority of senators, fresh from the embarrassing situation of the Thomas-Hill hearings only two years before, to confirm Guinier. Clinton failed to comprehend that it is always better to fight for your principles—especially when your principles are worth fighting for.

IN DEFENSE OF ANGELA DAVIS

More than a quarter-century ago, African-American scholar/activist Angela Davis first came to public attention. The young philosophy professor was dismissed from her faculty position at the University of California, Los Angeles, in June 1969 by California Governor Ronald Reagan. The "grounds" for her dismissal had nothing to do with her scholarship or teaching effectiveness, both of which were outstanding. Davis's membership in the U.S. Communist Party—and her public commitment to black liberation— were the basis for purging her from higher education.

Less than one year later, FBI agents charged her with involvement in a shoot-out in a California courtroom that led to several deaths, including those of a judge and a member of the Black Panthers, 17-year-old Jonathan Jackson, the younger brother of the revolutionary prisoner George Jackson. Davis was named one of the country's "Ten Most Wanted Criminals." Once captured and imprisoned, she was constantly harassed and victimized. But a massive international campaign erupted in her defense. Throughout the world, the name of Angela Davis came to symbolize the racist nature of the U.S. criminal justice system and the naked political suppression of radicals within American society. In June 1972, after nearly two years of imprisonment, a California jury declared her innocent of all charges.

Since then, Davis has continued her commitment to political activism and scholarship. Since leaving the Communist Party several years ago, she has become a leading member of the Committees of Correspondence, a democratic and socialist organization involved in progressive political activism.

In 1995, a scurrilous and vituperative attack against Angela Davis, reminiscent of the demagoguery of the McCarthy era, surfaced again in California. That January, Davis was named to the University of California Presidential Chair by the university's President, Jack Peltason. Within days, State Senator Bill Leonard, a Republican, launched a vicious attack on the appointment. Leonard declared that Davis "was part of trying to create a civil war between whites and blacks." Several California newspapers joined the assault. One op-ed piece in the *Sacramento Bee* described Davis's work as "vulgar anti-Americanism and banal economic reductionism." Editorial writer Peter Collier demanded to know,

> Would those who think she deserves to be honored
> with a Presidential Chair also agree that someone such
> as Tom Metzger or David Duke should be given a ten-
> ured position? Is hiring a Stalinist such as Davis to
> teach social policy any less disgusting than finding a
> Nazi to teach eugenics?

This attack against Angela Davis is a smear against her outstanding record as a scholar and leading progressive intellectual. Her contributions to the literature of race, gender, and class in America have placed her at the very center of multicultural scholarship. Experts in the field appreciate her theoretical and historical work and unanimously praise her intellectual insights. Students and supporters of Professor Davis soon began a counteroffensive in favor of her appointment to the Presidential Chair, linking their activity to a defense of affirmative action, which was also under attack in California and throughout the country. Certainly, Davis should be supported on the grounds of academic freedom and the right of anyone, within any university, to the free and unrestricted expression of critical ideas from any political perspective.

The larger issue at stake transcends the personal example of Angela Davis. Throughout the United States, the far Right has consistently targeted black intellectuals and prominent progressive scholars representing the African-American community. Mass conservatism recognizes that it must delegitimate all potential and real voices of progressive opposition, within the academy and throughout society. The far Right seeks to wage ideological war on scholars advocating the principle of human equality.

The defense of Angela Davis is once again on our agenda, and we are challenged as never before to raise our voices in protest. For if scholars like Davis, who is committed to democratic activism, women's rights, and black equality, are silenced or removed from their jobs, it is only a matter of time before other progressives, from whatever sector of society, are targeted as well.

KENDRA ALEXANDER, FREEDOM FIGHTER

One of America's foremost advocates of human equality, social justice, and peace, Kendra Alexander, died tragically on May 23, 1993, in a terrible fire that destroyed her home in Berkeley, California. For the thousands of political activists and progressives across the United States and throughout the world whose lives she touched, her unexpected death evoked deep and profound sadness.

Alexander was born in 1946 and raised in Los Angeles. Her involvement in the black liberation movement began in 1965, when she joined the Congress of Racial Equality (CORE) to register African-American voters in Louisiana. Enrolling in Los Angeles State College, the young militant then joined W.E.B. Du Bois Clubs, a multiracial socialist youth organization. Like Angela Davis, Alexander developed commitments that led her to join the U.S. Communist Party. During these years, she also met and married Franklin Delano Alexander, another respected African-American activist.

Throughout the 1970s and 1980s, Alexander acquired a national and international reputation as one of this country's most influential progressives. She was a key leader in defending Angela Davis after her unjust imprisonment. She was active in peace, labor, and anti-racist organizations. Most outstanding, perhaps, was Alexander's extensive work in the anti-apartheid movement. She helped to establish the Bay Area Free South Africa movement and successfully supported San Francisco dock workers who refused to unload South African cargo in 1984. The late South African liberation fighter Chris Hani was a friend and trusted acquaintance of the Alexander family.

I first heard of Kendra Alexander during these years, long before we became friends. Like many other African-American leaders before her—such as Du Bois, Paul Robeson, and Benjamin Davis—she had become attracted to the politics of socialism. Alexander understood that racial discrimination and the fundamental inequalities suffered by African-Americans and other people of color were inextricably linked to the institutions of power, privilege, and private property within our society. To take a stand against racism and to affirm the equality of all human beings, Alexander believed, also meant an opposition to the economic exploitation of all working people.

Alexander rose in the national leadership of the Communist Party and was elected to that body's Central Committee. As disagreements grew within the party, Alexander became identified with demands for greater democracy and freedom of political expression. Because of her strong opposition, she was removed from her leadership position.

In 1992, hundreds of northern California activists resigned from the Communist Party in protest, Alexander and Davis among them. In July, many of these activists joined forces with independent progressives, trade unionists, feminists, blacks, and Latinos to create a new organization—the Committees of Correspondence. Alexander and I were elected national co-chairs of this formation.

Over the next year, I came to admire and respect Alexander. Within the national leadership of the Committees of Correspondence, she was clearly the most argumentative, insistent, and challenging member of our group. She was intelligent, dedicated, and always humorous. She never hesitated to let you know what she thought, or where she stood politically. And like many other strong black women I have known, she always argued the most with those whom she loved most deeply.

At the time of her death, Alexander was employed as a legislative aide to Berkeley City Council member Maudelle Shirek. She was instrumental in bringing together people from a wide range of political traditions and experiences into a unified organization. But the central reality of Alexander's entire public career was her strong love for black people and her deep desire to serve all of humanity.

She hated poverty and wanted to end it. She despised racism and sought to uproot it. She witnessed hunger and homelessness, and worked to abolish it.

Kendra Alexander's politics were guided by real feelings of love—for the children in her neighborhood, for the rights of all workers, for African-American people fighting for equality, and for all who continue to sacrifice and struggle for democracy everywhere. Black America has lost a great defender and powerful political advocate, a brave and gifted woman who personified the willingness to take a stand for freedom. And those of us who were Alexander's closest friends and associates will always remember the love she so tirelessly gave to all of us.

RETHINKING THE ABORTION DEBATE

With the appointment of Clarence Thomas to the U.S. Supreme Court in 1991, it seemed to be only a matter of time before *Roe v. Wade*, the landmark decision that liberalized this nation's laws concerning abortion, would be overturned by the court's conservative majority. The battleground would subsequently shift to the states, as "pro-choice" and "right-to-life" forces battled for the hearts and minds of the American public on this sensitive and emotional issue. Fear of *Roe*'s imminent reversal has faded with President Clinton's two court appointments, but the public debate over abortion will not die.

Much of the problem with this debate, I believe, is the narrow and confrontational manner in which issues have been framed. The media tend to refer to "pro-choice" advocates as being "pro-abortion," as if their activism favors the termination of most pregnancies. Many pro-choice supporters believe very deeply that abortion is *not* just another form of birth control, no more and no less. They understand that there is no abortion without human tragedy. The decision is never easy, and those who are tempted to claim otherwise trivialize and distort the issue. From the perspective of black history, the issue of state-funded abortions always raises the question of reproductive rights for low-income women and the terrible history of forced sterilization imposed on African-American women over many decades. As a pro-choice supporter, I recognize that these issues aren't as clear-cut as our allies sometimes claim.

Some right-to-life supporters advance the argument that the relative accessibility of abortion promotes attitudes of sexual promiscuity among young people. Certainly, irresponsible sexual behavior can culminate in unwanted pregnancies. Yet the solution suggested by these right-to-lifers, that banning abortions will reinforce abstinence and sexual "morality," makes absolutely no sense. Blaming abortions for casual sexual behavior and unwanted pregnancies is something like blaming dentists for tooth decay. Nevertheless, pro-choice defenders should recognize that many thoughtful and progressive citizens have deep personal reservations about abortion, at least in their own lives.

The real issue beneath the "pro-choice" versus "right-to-life" debate is whether our society can balance two distinct ideals. The first is the human right of procreative freedom, which includes the right to decide whether or not to have children, how many children to have, and how they should be nurtured. The second ideal is the value of social responsibility, the right of every society to set guidelines for human development, interaction, and growth. No freedom has ever existed without responsibilities and constraints. To insist upon a procreative doctrine that claims the absolute freedom of sexual expression without regard to the health or well-being of one's sexual partners or others, and the freedom of childbirth and nurturing without external checks, would be potentially destructive.

In this country, however, such constraints on procreative freedom are usually a function of one's race, gender, or income. Gender is obviously the most fundamental criterion for accountability. A male who unintentionally impregnates a woman is rarely compelled to pay child support, let alone physically co-reside and nurture first the fetus for the nine months of gestation and then the child from after its birth until its maturity. Women who are poor, unemployed, and/or nonwhite usually have relatively few options if they have unwanted pregnancies. An unplanned pregnancy can be a devastating economic event for the single, jobless female who is existing below the poverty line. The wealthy, white businesswoman who becomes pregnant will still retain many options, even if *Roe* is overturned. She will have sufficient funds and professional contacts to locate a gynecologist to make available to her the "morning-after pill" or to terminate the pregnancy medically. But an African-American or Latina woman from a working-class family—or the victim of incest or rape in Appalachia, perhaps—will not have the luxury of these alternatives. Once more, we will witness the terrible tragedy of the medical butchers of women returning to the alleys and side streets, taking advantage of their newfound opportunities with Roe's reversal.

The call for "right-to-life" is dishonest unless it considers the larger human context. We have all heard the arguments about the absolutist "right-to-life" of the human fetus. But what about the "right-to-life" of the child once she or he enters the real world? What of the right of all children not to starve? The right to decent, accessible health care, quality education, and decent shelter? Certainly the concept of right-to-life, the sanctity of human creation and existence, ought to require some rethinking about the death penalty. Why do many political conservatives advocate the rights of the "unborn," yet anxiously relish the thought of having other human beings executed when adult?

Within our culture, human sexuality is best expressed in loving, constructive relationships and in the context of social responsibility. Such relationships may be heterosexual or homosexual, and they may sharply differ in character and composition from those in traditional, patriarchal households. The key point is that household relationships that are not supportive and loving tend to be less nurturing for children.

Real procreative freedom balanced by social responsibility requires the preservation of safe abortions as an essential option, combined with more extensive sexual education. Without this option, a two-tiered system for terminating pregnancies will be the result—unsafe and brutal for the poor, minorities, and working people; safe for the privileged few. But our long-term obligation is recognizing the inescapable link between procreation, abortion, and the destructive effects of poverty, ignorance, and powerlessness.

So long as several million Americans live in the gutters and streets, 1.6 million Americans are incarcerated in prisons and jails, and millions more are unemployed, underemployed, or illiterate, the necessity for abortions will be greater. Create an environment that is less socially and economically destructive, a context for building loving relationships that are not based on violence or fear, and over time the number of abortions will be reduced. Let us resolve the abortion debate by doing more to support parenting and to make caring, loving relationships possible.

SECTION THREE

EDUCATION AND AFRICAN-AMERICAN YOUTH

A MESSAGE TO BLACK YOUTH

The black revolutionary writer Frantz Fanon once asserted that each generation, out of relative obscurity, must discover its own destiny. Then it has a choice: it may fulfill that destiny or betray it.

How can today's rising generation of African-American young people come to terms with their own destiny? What is the meaning of the challenges and opportunities that history has planned for them? What kind of ethics or moral anchor is required for group empowerment and collective advancement?

As a historian of black America, I know that the question of values and ethics is inextricably connected with memory and collective experience. What we can know about ourselves and how we define our own aspirations is informed by what we believe has been the meaning of our historical and contemporary experience. What we believe we can accomplish as individuals is often prefigured by the dimensions of community, by our sense of connection and responsibility to others, and by the values that inform the ways we treat others and expect to be treated in return.

As the years progress, what young women and men will discover is that the most lasting and rewarding educational experiences come not from specific information provided in classroom lectures or assigned textbooks, but from the values obtained in active engagement in meaningful issues. We achieve for ourselves only as we appreciate the problems and concerns of others—and only as we see our own lives as part of a much greater social purpose.

Philosophy as a discipline tells us about the search for meaning—why are we here, and what is the point of our existence? As African-American young people, you must ask hard questions of yourselves. What are the problems and pains, the struggles and challenges of my world, however that world is defined—from my block in my neighborhood to the global village of the planet? How can my skills, my intellectual gifts, my knowledge and training, be of some service to others in that community? How can my voice speak for those who are denied a voice in our society—whether by poverty or disease, by hunger or homelessness, by race, gender, sexual orientation, or physical ability? We can find real meaning in the work we perform when our efforts empower others, generating new human possibilities and new visions for those who do not have the opportunities we take for granted.

The Quakers have an expression: those who would fight against social injustice, those who take a stand for human freedom and equality, must "speak truth to power." So I would urge African-American young people, no matter what education you may attain, or vocation you pursue, or social, religious, and political affiliations you may have, to "speak truth to power." If you go forward to law school or professional school, acquiring skills of advocacy and technical information, speak truth to power by applying those credentials to a fearless examination of inequality and social injustice. If you become a teacher, teach in a manner that will empower your students to recognize oppression and racism, to liberate themselves from bigotry and inequality. If you become a journalist, writer, or poet, use your creative talents to unearth the cultural roots of contemporary social problems.

Speaking truth to power means standing for a set of principles and acting courageously, finding your own voice, struggling with joyful hope and a deep love for the promise of humanity. To continue our collective commitment to the struggle for freedom and equality, to revive the vision of Martin and Malcolm, is the generational challenge for young African-Americans.

YOUTH VIOLENCE AND GANGSTA RAP

I was sitting in my study, and the music from the bed-room of my younger daughter, Sojourner, descended down the steps. Over the dull hum of my electric typewriter, I could hear the menacing words of the popular rap artist Dr. Dre: "Rat-a-tat and a tat like that/Never hesitate to put a nigga on his back." In other words, the lyric urged young African-Americans to murder each other.

That's exactly what's happening to our young people throughout America. "Gangsta rap"—the music of Snoop Doggy Dogg, Dr. Dre, and company—only articulates the epidemic of violence in our streets, schools, and neighbor-hoods. In predominantly black Washington, DC, for exam-ple, in a three-year period (1988-1990), the number of juvenile homicide arrests nearly tripled. And elements of our young people's popular culture dangerously glorify vio-lence.

According to the Bureau of Alcohol, Tobacco and Fire-arms, there are more than 280 million guns in the United States; 2.5 million were purchased in just one recent year. The easy availability of guns is the central reason that fire-arms are the leading cause of death for black men between the ages of 15 and 24. If the next six years follow the same pattern, more black men will be murdered by other black men than the total number of U.S. troops killed in Viet-nam. That's nothing short of a war.

But this proliferation of violence is not just a black phe-nomenon—it affects whites, Latinos, Asian-Americans, and others. The number of juvenile murders has almost dou-bled over the past decade, and the rate of juvenile violent crime rose during the same time by over 40 percent. Ac-cording to the National Center for Juvenile Justice, a Pitts-burgh-based research institute, the murder-arrest rate among all children between the ages of 10 and 17 more than doubled, from 5.4 arrests per 100,000 population to 12.7 per 100,000. In 1991, 5,356 young people under age 19 were killed by firearms, or nearly 15 each day. Thou-sands more are wounded by firearms.

What are the economic costs of this epidemic of violence? According to the National Association of Children's Hospitals and Related Institutions, it costs more than $14,400 to treat each child struck down by gunfire, as of 1991. That's more than what it costs to pay for tuition at many four-year private colleges. That's hundreds of millions of dollars—not counting the emotional and social devastation to tens of thousands of families.

Our federal and state governments have responded to this crisis by addressing the symptoms, rather than the root causes, of youth violence. The congressional response has been to provide billions of dollars to hire new police officers and to extend the federal death penalty to cover 52 new offenses. At the state level, the laws have been changed to judge youth violence by adult standards. Legislators in several states have amended the laws in order to prosecute as adults teenagers as young as age 14. But changing these laws, building more prisons, and hiring thousands of additional police won't halt the violence.

Violence is only partially a question of values. We have to find creative ways to get our children and young people to resolve their differences in nonviolent ways. We have to get young people to respect themselves and to realize that when people of color murder and maim each other, only our oppressors' interests are advanced.

But that is not enough. Neither Latinos, nor African-Americans, nor poor people produce or profit from the proliferation of firearms in our communities. Neither do we reap the bulk of the massive profits from the international drug economy.

We must continue to crusade for drug-free zones in our communities, schools, and workplaces. We must target the collusion and complicity of the police against people of color in the economics of drugs. And we must condemn the false assertion that the racist death penalty in any way addresses the crisis of crime and violence in urban America.

As Marian Wright Edelman, leader of the Children's Defense Fund, has observed: "The deadly combination of guns, gangs, drugs, poverty, trauma, and hopeless youth is turning many of our inner cities into zones of destruction and despair." She adds, "I promise you that many of those youths will be shooting at *us* tomorrow. No gate will be high enough to protect us."

MINORITY SCHOLARSHIPS AND HIGHER EDUCATION

Over the Christmas holidays of 1994, I spent several days with my oldest daughter, Malaika, helping her to complete the admissions forms for colleges. A high school senior, Malaika was busily contemplating her options, just like a million other teenagers at that time of the year. Her criteria for considering one school over another included a review of the curriculum, the core requirements for graduation, the percentage of minorities on campus, and the range of cultural and social activities.

My criteria for considering colleges, like those of millions of worried parents, begin with finances. The tuition, room, and board costs for public colleges have more than doubled in the past dozen years. Most of the better private universities and colleges now charge far more than $20,000 each year for tuition, room, board, and fees. As the price of higher education soars, its accessibility to black, Latino, and low- and middle-income families declines. Back in 1975, about 32 percent of all African-Americans of college age, from 18 to 26, were enrolled in colleges and other post-secondary programs. Fifteen years later, the percentage of college-age African-Americans enrolled in such programs had fallen to 28 percent.

There are three basic ways to pay for a college education: loans, work-study, and scholarships and grants. Borrowing money to obtain an education is usually necessary, but it burdens students or their parents with debts that may take years to pay off. Work-study programs are an excellent way for students to earn their own money while enrolled in college. But work-study programs funded by federal dollars are often limited, and students usually can generate only a small part of their tuition.

Only about 2 percent of all scholarships are designated for minority students. Relatively few African-American students are awarded grants or scholarships that permit them to attend college without financial obligations. Yet in 1994, the U.S. Court of Appeals in Richmond ruled that the University of Maryland had no right to offer a scholarship program limited to African-American students. The decision was prompted by the lawsuit of Daniel J. Podberesky, a white man claiming Hispanic heritage, who had applied for Maryland's Benjamin Banneker scholarship and been rejected. Podberesky insisted that the scholarships should be made available to others. Unsuccessfully, the University of Maryland pointed out that only 30 students received Banneker scholarships annually and that the award had been created to compensate for past racial discrimination.

Millions of whites insist that minority scholarships are a form of "reverse discrimination," imposing unfair and unequal standards that penalize innocent whites. If this is so, then how do we explain the hundreds of thousands of scholarships, grants, and policies for whites in higher education that deliberately and systematically exclude blacks?

Many elitist colleges practice an admissions policy favoring "legacies," or the children and other descendants of alumni. At Harvard University several years ago, for example, about one-tenth of the prospective undergraduates applying for admission were legacies, and more than 40 percent of those who were finally admitted were legacies. At many universities, star athletes are given special consideration for admission, and standards for high school grade point averages and scores on standardized tests are reduced or eliminated.

As a 1994 *New York Times* article observed, most scholarships are designed for very special interests having little to do with ending discrimination. Here are just a few examples: Harvard University's Baxendale, Borden, Pennoyer, and Murphy scholarships may be awarded to any student with one of those surnames. Reed College's Opal Weimer TICE scholarship is "for a young woman who was a Girl

Scout for three years or more." Valparaiso University's Martin Luther Award gives $1,000 to $3,000 scholarships only to the "dependents of full-time Lutheran church workers." Juniata College gives four scholarships to "left-handed students with financial need." The University of Houston at Victoria awards full tuition and fees to "children of disabled firefighters and peaceofficers."

My daughter is entering college at a moment in history when programs for equal opportunity are being eliminated and when the national commitment to uproot racial discrimination is all but extinguished. A college education remains a prerequisite for a better life, especially for African-Americans and other people of color. As we fight for minority scholarships and related programs, we expand the basis for democracy and racial equality.

RACISM ON COLLEGE CAMPUSES

Throughout the United States, there has been an upsurge of racism in recent years, characterized by attacks against affirmative action and by the efforts of the Republican-controlled Congress to reverse programs and policies favoring minorities. But some of the most blatant examples of racial prejudice within society today can be found at universities and colleges.

Racial attitudes on U.S. college campuses began to worsen in the mid-1980s. Across the country, incidents of what seem to be racially motivated random violence, harassment, and intimidation of black, Latino, and Asian-American students by whites have been on the increase.

In the spring of 1986, the Kappa Sigma fraternity's chapter at the University of Wisconsin at Madison sponsored a party featuring what was termed a "Harlem room." Fraternity members wore black-face makeup and Afro-style wigs. Fried chicken and watermelon were served, and ugly graffiti were painted on the walls. The following year, also at the University of Wisconsin at Madison, the Phi Gamma

Delta fraternity held a "Fiji Island" party highlighted by a caricature of a black man with a bone through his nose. In the fall semester of 1988, the same university's Zeta Beta Tau fraternity featured a "mock slave auction," in which members donned Afro-style wigs and black-face makeup. These events at the University of Wisconsin sparked widespread condemnation on the campus as well as throughout the country.

Researchers in race relations began to suspect that these incidents represented a broader national trend, which university officials and law enforcement authorities had largely ignored. In 1987, the Baltimore-based National Institute Against Prejudice and Violence began to collect documented cases of racial harassment and violence against minorities on college campuses. From the fall semester of 1987 through the fall semester of 1990, about 300 campuses reported racial incidents.

Just a short list of such incidents is both sickening and shocking. At the University of Illinois at Chicago, in May 1990, a penis severed from a medical school cadaver was hung outside the door of an African-American female residence hall counselor. At the University of Texas at Austin, in April 1990, African-American students protested after one all-white fraternity painted a racist epithet on the trunk of an automobile and another fraternity printed a racist image on its T-shirts. At Teikyo Loretto Heights University in Denver, a dozen Japanese students were harassed and pelted with eggs, and several racists even urinated in front of them in public. At Brown University, students received hundreds of computer-printed fliers urging them to "keep white supremacy alive." At the State University of New York at Oswego in October 1989, racist and anti-Semitic epithets were written on the walls of the campus library, the student union building, one dormitory, and the walls of an underground tunnel.

White students who felt aggressively hostile to blacks and other minorities also began to demand the termination of courses in African-American studies and of a multicultural curriculum emphasizing diversity and tolerance. They argued that whites had become the "new minorities" on college campuses and insisted that "reverse discrimination" had relegated them to a second-class status. At Temple University in Philadelphia, a group of militant whites established a white student union, which for a time claimed 150 members. At the University of Florida in Gainesville, a group of angry whites also established a white student union, which called for the abolition of minority scholarship and internship programs. The white student union quickly established contacts with Tony Bastanzio, a former Imperial Wizard of the Ku Klux Klan, to help organize similar groups at campuses across the state.

Today it is estimated that one out of four minority students becomes a victim of racist harassment, intimidation, and/or violence. Wherever I travel across this country, hundreds of African-American students give accounts of instances of racist notes passed under their dormitory doors or of white college professors who crack racist jokes during their lectures.

But in general, patterns of campus racism are not primarily the blatant acts of bigots, nor are they racially motivated random violence. Far more important are the intricate patterns of discrimination that marginalize blacks, Latinos, and other students of color in campus life. Student government associations often do not adequately fund programs and events promoting cultural diversity. Deans' offices may emphasize the recruitment of minority students, but often do little to ensure their retention.

The only way to begin to reverse the trend toward further racial discrimination is to foster an environment of pluralism and diversity within educational institutions. This would include changes in the curriculum and required courses to reflect multiculturalism and the full richness of diversity within our society. It would mean supporting scholarship programs to increase access to college for blacks and Latinos, and increasing the numbers of minority faculty and administrators within white universities. Without vigorous efforts, the prevailing racist stereotypes and prejudices that are being allowed to grow on college campuses threaten the prospects for educational equality for African-Americans and other people of color.

EQUAL ACCESS TO HIGHER EDUCATION—
THE CASE OF MISSISSIPPI

Will black public universities in Mississippi survive into the 21st century? The U.S. Supreme Court's 1996 refusal to block the enactment of new admissions standards for that state's public universities threatens to destroy equal access to higher education for black residents. The new requirements being implemented might ultimately eliminate a half of the total enrollment at Mississippi's three predominantly black state-supported universities.

We need to remember the history of segregated education in the South to acquire a proper perspective on the current controversy. For generations, blacks were denied access to white schools; their teachers were paid much less than whites, and their school texts and educational materials were usually substandard. Jackson State University, Alcorn State University, and Mississippi Valley State University were created, in part, to preserve racial segregation in higher education. Yet despite their limited financial resources, these schools performed remarkably, providing access to quality education to tens of thousands of poor and working-class black people. Today, about 60 percent of all African-American students in the state attend these three institutions.

In 1992, the Supreme Court ruled that the state of Mississippi had to dismantle its dual system of education, which had set different standards for black and white admission to the state's eight public colleges. Under the new rules, any high school graduate with at least a 3.2 grade point average is automatically admitted to any of the state colleges. Students with a 2.5 average may be enrolled if they also score at least 16 on the American College Test, or ACT. Those students with a 2.0 grade point average are required to score at least 18 on the ACT. Of all high school graduates in Mississippi, 79 percent of whites score 16 or higher on the ACT; only 30 percent of all African-Americans score at this level.

With these new admissions guidelines, thousands of black people will be refused admission to the historically black colleges. Enrollments for the fall of 1996 may be 20 to 30 percent lower than in 1995. Jackson State President James E. Lyons stated that a "decrease of 500 students, a possibility for this fall, would cost the university $2.5 million."

Combined with the recent *Hopwood* decision in the U.S. Court of Appeals for the Fifth Circuit, the Mississippi case symbolizes the cynical manipulation of "race" in order to push blacks' educational opportunities backward. In the *Hopwood* decision, the court ruled that race could not be used as a factor in admitting students. Educator Elias Blake, Jr. astutely observed that the *Hopwood* case "is the closing of the doors to the elite universities and graduate and professional schools at the top." The Supreme Court's refusal to block the new admissions criteria in Mississippi "is about closing the door for the mass of blacks at the bottom."

All educators know that standardized tests don't tell us everything about the intellectual potential of students. If young people are taught for 12 years in substandard public schools, with limited resources, they will probably be less competitive in standardized tests. Using a single, arbitrary admission standard for everyone in effect penalizes young people who come from impoverished backgrounds and poor school systems. If a single standard is to be used for the sake of educational opportunity, then let it be applied equitably to all. For example, a more democratic method of college admissions would be to accept the top 20 percent of all graduating seniors from every high school in the state, based on the same grade point averages. Black and poor students who are valedictorians at their schools might score lower on the ACT than whites from privileged backgrounds who only have 3.0 averages. But hard work and merit should be rewarded equally at state-supported institutions, regardless of the unequal conditions for learning at public high schools.

What is absolutely certain about this latest educational controversy is that it has little to do with improving the quality of learning in the state of Mississippi and everything to do with destroying educational access and opportunity. We will not eliminate racism in our universities by pretending that "race" as a barrier to opportunity no longer exists, and that an arbitrary standard can be applied to groups with very different cultural, social, and political histories. In the interests of fairness, we must ironically use "race-conscious remedies" in the short run to eliminate racism in the long run.

JIM CROW AND THE BROWN DECISION REVISITED

The 40th anniversary of the decision in the case of *Brown v. Board of Education* was an occasion to recall the day in May 1954 when the Supreme Court, by a unanimous vote, outlawed racial segregation in America's public schools. From 1896 until that day, the *Plessy v. Ferguson* decision had justified strict racial segregation in thousands of school systems across the country. As we look back at that historic struggle to overthrow Jim Crow education, it is important that we examine both the strengths and the limitations of the *Brown* decision, particularly as we try to understand the meaning of "multiculturalism" and to uproot institutional racism today.

The legal foundations to overturn *Plessy* were drafted in the early 1930s under the leadership of Charles Hamilton Houston, a brilliant and intense law professor at Howard University. Over two decades' time, Houston and his gifted protégé, Thurgood Marshall, successfully attacked and challenged racist laws and regulations.

The *Brown* decision actually covered a basket of cases that had been brought to the Supreme Court. The "Brown" in this case was Linda Brown, a seven-year-old African-American girl living in Topeka, Kansas. She was forced to cross railroad tracks in a switching yard to attend the black school across town, while an all-white school was only blocks from her home. Linda's father, the Reverend

Oliver Brown, sued the Topeka school board, demanding that his daughter be admitted to the nearest elementary school.

One tactic employed by Thurgood Marshall and the NAACP Legal Defense Fund was the use of sociology. They presented the research of Kenneth Clarke indicating that racial segregation and stereotyping created an inferior sense of self-worth and psychological damage among young African-Americans. Clarke's original study had examined the impact of Jim Crow on schoolchildren in Washington, DC and New York.

But probably the most important single factor in the victory over school segregation was the presence of Earl Warren as Chief Justice. President Dwight Eisenhower named Warren to the court to replace Chief Justice Fred Vinson, who had generally favored separate-but-equal laws. As Republican Governor of California during World War II, Warren had ordered thousands of Japanese-American citizens into internment camps, but he was sharply opposed to racial segregation. His wartime willingness to suspend the civil rights of Americans of Japanese descent did not apply to the black schoolchildren of the South.

Warren used his influence among court members to consolidate a unanimous decision to outlaw *Plessy*. On May 17, 1954, speaking for the entire court, Warren declared:

> Does segregation of children in public schools solely on the basis of race, even though the physical facilities and other tangible factors may be equal, deprive children of the minority group of equal educational opportunities? We believe it does. To separate them from others of similar age and qualifications solely because of their race generates a feeling of inferiority as to their status in the community that may affect their hearts and minds in a way very unlikely ever to be undone. We conclude, unanimously, that in the field of public education the doctrine of "separate but equal" has no place.

Eisenhower was outraged by Warren's courageous decision, later lamenting that the California Republican's selection as Chief Justice was "the biggest damn fool mistake I ever made."

In the *Brown* era, liberal educators and social reformers argued that Jim Crow segregation was designed to perpetuate inequality. A half-century ago, the most glaring examples of inequality in the public schools were the sharply different material conditions that separated the races in terms of teachers' salaries, instructional materials, and the basic conditions of learning. In many southern states, the expenditures-per-pupil ratio between white and black students was four to one, or even greater. Black teachers would normally receive half or a third of the annual salaries of white public school teachers.

High schools in northern cities, such as Chicago and St. Louis, frequently denied admission to African-American students, at least up until the Great Depression. Older textbooks, used for years by white students and filled with outdated and even erroneous information, were distributed to black elementary and secondary schoolchildren. Black high schools, where they did exist, frequently did not have courses in physics, calculus, chemistry, or foreign languages. The equipment in the biological sciences was inadequate and often nonexistent. Within this Jim Crow learning environment, it is hardly surprising that many African-American students lagged behind their white counterparts.

We are frequently told that Jim Crow education is a thing of the past. But a study by the Harvard Project on School Desegregation illustrates how far we have retreated as a society from the vision of equality and social justice articulated by Dr. Martin Luther King, Jr. and the Civil Rights Movement.

In academic year 1991-1992, 66 percent of all African-American students and 73 percent of all Latino students attended predominantly minority schools. This was the highest concentration of black people in de facto segregated schools in nearly a quarter-century. The largest increases in racial polarization of public schools were found in Michigan, Maryland, New Jersey, Connecticut, Tennessee, and Alabama. The lowest proportion of whites in schools attended by African-Americans was found in New York state.

Gary Orfield, the chief researcher in the Harvard Project, was pessimistic about his finding: "The civil rights impulse from the 1960s is dead in the water."

One example of the continuing burden of racial inequality in our schools is found in Connecticut, the nation's wealthiest state. Today, the enrollment in 140 of the state's 166 school districts remains 90 percent white, with 80 percent of the African-American and Latino students concentrated in 10 percent of all school systems. As of October 1992, the public schools in Hartford, the state's capital and largest city, had an enrollment that was 93.1 percent minority. Across the Connecticut River in East Hartford, the public schools were 38.1 percent nonwhite. But the percentages in the public schools of Hartford's other suburbs was strikingly different: 7.6 percent nonwhite students in Newington, 6.7 percent in Wethersfield, 17.2 percent in West Hartford, and 8.3 percent in Glastonbury. Statewide, African-American and Latino students comprise more than one-fourth of the state's total public school enrollment.

For nearly 30 years, efforts have been under way to deracialize Connecticut's public schools. In 1966, a voluntary desegregation plan called "Project Concern" was initiated and 266 black inner-city students traveled daily to the white suburbs. Project Concern sent counselors to answer the questions of black parents whose children participated in the program. By 1969, about 700 children had taken part in Project Concern, which received federal, state, and foundation funding.

But problems surfaced almost immediately. Project Concern soon encountered severe budgetary problems. By the late 1970s, Project Concern reached nearly 1,200 children in 12 grades. But by 1992, enrollment had fallen to less than 700. Critics correctly called it an example of racial tokenism. Creating a one-way street for black children into the white suburbs perpetuated the illusion that integration in the classroom was identical with academic excellence. It did nothing to transform the curriculum or the dynamics of learning.

In April 1989, civil rights proponents filed a lawsuit on behalf of Hartford's black schoolchildren, *Sheff v. O'Neill*, charging that Jim Crow conditions existed in the public schools. To foster educational equality will require a fundamental change in how education is financed, and an infusion of capital and resources into predominantly minority schools.

We celebrate the *Brown* decision as a decisive blow against the totalitarian system of racial prejudice. *Brown* reinforced the concept of equality for all under the law. But in fairness to history, we must also recognize *Brown*'s limitations. Since 1954, we've found that *Brown* didn't end segregation, nor did it create integration. And we've found that integration itself is not the answer.

Providing a seat for a black child in a formerly white school does not, by itself, alter curriculum or course content of that school. It doesn't change the racial composition of the teachers and administrators of a school system. It doesn't challenge the Eurocentric, ethnic, and gender biases that underscore traditional pedagogies and systems of learning. The logic of *Brown* implied that blacks could not learn as well within an all-black environment—but the history of African-Americans proves that this is not true.

We must make a critical distinction between "desegregation" and "integration." The cultural assumptions behind *Brown* favored integration, the upward mobility of blacks within the so-called cultural mainstream. What we have learned since 1954 is that neither racial segregation nor integration *per se* creates the conditions necessary for an exchange of values and learning experiences between children of different backgrounds. The framework that respects the diversity of all people is not "integration," the loss of black identity, but "multiculturalism"—the full respect for our social differences while maintaining our political unity as American people. The *Brown* decision was only the beginning, not the end, in a long struggle to make a genuine democracy in the United States.

RICH SCHOOLS VERSUS POOR SCHOOLS

In 1988, George Bush promised the American people he would become "the Education President." Bush's Education Secretary, Lamar Alexander, liked to boast that the United States spends a "significant" amount of the national wealth on public schools. Yet in reality, the Reagan and Bush administrations waged a 12-year war against the promise of educational equality. The chief casualties in this assault against public schools were minorities and the poor.

First, let's separate Bush's educational polemics from actual programs. According to a recent report of the Paris-based Organization for Economic Cooperation and Development, U.S. spending for education lags behind the majority of western industrial nations. Out of 20 industrial countries, the United States ranks only 13th in its per capita public spending for education. Smaller countries like the Netherlands, Norway, and Denmark invest far more in their schools than we do. Children in Japan attend school nearly 60 more days each year than their American counterparts and score much higher in math and science than American young people at all ages. Japanese schools have a dropout rate of only 10 percent, compared to 27 percent in the United States.

America's largest urban school districts spend about $5,200 per pupil, which is nearly $1,000 less than suburban schools spend per student. But what's even more significant than the difference in funding levels is how these monies are allocated and the racial and class profile of the students who are being served.

The 47 largest urban school systems are all located in cities with more than 250,000 people. They have disproportionately large populations of color and many students with special needs. And although these schools are responsible for only 13 percent of the nation's total school enrollment, they have 32 percent of all Latino children and 37 percent of all African-American students. They also have 25 percent of all children living below the federal government's poverty line and 32 percent of all students with limited English ability. Such schools must spend more on health services, instruction in the English language, and remedial educational programs than suburban schools. Less money is left over for teachers' salaries, textbooks, libraries, new equipment, and computers.

By contrast, suburban schools not only have more money to spend, but they are also able to allocate their resources more generously on the tools that make learning possible. They spend $506 per student more than large city schools on classroom instruction, especially on books and reference works.

Why did the Bush administration do so little to close the fiscal disparity between struggling urban schools with deteriorating tax bases and the comfortable suburban schools that draw their students from the middle and upper classes? There's no question that race is a major reason for these differences. Fewer than one in four students who currently attends large urban school districts is white. The 47 largest city school systems only educate 5 percent of the country's white children. Perhaps this is the reason Bush could ignore the fact that less than 40 percent of urban students entering their junior year can do basic algebra. If a president's racial politics include Willie Horton and bashing affirmative action, it is not surprising that his agenda is "color blind" to the education difficulties of the inner-city.

Education is one of the few bridges that exist to help lead people from poverty, homelessness, and illiteracy toward a better life. We need to broaden that bridge with massive federal initiatives to improve the quality of ghetto schools, giving millions of black, Latino, and Asian-American youth a better chance for opportunity and equality.

NEW DIRECTIONS IN BLACK PUBLIC SCHOOLS

A generation ago, black educators and civil rights leaders were convinced that the desegregation of public schools would improve the quality of education for black students. The "separate but equal" concept was outlawed by the Supreme Court's *Brown* decision in 1954. Subsequently, the percentage of black southern schoolchildren attending schools that were at least half white increased dramatically, from 2 percent in 1955 to 45 percent by the 1970s.

But in the past two decades, progress toward improving black public education has been reversed. In many northern school systems, desegregation was thwarted by the mass migration of millions of white families from the central cities to the suburbs. Even in those cities where integration took root, the evidence that black children actually benefited from the experience was questionable. For example, an educational task force in Milwaukee reviewing the test scores of 15 high schools, 14 of which were integrated, found that African-American students achieve an average score of 24 on a reading examination, compared to the white students' average of 58. This implies that factors other than racial integration, such as income and parental involvement in the educational process, are more decisive in predicting student performance.

The crisis for black inner-city children in the public schools has finally reached such proportions that many innovative programs have been started to address their problems. One creative approach has been to launch supplemental educational projects within African-American churches. In 1987, the National Science Foundation agreed to fund an after-school tutorial project in 800 black churches located in 17 cities. The church-based project offers field trips to urban museums and science career days, manuals for helping parents teach their children basic scientific and mathematical concepts, and an introduction to the use of personal computers. In Chicago alone, more than 500 inner-city churches have initiated supplemental educational programs during the school year in math, science, and computer skills. During the summer of 1991, 10 churches ran similar programs involving 500 black and minority children. The Chicago projects also bring in professionals in the fields of math and science to serve as "mentors" to children, and invite speakers to talk about opportunities in these fields.

Other projects of this type throughout the country have added a humanities component, usually including an awareness of African-American history and culture, a discussion of personal ethics and moral values, and dialogues on social responsibility. Perhaps the best example of this trend is "Project Spirit," initiated by the Congress of National Black Churches and funded, in part, by the Lilly Endowment and the Carnegie Foundation. Project Spirit is a nine-city network of churches offering an after-school program to black children, featuring African-American history, moral teachings and spirituality, as well as science and mathematics. The Community Foundation of Southeastern Michigan has provided financial support to a similar project in Michigan involving more than 40 African-American churches.

Some educators have begun to argue that the high rate of failure for African-American youth in the public schools is attributable more to the structure of the curriculum and to the absence of a program instilling rigid discipline and self-respect among the students. The chaos outside the boundaries of the schools, the drugs and black-against-black violence permeating the African-American community, could not be kept out of the public schools unless they were radically transformed. Black educators have for decades argued that inner-city young men, frequently living in single, female-headed households, lacked black male adult role models in their lives. Examples of such men who were also integrally involved in their education might point black male teenagers and children onto more constructive paths.

In recent years, several schools in Baltimore, Miami, New York, and other cities have experimented with all-black-male classrooms in coeducational public schools. Most of these attempts have included alternative teaching methods, the direction of a black male teacher serving as a stern disciplinarian and role model, and a curriculum reflecting "Afrocentrism"—heavily focused on African-American and African history and culture.

But such projects are controversial—not least because of their sex segregation, which is prohibited by Title IX of the Federal Education Amendments of 1972. In Milwaukee, two Afrocentric public schools scheduled to open in 1991 were forced by school administrators to open their doors to girls as well as boys. In Miami, a proposal for an all-male school with an Afrocentric curriculum was canceled when the U.S. Department of Education warned that the school would be in clear violation of Title IX.

Black educators in Detroit had an even more ambitious and controversial proposal to save young black males and improve the quality of education. Dr. Clifford Watson, a black elementary school principal there, proposed the creation of three Afrocentric grade schools, involving 560 inner-city boys. The proposed names of these schools—Malcolm X Academy, Marcus Garvey Academy, and Paul Robeson Academy—were chosen to reinforce racial pride and cultural consciousness. The curriculum was designed to emphasize Afrocentric values and heritage; special Saturday classes and tutorials would be offered in specific subjects. Anchoring the concept would be the presence of articulate and culturally aware black male educators, serving as mentors, instructors, and disciplinarians. In the proposal, the Robeson Academy was to be all-male, with the other schools making this transition over a period of time. In February 1991, the Detroit school board reviewed the controversial proposal and approved it by a vote of ten to one.

Opposition surfaced from several quarters. The American Civil Liberties Union (ACLU) and the National Organization for Women (NOW) Legal Defense Fund went to federal court that August and blocked implementation of the plan, fundamentally on the grounds that it specifically discriminated against black female students. Howard Simon, Executive Director of the Michigan branch of the ACLU, argued against Watson's approach: "There is clearly a crisis, but the crisis is all urban schoolchildren. These schools may open up a whole new world for these boys. That world should be open to girls too."

Watson countered in television interviews that the manifestations of this urban crisis were particularly devastating to young black males, who comprised the overwhelming majority of those engaged in criminal activity and violence in the city, and 90 percent of all students expelled from the school system. Black feminists and others aligned with

NOW's Legal Defense Fund and the ACLU, according to Watson, were either "Uncle Toms" or the active agents of white supremacy.

Where some Afrocentric educators such as Watson err is in their argument that a system of instruction that specifically excludes black females will contribute constructively to an environment in which young black males can be saved. A coeducational setting could accomplish even more, all things being equal. Young black males could be challenged to interact with their sisters not from the basis of male chauvinism, but with respect. They could begin to acquire the values essential to a responsible approach to social relations, including sexuality and childraising. By segregating their project on the basis of gender, these educators indirectly contribute to the tensions and contradictions already creating problems between black males and females—which goes directly against the interests of the African-American community as a whole.

On balance, however, Watson's overall proposal merits serious consideration and support. As long as young blacks are unaware of their own history, literature, culture, and our political contributions to democracy, no genuine dialogue with whites is possible. Ethnic pride, self-awareness, and a seriousness of purpose in the classroom can help to end the violent and self-destructive behaviors of many African-American young people.

DIVERSITY AND DEMOCRACY IN HIGHER EDUCATION

The central social dilemma in American history has been the effort to reconcile a vast spectrum of cultures, classes, and communities—groups classified or identified by gender, sexual orientation, religion, and race—into a common political project called democracy. That uneven and often interrupted dialogue and debate have taken many forms: the abolitionist movement of the 19th century; the suffragist movement; the struggles for an eight-hour day and the right to organize collectively; the Second Reconstruction, the massive movement of nonviolence and civil disobedience led by Martin Luther King, Jr.; the renaissance of the feminist movement; and the Stonewall riot and the emergence of a gay and lesbian rights movement. These are only some of the examples of movements that began with the category of "difference," as defined both by ourselves and others, and from that site of identity and culture articulated a vision of what political society can and should be. At times, this dialogue has been civil and cordial; at other times, it has become violent and unpredictable when the exchange of perspectives and attitudes has completely broken down. The Los Angeles civil unrest of 1992, which resulted in the arrests of more than 20,000 people and the destruction of more than $1 billion in property, represents the collapse of the democratic dialogue. Instead of communication constructing bridges and opportunity and mutual understanding across the boundaries of class and color, a fault line appeared, revealing a deep social chasm within the fabric of society and fostering even greater alienation and anger among the oppressed.

How can the educational system create frameworks for understanding the tensions between diversity and democracy? Perhaps the place to begin is with Langston Hughes, the poet laureate of Harlem and black America, who constantly explored the love/hate relationship our people have felt toward American democracy:

I, too, sing America

I am the darker brother.
They send me to eat in the kitchen
When company comes,
But I laugh, and eat well
and grow strong.

Tomorrow,
I'll be at the table
When company comes.
Nobody'll dare say to me,

"Eat in the kitchen,"
Then.

Besides,
They'll see how beautiful I am
And be ashamed.

I, too, am America.

Hughes offers a powerful perspective on what the democratic project should be about. It isn't expressed in Jefferson's eloquent yet incomplete democratic arguments in the Declaration of Independence or in Lincoln's Gettysburg Address. When students are introduced to voices such as Hughes's, they learn about democracy from another perspective, not from the top down, but from the bottom up.

"Difference" is coded in any number of ways: by race and ethnicity, by gender and sexual orientation, by social class and income, by physical disability. The concept of difference seems to imply that some people are defined as the "norm," and that others occupy a space somewhere on the periphery. From this perspective, "overcoming difference" means forgetting about the real variations among human beings, trying to make those who are on the outside more acceptable, more "normal," like those on the inside. So a generation ago, liberal educators praised their black students when they exhibited the same behaviors or spoke the same language as their white students. Dwelling upon differences between people or groups was certainly divisive. Race was something to be overcome, or at least ignored. If blacks, Latinos, and other people of color could only manage to blend into the normal habits and customs of mainstream society and stop acting "differently," racial distinctions could disappear. Liberal educators viewed racism as a product of ignorance, rather than a logical social consequence of patterns of inequality and institutional discrimination.

But the category of difference in itself doesn't tell us much about why American society works the way it does. All Americans are, in certain respects, "different" from everyone else. But not *all* Americans have been routinely denied bank loans, refused accommodations in hotels, or had their houses of worship burned to the ground just because they were "different." Difference has social significance only when it tells us how and why certain groups have been denied basic economic opportunities and political rights while others have not. If we approach the study of diversity simply as an uncritical celebration of all cultures, we don't answer any of the real questions at the heart of the crisis in American democracy.

Let's think about the meaning of difference by looking for a minute at the issue of race. Most scholars agree that race has no validity as a biological or genetic concept. Race is a social construction, a product of ideology, prejudice, and power. For African-Americans, their consciousness of themselves was forged, in part, in the crucible of slavery and segregation, in the struggle for freedom. Identity, which is in a real sense the understanding and embracing of those things that make us unique, is the way we find our own voice. For oppressed people, for people who have experienced legal discrimination, the search for identity is a way to create culture and find meaning within the larger world.

Euro-American ethnics who came to this country certainly experienced hardships and in many instances, as in the cases of the Irish, Italians, and Jews, extreme intolerance and prejudice. Yet each successive group of Euro-Americans eventually was assimilated into the racial mainstream of whiteness. As the wonderful work of historian David Roediger points out, from its beginning America was a racialized society, where immigrants achieved socioeconomic and political empowerment by claiming the status of whiteness. As Roediger observes, "Working-class formation and the systematic development of a sense of whiteness went hand in hand for the U.S. white working class." Noel Ignatiev's recent historical study also explores "how the Catholic Irish, an oppressed race in Ireland, became part of an oppressing race in America." Although anti-black racism was the dominant paradigm for institutional discrimination, Asian-American, Latino, and Native-

American identities are all partially historical and cultural products of exclusion, segregation, the denial of full political rights, and economic exploitation.

Like African-Americans, Asian-American immigrants have experienced a profound encounter with discrimination. As early as 1854, the California Supreme Court ruled that Chinese immigrants weren't permitted to testify against whites. In 1882, the Chinese Exclusion Act banned all immigration from China. As Japanese immigration to the United States grew, discriminatory legislation was extended to include them. In 1913, California prohibited aliens who were ineligible for citizenship from owning property. The 1924 National Origins Act barred most Asians from migrating to the United States. With the outbreak of World War II, 110,000 Japanese-Americans were relocated to internment camps. It was only in 1952 that Asians born outside of the United States were permitted by law to become citizens. African-Americans have not been alone in their search for a nonracist democracy.

Conversely, the study of racial and ethnic realities today illustrates profound differences among minority groups. Most blacks and Latinos have continued to be subjected to severe socioeconomic discrimination and are under-represented in many professions, but many Asian-Americans are not. According to census surveys, in 1989 the median household income of Asian-Americans was $36,100, compared to $30,400 for non-Hispanic white households, $21,900 for Hispanic households, and $18,100 for African-American households. According to the Census Bureau's *1987 Survey of Minority-Owned Business Enterprises*, the number of Asian-American-owned businesses in the United States grew from 187,691 in 1982 to 335,331 in 1987, an increase of 79 percent. By 1987, about 6 percent of all Asian-Americans owned a business of some type, compared to 6.5 percent of all non-Hispanic whites, 2 percent of all Latinos, 1.5 percent of all African-Americans, and 1 percent of American Indians.

Similarly, in terms of access to higher education, there are also real differences among minority groups. Although African-American and Latino college enrollments reached 1.4 million and 1 million, respectively, by 1993, both were

heavily under-represented in terms of their general populations as compared to whites. Between 1976 and 1992, the
number of African-Americans who received both master's
and doctoral degrees actually declined. Conversely, during
these same years, access to higher education for Asian-
Americans increased significantly. From 1976 to 1993, the
number of Asian-Americans enrolled in colleges and universities soared from 198,000 to 724,000. In the academic
year 1992-1993, Asian-Americans received more doctorates
(1,580) than either African-Americans (1,350) or Latinos
(830), and earned more professional degrees (5,160) than
either blacks (4,100) or Latinos (2,980). So, while the overall proportion of degrees earned by racial ethnic minorities
has sharply increased, the actual status of individual
groups varies significantly. These statistics may explain
why Latinos and African-Americans overwhelmingly support affirmative action programs and minority scholarships
in higher education, while a large percentage of Asian-
Americans do not.

A curriculum for diversity must do more than relate the
individual stories of these racial ethnic minorities. It must
integrate their cultural perspectives, divergent socioeconomic experiences, and political histories into a broader,
richer discussion of the commonalties and differences
among cultures and values, the tragedies and triumphs in
the making of American society. There is a creative tension
between particularity and universality as we make the connections among these groups in literature, art, music, the
development of family and kinship networks, and a host of
other areas. But where tension and honest dialogue exist,
where there is recognition of difference and commonalty,
the environment for learning is extraordinary.

*   *   *

The "politics of diversity" is never easy on a college campus. At Columbia University, for example, the academic
year 1995-1996 will be remembered as "the year of ethnic
diversity." After a series of slow negotiations over several
years, Columbia students favoring the adoption of courses
and programs in ethnic studies initiated protests against

the administration. In early February 1996, demonstrators briefly occupied the office of Columbia Dean Austin Quigley. On April 1, four students announced the beginning of a hunger strike to force the administration to establish an extensive ethnic studies curriculum and program. Student organizers had already distributed an "Ethnic Studies Manifesto," which presented an articulate and well-conceived argument for their demands. The Manifesto called for the establishment of a Department of Ethnic Studies within the School of Arts and Sciences and for

> the reconstitution of the so-called Core Curriculum, which supports white supremacy by way of a Eurocentric academic program, to significantly include philosophies, literature, music, and art of ancient African, Asian, Native American, and other non-European peoples.

Columbia's administration was not unsympathetic to the basic argument that its traditional Eurocentric curriculum and academic programs had to be transformed. In fairness, over the preceding decade, more resources and support had been extended toward the enrichment of cultural diversity at Columbia than in its entire history. In 1986, there had been only five academic courses in topics relating to African-American Studies, and only six courses on Latin America, all within the Department of Spanish and Portuguese. In 1993, the Institute for Research in African-American Studies was established, and the undergraduate program in the African-American experience was expanded. Within three years, the number of majors and concentrators in African-American Studies rose from zero to more than two dozen. In academic year 1995-1996, the African-American Studies curriculum offered nearly 50 courses through 10 departments, and there were also more than 30 courses offered in Latin American Studies-related topics. Columbia College's 75-year-old Core Curriculum was also modified to reflect a greater appreciation of multicultural themes.

The essential difficulty for the administration was that its efforts to revise the curriculum on multicultural grounds had done little to address the growing field of Asian-American Studies. For nearly 50 years, Columbia had offered an Asian humanities curriculum, but these programs in East and South Asian culture and languages only indirectly addressed the cultures, social development, and history of people of Asian descent in the United States. In the 1980s and early 1990s, as the number of Asian-American students at Columbia grew rapidly, the demand for courses and faculty reflecting their own experiences increased. By academic year 1994-1995, Asian-Americans comprised 18 percent of the college's student body, but Asian-American Studies had no full-time faculty and offered only four courses.

As the conflict intensified, students revised their demands, calling for the establishment of the "Department for the Study of African, Asian, Latino and Indigenous Peoples in the Americas," for participation in the process of hiring faculty, and for changes in the Core Curriculum. On April 5, Columbia University President George Rupp responded personally in an open letter, emphasizing that Columbia would continue to marshal "significant scholarly and curricular resources toward continuing and further developing our study not only of European but also of African, Asian, and Latin American traditions in the United States." Their disagreement was essentially about "the means to that end." Rupp explained that there was "no likelihood of significant support" for a department of ethnic studies, adding, "Nor do I personally consider that proposal the most effective way to reach the goals we share."

By the ninth day of the hunger strike, Columbia administrators thought they had achieved the basis for ending the confrontation. The college's Committee on Instruction formally approved the establishment of a Latino Studies major and announced that it had "made progress" in developing Asian-American Studies. A small group of faculty believed that they had reached a tentative agreement with some student leaders. But by the afternoon of April 9, a core group of students remained unwilling to compromise. Hunger striker Marcel Agueros, a Columbia College senior, characterized the administration as "ridiculous and disrespectful to us and our cause." At 4:30 pm, about 150 students occupied the rotunda of Low Library, completely shutting off all access to the building. At 11:00 the next morning, New York City police entered the building, and students were warned that they would be subject to arrest as well as disciplinary action by the university if they refused to leave. After 10 minutes, police began their arrests, and 22 people were taken into custody. The following day, about 30 students received letters warning them of pending disciplinary action due to their involvement in the Low Library occupation.

The arrests seemed to polarize the campus. Hundreds of students who had been apathetic or uninvolved in the campus debate over diversity became sympathetic toward the demonstrators. On Thursday evening, April 11, several hundred students seized control of Hamilton Hall. Many influential voices, both inside and outside Columbia, immediately urged the administration to come down hard against the campus dissidents and to restore order, even at the price of more arrests. Instead, President Rupp wisely decided to pull back from the confrontation and offered the students a process for a negotiated settlement. Several faculty known to be sympathetic to the students' concerns presented the administration's proposal. After some debate, the students agreed to negotiate with the administration. For the next 48 hours, Hamilton Hall remained occupied, as negotiations continued.

By Monday, April 15, a tentative agreement had been reached, which essentially represented the most liberal position the university administration was prepared to accept. In brief, the agreement called for the appointment in 1997 of two new tenured faculty who would serve as the directors of the Asian-American Studies program and Latino Studies program. A junior, tenure-track appointment would be made in Asian-American Studies, and a fundraising effort would be undertaken by the university for a tenure-track Latino Studies scholar. Students would be "actively involved" in all search committees, including interviewing candidates and making recommendations for finalists. Both programs would be allocated physical space on campus, which could possibly include "their transformation into a center of ethnic studies." Students involved in the campus protest would "not be expelled or suspended, nor will the graduation of any seniors among them be delayed." Students who participated in the Low Library and Hamilton Hall sit-ins would be "subject to the sanction of censure...for two years or until they graduate from their current program of enrollment, whichever occurs first." In return for these concessions, the student protesters would agree to leave Hamilton Hall, to end all "further disruptions," and to call off the hunger strike.

The administration's representatives signed the compromise agreement; the students' representatives refused, and consulted with their constituency in Hamilton Hall. By Monday afternoon, it had become extremely clear that the administration had now gone as far as it was prepared to go. The New York police would be called in soon to clear the building. If this were to occur, none of the provisions in the agreement would remain in effect. Many students would have been expelled or suspended. Several faculty actively involved in the African-American Studies program tried to persuade the students to accept the compromise. Most of the students who had participated in the demonstrations were bitterly disappointed with the terms reached by the negotiators. For hours, they debated the agreement, requesting additional time. At one point, the majority of students overwhelmingly rejected the agreement. Forty students offered to risk arrest if the majority of the students in the building agreed. But most students recognized that the continued occupation of Hamilton Hall would force the university to withdraw the offer. Reluctantly, the students accepted the terms. The hunger strike was officially over, and the occupation of Hamilton Hall ended.

In retrospect, there were three things about the entire event that were particularly striking and that speak to the difficulties inherent in a project of diversity in a campus community. Although Columbia's administration had successfully averted a public relations disaster, it again alienated many members of the community by insisting to the press that it had made absolutely no concessions to the protesters. In the *New York Times*, an official claimed that the university "had already begun to pursue most of the proposals contained in the settlement." None of the principal demands of the protests, including an ethnic studies department and fundamental changes in the Core Curriculum, were granted. Even the *Wall Street Journal* praised President Rupp and Columbia's administration for defending the classical Western Civilization canon against the "childish histrionics" of radical multiculturalists. In truth, the campus protests accelerated by at least three years the curricular and programmatic reforms for diversity that were already under way. To some extent, the university still suffers from what President Rupp has described as "a defensive orientation" since the disruptive 1968 campus strike at the height of the Vietnam War.

Most of the student protesters were earnest and idealistic, and were motivated by a genuine desire to achieve a multicultural academic environment. Yet, the vast majority of students on campus, and even most students of color, did not participate in the demonstrations or protests. Many Euro-American students weren't convinced that the ethnic studies agenda was relevant to them. At times, there was also a distinct tendency among some student activists to advance a perspective of "essentialism": that only by increasing the number of Latino faculty could a Latino Studies program be established; only by hiring black professors could the African-American Studies major be expanded. The danger here is what literary critic Gayatri Spivak calls "identitarianism": that only the oppressed can advocate the interests and perspectives of the oppressed; that feminist scholarship can only be written by women; that only blacks know what racism is. Any successful approach to diversity must uncompromisingly reject "identitarianism." Ethnic studies certainly has a special meaning to racial ethnic minorities in terms of personal history, culture, and experiences. But ethnic studies must be for everyone. Black studies makes a critical contribution toward interpreting and understanding the American experience, regardless of race. Literature and texts of diversity and multiculturalism can be taught well by anyone who possesses the intellectual interest, scholarly passion, and enthusiasm for this work.

We should not confuse a curriculum for pluralism and diversity with a program of affirmative action and equal opportunity hiring. A diverse curriculum and student service programs will enhance an institution as a place where minority faculty and students will want to come. But "multiculturalism" is no substitute for affirmative action. There is a pattern of racial apartheid in the hiring, promotion, and tenure patterns of many major universities, which can only be reversed through aggressive policies to recruit and retain faculty and administrators of color. But in the classroom, faculty who are black will and can teach Shakespeare and Milton, and faculty who are white may teach Toni Morrison and James Baldwin. The majority of students in my Introduction to African-American Studies lecture course are white. A dialogue on diversity must be inclusive, not exclusive.

But the most striking feature of the recent campus protest was its disconnection from the real and immediate problems of people of color in our city and within our own neighborhood. One of the central themes of black, Puerto Rican, and Chicano student militancy of the 1960s was the crucial link between campus activism and community struggles. A decade ago, when student activists at Columbia protested against the university's investments in companies engaged in business with South Africa, their mobilization was connected with a broad national debate over apartheid. "Multiculturalism" and "diversity" are not abstractions related solely to matters of curricula and faculty appointments. Rather, the larger issue is the relationship between the university as an institution of elitism and privilege, and the black, Latino, Asian, and impoverished neighborhoods of the city. Many of the more radical and progressive students involved in the strike had established important contacts in Harlem and the Bronx, especially around issues of police brutality. But the majority of student activists didn't relate in any meaningful way to the large communities of color or conceive of ethnic studies as an intellectual project involving an active engagement in the larger world.

Our scholarship and teaching on topics of race and ethnic diversity should be intimately connected with the contemporary challenges and perspectives of people of color. In other words, a multicultural curriculum must speak to the cultural diversity and social complexity that is all around us. Learning should illuminate and inform our relationships across racial, gender, and class boundaries. For Columbia, that relationship must begin with Harlem. At this moment, budget cuts threaten to lay off several thousand doctors, nurses, and health-related and social services workers in Harlem, which will have devastating consequences for the community. In 1993, Harlem's infant mortality rate of 25.2 per 1,000 live births was one of the highest in the United States. The majority of African-American males born and raised in central Harlem do not reach the age of 55. With labor force participation rates at only 55 percent, unemployment and poverty are widespread. More than 40 percent of all Harlem residents live below the federal government's poverty line. Nearly two-thirds of all Harlem households consist of single mothers with children. Harlem's murder rate for males is 10 times the national average.

Studies in race and ethnicity at Columbia will not by themselves provide fundamental solutions to Harlem's problems. But Columbia students will be able to appreciate that for most minorities, the crises of racism, poverty, hunger, and social inequality aren't abstractions. Columbia as an institution can become more actively engaged in developing constructive alternatives to empower the urban community. In this manner, racial and ethnic studies potentially provide a bridge between theory and action.

*   *   *

What is the connection between the values of diversity and democracy? A curriculum committed to pluralism and intercultural values gives us a sense of human possibility, inquiry, and creativity. Democracy as a political project starts from the theoretical premise that all human beings have value, that they are "created equal" and have "inalienable rights," and that all participants within the polity should be heard, should express themselves freely, and should be able to take part in the fundamental decision-making process. Democracy, in its ideal state, creates an environment of tolerance for diversity and a willingness to work with others to achieve common goals. In this sense, democracy and the university are linked, because a democratic system is supposed to nurture pluralism, individual initiative, and creativity, expanding the boundaries of imagination.

Today we take for granted that a democracy cannot work when certain classes, racial groups, and entire populations are deliberately excluded from full participation within the apparatus of governance, when their voices are not valued, and when their humanity is challenged. This has not always been true. For within the long memories of African-Americans and other people of color, our sojourn through American democracy has been at best a bittersweet affair. The democratic ideals of this country have resonated at their deepest cultural core in the political imagination of black folk. Martin Luther King, Jr.'s 1963 "Letter from the Birmingham Jail" is crafted with a passionate love for what American democracy could be for all Americans. The great abolitionist Frederick Douglass, who in 1852 delivered his moving address "What to the Slave is the Fourth of July?," raised the same set of searching questions about the profound contradictions within the American political system as they related to African-Americans:

> I say with a sad sense of the disparity between us, I am not included within the pale of this glorious anniversary! Your high independence only reveals the immeasurable distance between us. The blessings in which you this day rejoice, are not enjoyed in common. The rich inheritance of justice, liberty, prosperity, and independence, bequeathed by your fathers, is shared by you, not by me. The sunlight that brought life and healing to you, has brought stripes and death to me. This Fourth of July is yours, not mine. You may rejoice, I must mourn.

The quest for black freedom has always been an attempt to redefine the democratic social contract to include us, to permit us to become full partners in the structure of political and social power.

Today, social commentators frequently characterize race relations in the United States as being at an all-time low. In recent years, a series of public confrontations and events has accelerated racial polarization, from the Los Angeles civil unrest of 1992 to the trial of O.J. Simpson. Elements within the political system have deliberately manipulated racial and ethnic stereotypes and prejudices on a range of contemporary public policy issues: immigration and the 1994 debate over Proposition 187 in California, welfare "reform," the death penalty, minority economic set-asides, and affirmative action. At times we seem to live in parallel racial universes, where we speak the same language, but perceive reality in fundamentally different ways. There are voices within the black community calling for us to turn inward, toward racial essentialism and chauvinism, away from our long history of democratic involvement, pluralism, and coalition-building. And there are also powerful voices of white reaction: from conservative scholars who claim that a "civilization gap" exists between blacks and whites, who argue that slavery was actually a good experience for African-Americans, to politicians who would completely dismantle civil rights, equal opportunity, and affirmative action, who think that building more prisons will solve the problems of urban crime, poverty, and social alienation. It is time to go beyond black and white, the confrontational stereotypes and prejudices of the past, toward a democratic conversation based on pluralism, civility, and equal justice.

How can we find a common social vision and political language that can reduce and eventually eliminate the boundaries that separate us, that create the parallel racial universes? Our common goal must be the deconstruction of the idea of race itself, the elimination of all forms of racial inequality. As the great reggae artist Bob Marley put it: "Until the color of a man's skin is of no greater consequence than the color of his eyes, there'll be war." I agree. But the question is, *how do we get there?* We will not get there by pretending that race and racism have magically declined in significance in recent years. We cannot get there by asserting that black and Latino inequality is caused by a "culture of poverty," by "civilization gaps," or by biological and genetic shortcomings.

There is no question that government is part of the solution in helping to create the conditions where all citizens, regardless of color, can be productive members of society. But we can also do more to nurture and create social spaces for civic conversation and exchange between racial and ethnic groups inside civil society. By increasing intercultural and intracultural exchanges and dialogues at local levels and within neighborhoods, we may begin gradually to overcome the stereotypes that are the basis of bigotry. By strengthening the capacity of individuals and groups to participate in and influence public institutions to reflect their own cultures, values, and traditions, we enrich the pluralistic character of democracy.

Through programs in higher education, we can pursue a dialogue that recognizes both the profound diversity and the commonality of the American people. We are all Americans, yet we may speak different languages, have different faiths, different economic and social backgrounds, different educational experiences, and very distinct historical memories and traditions. Yet "difference" and "diversity" do not have to be translated into inferiority and subordination. "Difference" provides an opportunity for learning about others and ourselves. The exploration of difference helps us to understand what values we hold in common.

The urgency of this dialogue is created largely by demographics. The combined populations of racial ethnic minorities—African-Americans, Hispanics, Asian-Americans, Pacific Island-Americans, and American Indians—is growing more than seven times faster than the population of non-Hispanic whites. Much of this population explosion has occurred in only a half-dozen states. Between 1980 and 1990, the number of racial and ethnic minorities in the nation's most populous state, California, increased 61.1 percent, to 12.7 million. While New York's total population grew barely 2.5 percent in the 1980s, the state's minority population grew by 25.9 percent, to over 5.5 million. Florida's minority population during that decade reached 3.5 million, an increase of 52.3 percent. In 1990, Texas's minority population was at 7 million, growing at twice the rate of the state's overall population. Nationwide, in 1990, racial ethnic minorities accounted for 60.6 million Americans, representing about 24.4 percent of the country's total population. By the year 2000, that percentage will have increased to nearly a third of the U.S. population. According to demographers, by 2060 whites will have become just one minority in a land with no majority race/ethnicity. Issues of multicultural diversity will become increasingly central to every aspect of American life.

America has always been a land of diversity. From the establishment of the United States, there was a cacophony of languages, traditions, ethnicities, and nationalities. At its best moments, this nation has embraced that rich tapestry of humanity, the diverse and colorful threads representing the spectrum of cultural possibilities. But far too often, we have interpreted "difference" as a synonym for divisiveness, threatening the values and interests of those elites that have attempted to define the mainstream. We still tend to perceive those who are unlike ourselves as the "Other," as potential enemies of the natural order. And in a society deeply stratified by race and poverty, the Other frequently has a black or brown face, or speaks a language other than English. The Other dwells in the ghettos or barrios of our central cities. The Other fills our prisons, labors as a farmworker in our fields, or stands in unemployment lines. The Other lives in public housing or survives on Aid to Families with Dependent Children. If we are to resolve the central dilemma of American life, of whether and how diversity can be reconciled with the fullest meaning of democracy, we must begin a new, honest dialogue among all voices within our society. We must understand and embrace the Other as ourselves.

YOUNG, GIFTED, AND BLACK— THE PROMISE OF BLACK YOUTH

People of all races, ethnic backgrounds, and social classes frequently say that "young people are our most important resource." For people of color, and especially for African-Americans, our ideas about youth are affected profoundly by our collective memories, by the historical meaning we have drawn from the ordeals our people have experienced in the past, and by the challenges that confront us in the present. African-Americans see the promise of our young people as the brightest representation of the collective progress of black people in this country, what we have achieved and what we can become. We desperately want our children's lives and futures to be better and more fulfilling than our own lives have been. We want to feel that the burden of racism and social inequality will be lifted from the shoulders of our daughters and sons, as they prepare to enter the workplace and society. We believe that every African-American child is, in his or her own special way, gifted and deserving of every opportunity life has to offer.

The belief in the promise of black youth is also connected with the struggle to achieve freedom within U.S. society. Each successive generation of young African-Americans has made a vital contribution in the fight to destroy discrimination and inequality. In the 1940s black young people challenged segregation laws by joining the Southern Youth Congress and CORE. In 1960, black college students sparked the sit-in movement across the South. Black young people were in the vanguard of social change in the Student Nonviolent Coordinating Committee (SNCC).

Growing up black in white America has always been a challenge, but never more so than today. To be young and black in the 1990s means that the basic context for human development—education, health care, personal safety, the environment, employment, and shelter—is increasingly problematic. To be young and black today means fighting for survival in a harsh and frequently unforgiving urban environment.

In April 1995, the Institute for Research in African-American Studies at Columbia University, which I direct, held a major conference on "The Crisis of Black Youth." We listened to many representatives from community-based organizations, civic associations, academic institutions, churches, businesses, labor unions, and government. All of us felt keenly the urgency to educate our community about the problems of its young people. What emerged from this process between and among black folk was a preliminary blueprint, with several points of departure, for the survival, development, and empowerment of African-American youth.

The place to begin is within the black American community: our houses of worship and expressions of spirituality, our fraternal societies, social clubs, labor union locals, women's groups, tenants' associations, block clubs, youth organizations, and hundreds of informal and voluntary networks. Within our communities we must coordinate programs and youth-sponsored projects across institutional and organizational lines. We need to start youth internship programs designed specifically to bring young people into contact with community-based problems.

In the black community, we also need greater family awareness around youth-related issues. By "family," we shouldn't mean the standard definition of a nuclear, two-parent household, located in the suburbs. A family is a kinship network that shares resources, provides for the nurturing and guidance of its members, and is reinforced by love and respect. Our families are the chief foundation for the healthy development of young people. We need to foster the value and importance of building strong families as part of our strategy to save our children.

Young black people can be motivated through cultural appreciation and awareness. Music, poetry, theater, dance, athletic competition, and other activities provide young people with a vibrant sense of their creativity and human potential. A blueprint for African-American youth development should include new public policy initiatives addressing a host of basic urban problems: intervention to reverse the deterioration in the quality of public education, prevent teen pregnancies, halt the escalation of street violence, and curb access to handguns in our neighborhoods.

There is a renewed spirit of self-reliance among African-Americans today, promoting the idea that any basic societal changes favoring blacks will have to be achieved by ourselves. Self-initiative is, of course, essential to any people's progress. We need to build strong black institutions of all types. But we should never forget that the overwhelming majority of black people work hard every day, pay their taxes, and therefore, have a right to demand that the government and policymakers address their problems. Government action is vital to the prospects of black youth.

Most important, we need to cultivate the full leadership potential of our young people. Young African-Americans need to develop their ability to make critical choices, to have a full understanding of their communities. We need to support the creation of young people's organizations designed to articulate their perspectives.

A generation ago, the brilliant playwright and author Lorraine Hansberry captured the power and promise of what it meant "to be young, gifted, and black." Today, as the black community struggles to save its children, we cannot surrender that vision; we cannot sacrifice the promise of our youth on the altar of government cutbacks, illegal drugs, handgun violence, substandard housing, and teen pregnancies.

THE EMPIRE STRIKES BACK— CONSERVATISM AND RACISM IN THE 1990S

WHY VOTERS ARE ANGRY

The disclosure in early 1992 that hundreds of members of Congress had written thousands of bad checks struck an emotional cord of outrage across the country. Transcending ideological and partisan boundaries, citizens felt deeply betrayed by their elected officials. The media dubbed this latest scandal "Rubbergate" and newspaper editorials denounced the entire affair.

A *Newsweek* poll revealed that 78 percent of Americans interviewed would be unlikely to reelect their members of Congress if they were among the worst offenders. From the vantage point of African-American politics, several of the worst offenders were prominent blacks: Harold E. Ford of Tennessee, William Clay of Missouri, and John Conyers of Michigan. The worst African-American offender was Chicago Congressman Charles Hayes. Despite his long and admirable record as a defender of trade union and progressive interests, Hayes was turned out of office by former Black Panther and South Side alderman Bobby Rush, who used the check-bouncing issue to his advantage.

There are many different reasons why millions of Americans believe their political system no longer works. Three factors are central to the current public mood of pessimism.

First, most Americans have lost confidence in the politicians of both parties in Congress. Throughout much of the 1980s, Congress's "job rating" in public opinion polls was about a third negative. But in the late 1980s and early 1990s, the political system suffered through a series of scandals and shocks. Congress hiked its salaries during an economic recession; Democratic congressional leaders Jim Wright and Tony Coelho were forced to resign; senators were implicated in the massive savings and loan scandal, costing taxpayers billions of dollars. Finally, the public fiasco of the 1991 Clarence Thomas hearings outraged many liberals, because it starkly showed the Senate to be what it is: an exclusively white, overwhelmingly male establishment completely out of touch with women and their rights. Congress's negative rating soared above 70 percent.

Second, voters are alienated because the middle class, the bedrock of the American electoral system, is in social and economic crisis. About 63 percent of all U.S. families of four earn between $18,500 and $74,300, which is the group that perceives itself as the "middle class." Since the mid-1970s, the real incomes of most of these families have leveled off, while many have fallen sharply. Families are able to get by only because millions of spouses who used to stay home have entered the labor market and bring home extra income. Others have fallen into the ranks of the working poor and even the homeless.

Millions feel an acute sense of confusion and betrayal. The system once perceived as victorious over the "Evil Empire" is revealed as hollow and helpless. Thirty-seven million Americans lack medical care, millions go to bed hungry every night, and millions of manufacturing jobs have disappeared, while Washington does nothing to halt the decline in living standards.

Third, the electorate is angry because the gap between the economic and political leadership and ruling class, on the one hand, and the vast majority of American workers, on the other, is expanding. During the Reagan-Bush years, the upper 1 percent pocketed 60 percent of all income growth. While poor children starved and the indigent froze in vacant buildings, America's "rich and shameless" made billions, thanks to the 1981 Reagan tax cut.

In Japan, the gap between the salaries of executives and workers is much less than in the United States. In 1991, while Chrysler lost millions of dollars, the auto manufacturer paid Lee Iacocca $4.8 million. Profits are going to the salaries of fat executives rather than to investment in new technologies and machinery to create new jobs.

Today's outrage against the politicians and the government may mean an end to the politics of conformity. Whether this political anger yields constructive and progressive changes within the system, however, remains to be seen.

PLAYING THE RACE CARD

The 1991 gubernatorial election in Louisiana highlighted once again that "race" is still the most decisive element in American politics. African-American voters in record numbers came to the polls to defeat neo-Nazi and former Ku Klux Klan leader David Duke, who had campaigned on a platform of thinly veiled racism.

But if blacks had stayed home, Louisiana's white voters would have placed Duke in the governor's mansion. According to voter surveys, about 55 percent of all white voters supported Duke over three-term former Governor Edwin Edwards. Duke's greatest concentration of support came from whites who had suffered most in the state's economic recession: 68 percent of whites with a high school education or less voted for Duke; 69 percent of the white "born-again Christians" and 63 percent of whites with family incomes between $15,000 and $30,000 favored Duke. Conversely, only 30 percent of whites who earn more than $75,000 annually voted for the former Klansman. This shows that race can be highly effective in exploiting white working-class discontent.

Both the Democrats and the Republicans were aware that race would be a crucial factor in determining the 1992 presidential race. The Democratic candidates were going into the election as distinct long-shots for several reasons.

First, despite George Bush's decline in popularity, incumbent presidents of either party rarely lose. Second, Republicans have received a majority of whites' votes in every presidential election but one since 1948. No matter who the Democrats nominate for the presidency, any candidate will have the same difficult task: pulling together northern white ethnics and white workers from the South while courting African-American and Latino voters. The only recent Democratic candidate who achieved such a coalition was Jimmy Carter in 1976, but even he failed to gain a majority of the white vote nationally.

The Republicans and Bush had already begun to respond by playing the "race card," the deliberate manipulation of racial prejudice for partisan political purposes. By first vetoing and later signing a weakened civil rights bill, Bush postured in the shadow of Duke. C. Boyden Gray, Bush's counsel, attempted to force the president to sign a policy statement that would have ended the use of racial preferences in federal government hiring policies. Although Gray's statement was repudiated, the controversy it provoked among civil rights and congressional leaders illustrated once again that Bush had absolutely no commitment to the fight against discrimination.

Bush knew that if two-thirds of all white Americans were to support him in 1992—the same percentage backing Ronald Reagan in 1984—he would win the White House without a single black or Chicano vote. By pandering to white racism, Bush solidified his support among fearful, frustrated whites—the millions of jobless, discouraged whites seeking simplistic explanations for their poverty and economic marginality.

By playing this race card, Bush created an environment in which thousands of minorities might lose their jobs or fall victim to racist harassment. But Bush couldn't care less. His only worry about the race card was his competition on the Right, within his own party. By threatening to run for president, reactionary journalist Patrick Buchanan pressured Bush into more conservative policy positions. Duke even suggested that he and Buchanan run as a conservative "tag team" to challenge Bush.

But all speculation concerning the demise of Duke as a national presence due to his electoral loss in Louisiana was highly exaggerated. Duke flourished because Bush had prepared the ideological and cultural terrain. In political terms, Duke was Bush's illegitimate son and heir. Duke was the child whom the president desperately wanted to disown, but Duke's political features of hatred and hostility to civil rights bore too striking a resemblance to those of his father.

The race card will continue to be decisive in American politics so long as white Americans vote according to their perceived racial interests and not in concert with their basic material interests. Millions of white Americans are unemployed, just as Latinos and African-Americans are. Millions of white women do not receive equal pay for equal work and experience discrimination on the job, just like minorities. If a Democratic presidential candidate had the courage and vision to attack the lies behind the race card, and carried an aggressive message of social justice, the Republicans wouldn't have a chance.

THE POLITICS OF HATE

What do David Duke, Pat Buchanan, Dan Quayle, and George Bush have in common? That was the burning question of the presidential campaign of 1992. The answer transcended their allegiance to the bankrupt policies of the Republican Party. The answer: their manipulation of the "politics of hate."

Former Nazi and Ku Klux Klan leader David Duke denounced the "welfare underclass" and called for equal rights "even for white people"—ignoring the massive economic and social evidence that blacks and Latinos have actually lost ground compared to whites since the 1970s. Duke carefully neglected to mention that there are more white Americans on welfare than there are African-Americans.

Republican presidential candidate Patrick Buchanan never tired of bashing what he termed the "Israeli lobby," and openly expressed his solidarity with white supremacists in South Africa. Dan Quayle attacked people on welfare—without a coherent explanation of why, after 12 years of Reagan-Bush stewardship, no fundamental welfare reforms had been implemented. George Bush was perhaps the worst offender because he privately realized the consequences. Unlike Duke, who didn't mask his hatred, Bush manipulated racial symbols like "Willie Horton" and "reverse discrimination," while cynically disavowing any racist intentions.

But the most striking event in the early stages of that year's presidential campaign was the emergence of Patrick Buchanan on the electoral scene. This conservative television commentator, this former Nixon and Reagan speech writer who possessed no previous electoral experience, ran an unexpectedly strong race against Bush in the New Hampshire primary.

Battering Bush at every opportunity, Buchanan ran on one central theme: dumping George Bush and putting America first again. Every difficult question presented to Buchanan yielded a simplistic answer. The federal government's too big and too bureaucratic, you ask? Buchanan responded that he would "freeze federal hiring," consider "cutting farm subsidies," permit private firms to compete with the U.S. postal service, and "sell off power stations and airports." If Congress refused to play ball, Buchanan would "let the government shut down," permitting a "political bloodbath." For the corporations, Buchanan favored the total elimination of capital gains taxes. He explicitly condemned Bush for increasing the minimum wage by a third and for supporting the Americans with Disabilities Act. Buchanan denounced affirmative action and considered multicultural education a sinister plot to destroy Western Civilization and culture.

But the greatest controversy surrounding Buchanan concerned his espousal of racist and anti-Semitic views. Attacking the 1991 Civil Rights Act, Buchanan insisted that the "sons of middle America pay the price of reverse discrimination." White-owned small businesses lose contracts "because of minority set-asides." Buchanan vowed, if elected, to purge the federal government "agency by agency, and root out the whole rotten infrastructure of reverse discrimination, root and branch."

Buchanan's reputation as an apologist for anti-Semitism is equally well known. He joked publicly that Congress was "Israeli-occupied territory" and dismissed Democrats as "poodles" of the Israeli lobby. Vigorously opposing the imminent war against Iraq, Buchanan explained in 1990 that only the Israeli defense ministry and its "amen corner" inside the United States really wanted war.

As *New York Times* columnist A.M. Rosenthal later observed, Buchanan was slyly warning white America to "watch out, the Jews are trying to drag you into war for foreign purposes." Combining these statements with Buchanan's equal hatred of multiculturalism and his love of tax cuts for the rich, the death penalty, and Clarence Thomas, one has a profile of a rigidly reactionary ideologue who substitutes stereotypes for analysis. When Buchanan shouts "America First" from the campaign podium, what he's really saying is "White Upper Class America First—Except Jews."

So Buchanan, aided by teammates Duke, Quayle, and Bush, spread the bitter seeds of racial and social bigotry, harvesting their fruits of hatred for partisan political purposes. And the consequences of the politics of prejudice were an increase in hate crimes all over America.

Back in 1980, the Anti-Defamation League of B'nai B'rith recorded 489 instances of anti-Semitic vandalism, threats, and assaults throughout the United States. By 1991, the number of reported anti-Semitic incidents had soared to 1,879; in California alone, there were 124 hate crimes targeting Jews, including the bombing of a synagogue. The number of neo-Nazi hate groups increased from 160 in 1990 to 203 in 1992.

Blaming Jewish people for the world's problems has long been a tradition on the ultra-right. Listen to Pat Buchanan's glowing description of Adolf Hitler: "Though Hitler was indeed racist and anti-Semitic to the core . . . he was also an individual of great courage, a soldier's soldier in the Great War, a political organizer of the first rank, a leader steeped in the history of Europe." This thinly veiled admiration for authoritarianism influences the political behavior of many alienated white voters, who want a convenient scapegoat to explain away their troubles.

Politically motivated hate crimes against gay men and lesbians were also increasing, for similar reasons. According to the U.S. Department of Justice, thousands of assaults against lesbians and gays are recorded every year. In 1990 alone, there were 563 assaults against lesbians and gays in California, 529 in Illinois, 387 in Ohio, 268 in New York, and 997 in Texas. North Carolina, the home of the notorious homophobe Jesse Helms, led the nation with 1,204 hate-motivated attacks on gays and lesbians.

We must make a critical distinction between the personal beliefs and the political activities of officials or candidates seeking office. It is very unlikely that Bush personally hates all blacks, Hispanics, and Asian-Americans. It is improbable that Buchanan despises all Jewish people. Rather, the source of their hatred is politically inspired. Buchanan's anti-Semitism and Bush's pandering to racism are the products of political ambition. Neither would lead a lynch mob or deface a Jewish cemetery—but some of their zealous followers on the far Right undoubtedly would.

As 1992 wore on, it was no exaggeration to describe the behavior of Republicans as "howling from the cave." If anyone needed a reason to vote for Bill Clinton that November, she or he needed only to watch in horror as the Republican Party met in convention that summer in Houston. Beneath the colorful red, white, and blue banners, the party was kidnaped by its fanatical right wing. The bigotry, intolerance, and sanctimonious behavior exhibited at the podium transcended even the political backwardness of the Reagan administration.

Some scenes from the convention reminded me of the fanatical rallies in Munich and Berlin six decades ago: loudspeakers bombarding the audience with patriotic music; and the freshly scrubbed white faces of the Young Republicans, their blue eyes glazed over in fixed expressions.

The message was unambiguously clear: there are no problems in "our America," no poverty or hunger, no sexism or illiteracy, and no AIDS epidemic. The 37 million Americans who don't have any medical insurance don't exist. There's no pollution problem, only environmental extremists who want to overregulate our bountiful natural resources. There's no discrimination, except when minorities and bleeding-heart liberals demand "quotas" and policies for "reverse discrimination," which unfairly hurts innocent white victims. A social explosion like the one in Los Angeles earlier that spring is an example of liberal cultural values and the breakdown of morality among ghetto residents. All freedom of choice regarding abortion is forbidden—even in instances of rape and incest.

The convention delegates were overwhelmingly white and economically privileged. Out of more than 2,200 delegates and 2,200 alternates, only 103 delegates and 94 alternates were African-Americans. By contrast, at that summer's Democratic convention in New York City, 771 delegates were African-Americans, nearly 18 percent of the total.

In Houston, black Republicans were supposed to be seen but rarely heard. None was in a policymaking position inside the Bush campaign or Republican leadership. When Allen Keyes, the black Republican candidate for the Senate in Maryland, pleaded for weeks to be invited to speak at the GOP convention, he was ignored. White officials refused to answer his many letters and telephone calls. Only when Keyes complained openly to the press was he permitted to speak on stage. Despite his conservatism, Keyes attributed his mistreatment to what he termed "the residue of racism."

The convention's speakers, with few exceptions, were a parade of bigotry. California Attorney General Dan Lungren gave a "law-and-order" appeal to covert racism that could easily have been delivered by David Duke. Pat Robertson thundered that the 1992 presidential campaign was a moral crusade against immoral enemies. Former Education Secretary William Bennett attacked "rampant promiscuity." Marilyn Quayle spat venom at her husband's critics. With a sneer masked as a smile, she declared that not all Americans during the 1960s "took drugs, joined in the sexual revolution, or dodged the draft." In Marilyn Quayle's eagerness to refight yesterday's battles, she forgot that young Danforth had deliberately joined the National Guard to duck going to Vietnam.

But the Republican convention's "Prince of Hatred" was Pat Buchanan. In the *New York Times*, novelist Stephen King described this master of demagoguery as looking "like

a bulldog that has just enjoyed a good meal—a child, perhaps." Buchanan blasted the civil rights of homosexuals,
denouncing the Democrats as "pro-lesbian and pro-gay."
He described African-Americans who took to the streets in
Los Angeles last spring as a violent "mob" and called for
additional programs to help "our people"—meaning whites.

Buchanan also aimed his anger at Hillary Clinton, declaring that she believes "12-year-olds should have the
right to sue their parents" and that she had once "compared marriage and the family as institutions to slavery
and life on an Indian reservation." These are gross distortions of Hillary Clinton's statements on children's rights.
But rogue elephants like Buchanan bitterly recall that she
had worked as a lawyer back in 1974 for the House Judiciary Committee, which recommended the impeachment of
President Richard Nixon. By lying about Hillary Clinton,
Buchanan is trying to settle old scores.

Most moderate Republicans were ashamed and even outraged by this sorry spectacle. At least 16 of the 43 GOP
senators and 70 of the 166 representatives did not attend
the convention. New Hampshire Senator Warren Rudman
explained, "This image of a far-right party, this is not the
party I belong to." The party of Lincoln, Willkie, and Eisenhower is now a cesspool of reaction and racism. The frightening message from Houston was little more than the
glorification of hatred. Now we finally understand what
Bush meant when he vowed that he would "do what I have
to do to be reelected."

Hatred cannot be barred from politics unless we begin to
take steps to uproot discrimination throughout society as a
whole. This means actually empowering the oppressed and
supporting multicultural education to facilitate dialogue
and understanding. It means endorsing greater pluralism
in the ethnic, gender, and racial composition of our political, corporate, and media leadership. Hatred is a by-prod-
uct of fear, and so long as white Americans are easily
manipulated by the demagogues of bigotry, our real problems will go unanswered. The politics of hate will continue
to triumph.

FREE TRADE OR CLASS WARFARE

When President George Bush called for a "New World Or-der," he meant something more than the death of Soviet communism. The New World Order also promised the end of international barriers restricting trade and corporate in-vestment among nations.

Europeans have initiated the European Union to elimi-nate customs duties, create a common currency, and even-tually form a strong federal government. The free trade agreement reached in 1992 by Canada, Mexico, and the United States meant fundamental changes in the economic relations among these countries as well. In brief, the plan was to gradually eliminate all customs duties on products traded among these nations; open the closed insurance, banking, and securities industries of Mexico to competition and investment from Canada and the United States; and establish trilateral boards to resolve disagreements con-cerning environmental standards. Bush proudly pro-claimed the North American Free Trade Agreement as one of the greatest achievements of his presidency.

Most economists and media generally endorsed the trade agreement. Every U.S. president since the Great Depres-sion had supported the principle of free trade, and Bill Clinton announced his qualified approval a few months be-fore the election. The fierce battle for its ratification then became a touchstone of *his* presidency. Theoretically, the elimination of trade barriers meant that consumers throughout North America would be able to purchase many goods at lower prices, and the savings would generate new jobs. Gary Hufbauer and Jeffrey Schott of the Institute for International Economics estimated that within three years, the trade accord would create 325,000 new jobs inside the United States, with a loss of about 150,000 jobs. Other economists were even more optimistic. Researchers at the University of Michigan asserted that the jobs of only 15,000 to 75,000 would be lost with the North American trade pact.

But there were several fundamental problems with these rosy estimates. Twenty-five years ago, U.S. trade—the total amount of all imports and exports—represented only 10 percent of America's gross domestic product. By 1992, though, trade accounted for 25 percent. Thousands of U.S. companies were shutting down factories in cities like Cleveland, Detroit, Baltimore, and St. Louis, and relocating outside the country, where wages were usually lower and fewer environmental protection laws existed. For example, back in 1960, nearly all of Motorola's employees worked inside the United States; in 1992, only 44 percent of Motorola's 100,000 workers were in America. Since 1984, American Telephone and Telegraph (AT&T) had eliminated 21,000 blue-collar manufacturing jobs in the United States, according to *Business Week*. During the same period, AT&T created 12,000 mostly lower-paying jobs in foreign factories. Countries in which workers earn low wages attract labor-intensive businesses from the United States.

We can understand the problem better if we divide the U.S. labor force into several groups. For college and professional school graduates, jobs and incomes will probably increase because of free trade. The increase in trade and investment means that U.S. businesses will require a more highly trained, better educated, white-collar labor force: more engineers, managers, designers, and technicians. From 1979 to 1992, the real incomes of American college graduates rose 8 percent.

Conversely, the real incomes of workers with less than a high school education declined 20 percent during that time. Those with a high school education or less are more likely to be hired in blue-collar, semi-skilled, and manual labor positions—and it is precisely their wages that stand to be cut even further by the free trade agreement. Sixty-four million U.S. workers have a high school education or less. Without a massive federal educational and vocational retraining program, the economic futures of many U.S. families are in jeopardy.

The greatest danger of this agreement is its potential to accelerate the class polarization of American society. As millions of poorly educated young people are left behind by the new technologically advanced job market, they could become alienated and angry. Today's urban unrest, driven largely by racial conflicts, may be turned into class warfare between the increasingly affluent "haves" and the economically depressed "have nots." With unstable political systems, massive violence, and extremes of wealth and widespread poverty, Harvard economist Richard B. Freeman warned, the United States could evolve into "a class society like those in Latin America.... That's the direction we're headed."

WHAT CLINTON OWED US—AND WHY HE DIDN'T PAY UP

The presidential campaign of 1992 seemed, in many respects, to be a replay of 1976. In both campaigns, a moderate Democratic governor from a southern state emerged from the middle-class hinterland to seize his party's nomination from the liberal establishment. An embattled, frustrated Republican president presided over a major economic recession, sending his popularity ratings into the basement. The Republican incumbent was challenged unsuccessfully by a leader of the right wing of his own party in the primaries. In November 1976, Jimmy Carter narrowly defeated Gerald Ford. In November 1992, Bill Clinton narrowly defeated George Bush.

The historical analogy breaks down when we consider the social and ideological forces behind Carter and Clinton, respectively. When Carter ran in 1976, the Democrats had won 7 of the previous 11 presidential contests, and the national disgrace of Watergate and Nixon's almost-impeachment had just tarnished the Republicans. Nevertheless, despite implementing a number of conservative policies, Carter was never able to transform the Democrats into an explicitly "centrist" party.

But after more than a decade of Reaganism, the political cultures of both major parties had shifted decisively to the right. It was in this context of reaction that Clinton and his conservative cabal, the Democratic Leadership Council (DLC), seized control of the party's national apparatus. Their conservative agenda represented a sharp break from New Deal/Great Society liberalism.

Clinton's basic strategy was to speak primarily to two key constituencies: "Reagan Democrats," the blue-collar white workers who abandoned the party of Roosevelt and Kennedy over affirmative action, busing for school desegregation, and welfare; and younger, suburban, white professionals who were attracted to the candidacies of Gary Hart in 1984 and Paul Tsongas earlier in 1992. The DLC's objective was to win the support of at least 47 percent of the overall white electorate. Clinton was painfully aware that the Democrats had captured the majority of whites' presidential votes only once since 1948. In the three presidential elections of the 1980s, Republican candidates won 33 million more votes than Democrats, with an eight-to-one margin in electoral votes.

This explained Clinton's determination to avoid being characterized as a "tax-and-spend liberal" in the Kennedy-Mondale-Dukakis tradition. Preaching "family values," "patriotism," and "personal responsibility," he frequently sounded like Republican evangelist Pat Robertson. Jack O'Dell, chief strategist for the Rainbow Coalition, suggested that a Clinton presidency would be roughly similar to that of Harry S. Truman.

For progressives, the real question presented by the Clinton-Bush electoral contest came down to a simple choice: do I vote for Clinton or do I stay home on November 3? At times, as I watched a Clinton speech on C-SPAN, his words almost made sense, but I knew he wasn't talking to me. I feared that a Clinton White House would be even further to the right than Jimmy Carter's. Despite these misgivings, I still advised African-Americans, other people of color, and progressives to criticize Clinton, but beat Bush, in 1992.

The question was whether a substantial, critical distinction could be made between a Clinton-Gore administration and a second term for Bush and Quayle. Millions of women, threatened with the loss of their freedom of choice on the issue of abortion, certainly understood the dangers of a Bush victory. People of color recalled that Bush had vetoed the 1990 Civil Rights Act and turned Willie Horton into Dukakis's unofficial running mate. Advocates for the poor realized that the Bush administration consistently rejected legislative proposals to address the crisis of hunger. The 37 million Americans without health insurance thought they had much to gain from Clinton's promises on health care.

But Clinton distanced himself from the black electorate and its concerns. He had no high-ranking blacks in his campaign organization, and his spring 1992 golfing excursion at an all-white country club was racially insensitive and politically stupid. And it was certainly possible for Clinton to snatch defeat from the jaws of victory, were more than 50 percent of black voters to stay home in November. African-Americans had to vote against Bush, and that meant voting for Clinton—but we should have been prepared to struggle every day against the conservative policies a Clinton administration was likely to adopt.

Clinton's win that year was analyzed and reanalyzed in the weeks following the election. Bush received only 38 million popular votes, 37.5 percent of the overall electorate. This was the lowest percentage of the popular vote recorded by an incumbent president seeking reelection in 80 years.

Clinton carried many states that normally vote Republican, such as New Jersey. Conservative Democrats attributed Clinton's strength to his move away from traditional liberalism and his embrace of centrist policies such as the death penalty. We were told by political experts that Clinton appealed successfully to white suburban voters, who made the critical difference in the election.

How true is this analysis? Close study of Clinton's real constituency reveals that his prime supporters were racial and ethnic minorities, working-class and poor people, and people who depended heavily on governmental programs, such as welfare, student loans, Social Security payments, and other social services. According to exit polls, 82 percent of all African-Americans who voted selected Clinton, the highest level of support the Democratic candidate received from any group. Clinton also received substantial support from Jewish voters (78 percent) and from Latinos (62 percent). The intolerant, homophobic character of the Republicans' national convention was critical in mobilizing millions of American lesbians and gays behind the Democratic nominee. Clinton's lesbian/gay vote in the election was estimated at about 75 percent.

Working-class people and the poor were also vital to Clinton's victory. Americans earning less than $15,000 annually supported the Arkansas Democrat by 59 percent. Other key groups in this category include members of trade unions and their households (55 percent), the unemployed (56 percent), and women without a high school diploma (58 percent). A plurality of Americans over the age of 60 (50 percent), full-time students (50 percent), and first-time voters (49 percent) endorsed Clinton over Bush and Perot. The only upper-income Americans clearly aligning themselves with Clinton were those with postgraduate university educations, who supported Clinton by 49 percent.

Bush's core supporters were strikingly different—overwhelmingly white, economically privileged, and culturally conservative. Bush scored best among "born-again Christian" evangelicals (61 percent), southern white males (48 percent), conservatives (65 percent), and people earning more than $75,000 annually (48 percent). If African-Americans and Latinos had stayed away from the polls, Bush would have received a narrow electoral college and popular vote victory. A plurality of white voters went for Bush (41 percent) over Clinton (39 percent) and Perot (20 percent).

The overwhelming backing of blacks meant that Clinton was able to carry a number of states in which the majority of white voters favored Bush. For example, Clinton's narrow victories over Bush in Georgia (44 versus 43 percent), Louisiana (46 versus 42 percent), Tennessee (47 versus 43 percent), New Jersey (43 versus 41 percent), and Ohio (40 versus 39 percent) were attributable to strong support by the African-American electorate. Latinos in New Mexico (38 percent of the state's voters), California (26 percent), and Colorado (13 percent) gave Clinton crucial support, helping him to win those states.

The major pluses from the 1992 elections were the unprecedented gains scored by women, Latinos, and African-Americans. Despite them, however, we still had—and have—a long struggle ahead to achieve a genuinely multicultural democracy. Clinton should have understood, clearly and forcefully, that without the crucial support of African-Americans, Latinos, working people, gays and lesbians, environmentalists, and others, he would be back in Arkansas instead of in the White House. But long before the inauguration, there was plenty of evidence that Clinton didn't get it.

After winning the presidency, Bill Clinton woke up to a new reality—the inescapable fact that running for office is fundamentally different from the task of governing. To get elected, politicians have to build coalitions with a widely divergent set of interest groups. You make promises you know you can't keep in order to win. But once in office, you are forced to make hard choices, and you can never please everyone. Conservative interest groups, which are always well organized, can easily influence the behavior of moderate and liberal elected officials. At the economic conference held in Little Rock right after the election, Clinton tried to maintain this difficult balancing act. He appealed to traditional liberals and minorities on some issues, while simultaneously catering to Wall Street and the corporations.

To reconcile these conflicts between his electoral base and his more conservative governing coalition, it seemed conceivable that Clinton might borrow a page from the governing strategy of Richard Nixon during 1969-1973. Nixon narrowly won a three-way presidential race in 1968, receiving only 43.4 percent of the popular vote. Nixon realized that his administration had to copy key aspects of the racist southern agenda of rival George Wallace of Alabama, who received 13.5 percent of the vote on the American Independent ticket.

Nixon made overtures to Wallace Democrats by nominating two southern judges, Clement F. Haynsworth, Jr. and G. Harrold Carswell, to the Supreme Court. Although their nominations were rejected, Nixon was able to establish a rapport with southern racists. Going further, Nixon advocated a halt to school desegregation and an end to advances in civil rights, a policy that became known as "benign neglect." His administration violated civil liberties and used the rhetoric of "law and order" to crush black urban rebellions. By maintaining his traditional Republican base in the suburbs, country clubs, and on Wall Street, and by incorporating racial/cultural conservatives and former Democrats such as Jesse Helms and Strom Thurmond into his governing coalition, Nixon built the "Silent Majority." In 1972, his coalition received 60.7 percent of the popular vote, crushing the liberal Democratic candidacy of George McGovern.

In 1992, I speculated that Clinton might try a similar political maneuver, only with different constituencies, in an attempt to keep his core Democratic electoral base—African-Americans, Latinos, Jewish Americans, labor, and so forth—while reaching out to two groups: the Perot electoral bloc and the white suburban, upper-middle-class voters who usually back Republicans. For his core constituency, Clinton could initiate a number of reforms chiefly on social policy, which don't cost much to implement. Such a policy would recognize that the centerpiece of his domestic agenda would be unavoidably costly: the restructuring of the nation's health care system. But one of the examples I cited as an "inexpensive" policy was Clinton's promise to abolish the homophobic restrictions on lesbians and gays in the military—a promise no more fulfilled than the more "expensive" promise of health care reform.

On economic matters, it was clear even in December 1992 that Clinton would turn his attention to Perot's voters, to diffuse a potential third party movement. The selection of Texas Senator Lloyd Bentsen as Treasury Secretary indicated just how conservative Clinton's economic policies would be.

What was the task of liberals and progressives at that point? To shed no tears for George Bush—his defeat had been absolutely essential to reverse 12 years of reaction, racism, and neglect. But we should not have harbored any illusions about the new Clinton administration. Despite the appointment of several prominent liberals to his cabinet, Clinton needed to be pushed, forced, and pressured by minorities, women, labor, gays and lesbians, and other liberal groups. As I said then, "Unless we mobilize immediately, the Clinton administration could look more like Richard Nixon's than like Franklin D. Roosevelt's."

It did not take President Clinton long to begin the process of betraying his core constituency.

The abandonment of Lani Guinier as his choice to head the Civil Rights Division of the Justice Department was an outstanding example of presidential weakness and failure of political courage. Yet from the perspective of conservative and moderate Democrats, Guinier was just the latest version of Sister Souljah, just another African-American woman who could be sacrificed to advance the white southern Democrat's flagging political fortunes.

Clinton was trying to rebound from the series of incredible political and personal blunders that plagued his first few months in office—including the mini-scandal in the White House travel office and the ridicule generated by his overpriced haircut. But in the immediate aftermath of the flap over Guinier, the path Clinton chose to stabilize his plunging political fortunes was to turn sharply to the right.

He selected a moderate Republican, David Gergen, to serve in a powerful post as White House adviser. Gergen's primary credentials included working as a political insider for the Nixon, Ford, and Reagan administrations. Gergen's role was to "moderate" the Clinton administration's image to white, upper- and middle-class America.

The next few weeks saw such moves as these: Clinton delivered an address on welfare that was interpreted as a capitulation to the conservatives. Despite promises to increase the minimum wage above the level of $4.25 an hour, Clinton retreated from his commitments to labor and blacks. Clinton expressed a willingness to work out his budget plan by increasing tax cuts and reducing social expenditures. On the issue of urban jobs, Clinton failed miserably to deliver anything to the central cities.

Despite Clinton's embrace of the political label "Democrat," his administration rapidly transformed itself into a bastion of what used to be called "liberal Republicanism," the politics of Nelson Rockefeller, Jacob Javits, Charles Percy, and other former GOP leaders. The programs Clinton seemed to favor for addressing social problems were modest at best, and, by repudiating the Guinier nomination, he once again distanced himself from the black community.

Part of the reason for Clinton's lurch to the right could be summed up in two words: Ross Perot. The Texas billionaire had become Clinton's major political enemy during the spring of 1993, constantly attacking the North American Free Trade Agreement as a political sellout of American workers to the multinational corporations. Clinton was elected with less than 43 percent of the popular vote, and Perot's constituency was perceived by Gergen and other moderate Clinton aides as absolutely crucial to the outcomes of the 1994 and 1996 elections. By moving to the so-called political center, Clinton tried to incorporate the anti-tax, anti-big-government message of Perot, appealing to elements of white, middle-class America that failed to vote for him in the 1992 election.

The other significant factor behind Clinton's move to the political right was the failure of traditional liberal and progressive constituencies to join forces and demand a higher level of accountability and commitment from the new administration. The civil rights, women's rights, labor, and environmental organizations didn't move aggressively enough to pressure Clinton from the left.

CLINTON'S ECONOMIC AGENDA

President Bill Clinton's 1993 economic plan was the first moderate alternative to the elitist and unequal "trickle-down" policies of Presidents Ronald Reagan and George Bush. Clinton spokesman George Stephanopoulos correctly characterized the new administration's budget proposal as a "reversal of Reaganomics, a reversal of the last 12 years." Unfortunately, Clinton's tax and stimulus package didn't go far enough to reverse the poverty, hunger, and income inequality generated by the policies of Reaganomics.

The essential presumption of "Clintonomics" was an effort to halt the spiraling growth rate of our $4 trillion national debt, while creating some new programs and services to invest in the long-term productivity of the country. Reagan had argued for years that it was possible to cut taxes, increase Pentagon spending by billions of dollars annually, and still balance the federal budget. In reality, the 1980s were a decade of unrivaled prosperity and greed for the wealthy, while lower-income people experienced a decline in their real incomes. Clinton's plan, in effect, announced, "The show's over, and now someone has to pay these overdue bills."

Clinton proposed to raise taxes and reduce government spending in more than 150 programs. These actions would theoretically have reduced the annual deficit from over $300 billion in 1993 to $140 billion by 1997. Over a five-year period, the deficit reduction was to come equally from spending cuts in the federal budget and from tax hikes.

The president's new economic plan initially received overwhelming support from most Americans. One CNN/*U.S.A Today* poll indicated that 79 percent of all Americans endorsed the basic concepts in Clinton's plan. The reason for such enthusiastic backing was simple: the plan demanded the greatest sacrifices from American households earning more than $100,000 annually. The "class arithmetic" behind Clinton's approach divided Americans into three very broad groups—low-income families (from the unemployed to those earning up to $30,000 annually), the middle class (households earning between $30,000 and $100,000), and the well-to-do (upper-income households with more than $100,000 annually). About 65 percent of all income tax returns come from Americans who earn below $30,000 annually. Because of their relatively low wages, however, they contribute only 15.6 percent of total federal income taxes. Under Clinton's plan, this lowest income category would have paid no new taxes.

About a third of all taxpayers are in the middle-income group, earning from $30,000 to $100,000 each year. They contribute nearly half of all federal taxes collected annually. They also have high voter-participation rates, and millions of them were attracted to the candidacy of Ross Perot in 1992. This group basically decides presidential elections in America, and Clinton was acutely aware that his 42 percent of the popular vote was insufficient to win reelection.

So for this middle-income group, Clinton's plan called for modest sacrifices, at most. New taxes on energy would cost these families roughly $100 to $200 a year. Middle-class seniors would be affected by new taxes on Social Security pensions, but most households would end up paying only an extra $30 to $40 per month.

Only 4.4 percent of all U.S. households earn more than $100,000 a year. But these three million taxpayers generate roughly 35 percent of the entire federal revenue. Clinton's plan placed 70 percent of the proposed tax increases on this group. Despite Republican criticisms that Clinton's plan was too restrictive on businesses, many corporate and financial leaders were publicly enthusiastic about the administration's strategy. The bond market was overjoyed with Clinton's stated commitment to cut the federal deficit, and interest rates fell sharply to the lowest levels in more than 15 years.

Why were so many rich people relieved by Clinton's economic program? They were relieved that he didn't go far enough to reverse the massive transfer of wealth that occurred in the 1980s, in which the middle classes and the lower classes gave billions to the upper classes. According to Professor Ralph Estes of American University, the author of *Who Pays? Who Profits?*, the wealthiest 1 percent of all Americans, in 1983, held 31.3 percent of the country's total wealth. By 1989, the top 1 percent held 37.1 percent of all wealth. The top 1 percent actually owns and controls more wealth than the bottom 90 percent of all Americans combined. And Estes notes that if the same rate of change were to keep up for the next 35 years, the top 1 percent would actually control the *entire wealth* of this country. Clinton's economic plan offered nothing to reverse this vast concentration of wealth for those at the top.

The basic political strategy behind President Clinton's new economic program rested on two basic observations: that middle-class taxpayers generally decide elections, and that most Americans are willing to make modest sacrifices, but want the pain to be allocated more equally across society. People were generally aware that the Reagan-Bush years had been a massive rip-off by the wealthy, with the top tax rates falling from 70 percent of taxable income in 1981 to 28 percent of income in 1988.

The key political architect of this approach was Stan Greenberg. In a brilliant 1991 article in *The American Prospect* magazine, Greenberg astutely observed that Reagan had constructed a "top-down" coalition of wealthy voters, entrepreneurs, and the largely white middle class. His social and fiscal policies clearly favored the well-to-do at the expense of trade unions, minorities, urban residents, and the poor; nevertheless, the vast majority of white middle-class people endorsed Reaganism. About two-thirds of all whites, regardless of income, voted for Reagan's reelection in 1984. Many middle-income people believed that too much had been given to the poor and racial minorities under Democratic administrations, and that they would be better off under an administration that openly and unashamedly favored the rich.

Anticipating Clinton's 1992 campaign, Greenberg argued that the Democrats had to advocate a "new class politics," which would divide the middle class from the rich. The Democrats had to "defend and enlarge social insurance initiatives that reach the lower and middle classes rather than constructing safety nets that protect only the poor." Thus when President Clinton called upon the rich to "pay their fair share" of federal taxes, he was consciously appealing to the interests of middle- and lower-income voters alike.

This "new class politics" strategy represented a major advance over the Democratic Party's tendency to attempt a revival of the old Roosevelt "New Deal" of the 1930s and 1940s. Yet this strategy wasn't sufficient to address the massive human problems experienced by the working poor, the unemployed, and the homeless—Americans who don't vote in large numbers, yet who represent a major social crisis for our whole society.

For example, 37 million Americans—white, Latino, and black—have no health insurance at all. And, according to the Congressional Budget Office, unless programs for funding health care change, our national health expenditure will triple by the year 2003, to an estimated $672 billion annually. In the long run, only a comprehensive system of national health care, modeled on the Canadian system, will really address the health crisis for millions of people.

Clinton should have been pushed toward a more progressive economic agenda for this country, one which really reverses the legacy of Reaganomics rather than nibbling around the edges. The taxes of the wealthy should be increased to a minimum of 50 percent. Most of the industrial world, after all, taxes its wealthiest citizens at much higher rates than we do. Japan's top tax rate is 50 percent, Germany's top rate is 53 percent, and France's top rate is nearly 57 percent. To cut federal expenditures even further, we need to accelerate reductions in the Pentagon budget. And on the revenue side, we should consider eliminating the home mortgage interest deduction, the sacred tax shelter of the middle and upper classes.

Clinton's "new class politics" represented a step in the right direction compared to Reaganomics, but it was woefully inadequate to address the economic problems of most Americans.

OKLAHOMA AND THE SPECTER OF TERRORISM

In the wake of the Oklahoma City bombing of 1995, with a death toll exceeding 130, law enforcement officials and politicians scrambled to stake out positions to reassure a public frightened by the specter of terrorism. What made the explosion at the city's federal building so emotionally devastating to millions was not just the stream of tragic photos of mutilated and bleeding children, of grieving parents, wives, and husbands. It was the bold and previously inconceivable notion that Middle America itself was completely vulnerable to acts of terror. Everyone understands that the rules of the game in a major metropolitan center like New York City are different. The World Trade Center bombing did not surprise Middle America. But in the realm of cultural politics, a terroristic attack in Oklahoma City was like bringing Hamas or the Irish Republican Army into the living rooms of *The Brady Bunch* and *Leave It to Beaver.*

It was not surprising that the basic responses of the Clinton administration were political gestures to, simultaneously, the Left and the Right. After some initial speculation—completely false—that the bombing was somehow the work of Arab or Middle Eastern "terrorists," it became clear that those responsible were part of a widespread underground of home-grown, right-wing militia. These armed vigilantes share racist and extreme anti-government ideologies. Several days after the bombing, Clinton attacked the voices of the radical Right on talk radio for nurturing extremist and intolerant viewpoints. For the next few weeks, the debate in the media shifted back and forth between those conservatives, like Rush Limbaugh, who viciously condemn liberal democracy and government, and those who supported Clinton's basic argument that the polemics had gone too far.

Meanwhile, the Clinton administration also moved in the opposite direction. Months before the Oklahoma bombing, Clinton had proposed the Omnibus Counterterrorism Act, which was supposedly aimed at foreign terrorists who might threaten American lives and property. But a little-publicized provision of the Act would permit the president to designate any foreign organization as a terrorist formation. Therefore, any American solidarity group, local or national support organization, or even an individual, who gave money or material support to such a group would be in violation of the law. Even if the funds raised by Americans went specifically and solely to support nonviolent, humanitarian purposes, such as health care, education, or clothing, donating the money would be a crime.

For black and progressive Americans, the implications of this bill should be immediately clear, if we recall what happened in the anti-apartheid movement in this country. Thousands of us were arrested in 1984-1986 protesting the Reagan administration's immoral policy of "constructive engagement" with the apartheid regime; more than one million Americans donated food, clothing, money, books, and other resources to the African National Congress (ANC) led by Nelson Mandela. The U.S. government maintained that the ANC was a "terrorist" organization for years. If Clinton's bill had been law back then, we would have been committing a crime to provide support for the ANC.

Meanwhile, nobody is saying what is really important about the growing phenomenon of neo-fascist, racist militias all over the country. There are more than 100,000 white men with guns who go target-shooting each weekend, motivated by extreme hatred of the government, and by contempt for black people and their interests. This is the extreme right wing of the mass white conservatism that occupies both houses of Congress and is represented nationally by Newt Gingrich. Outside the electoral political arena, this extremism is reflected within the National Rifle Association (NRA). Just days before the Oklahoma City bombing, for example, an NRA fundraising letter sent to thousands warned of "jack-booted government thugs" who "seize our guns, destroy our property, and even injure and kill us." Republican presidential candidate Robert Dole justified the inflammatory language of the NRA's fundraising letter, declaring that "I don't believe anybody can rile [terrorists] up."

Black Americans and other progressive voices in America must vigorously oppose and denounce Clinton's latest capitulation to conservatives, the Omnibus Counterterrorism Act. A generation after the FBI's COINTELPRO operation, which destroyed civil rights organizations and assassinated black leaders, we should not let the government once again have the legal power to silence critics, regardless of their ideologies. But we should also make the point that the Oklahoma bombing and those who applaud such acts of terror and violence are directly tied to the politics of the extreme Republican Right.

THE THIRD WAVE OF REACTION

The November 1994 elections gave the Republican Party control of both houses of Congress for the first time in 40 years. The Republican victories placed President Clinton even further on the defensive, as his administration scrambled to regain the initiative around public policy issues. Regrettably, the Clinton administration has moved toward accommodation with the Right around many issues, from prayer in the public schools to welfare reform.

Let us be frank, however: the key factor in the smashing success of the far Right is the core reality of racism within American politics and society. Race and to a lesser extent gender were primary factors fueling the victories of Republican congressional candidates in 1994.

According to Voter News Service exit polls, the overall vote in the elections of 1992 was divided 54 percent to 46 percent in favor of the Democratic candidates. White males that year tended to favor Republicans by a slight margin, 51 percent versus 49 percent. In 1994, the general electorate favored Republicans marginally, 51 percent versus 49 percent. But significantly, white males as a group overwhelmingly endorsed Republicans by a margin of 63 to 37 percent. Since white males comprise 42 percent of all voters, their nearly two-to-one endorsement of the Republicans was chiefly responsible for the disastrous Democratic defeat.

A breakdown of the white male vote by income and education is even more revealing. A majority of white males who have less than a high school education and less than $15,000 annual income voted Democratic. Conversely, 70 percent of white males who earn at least $75,000 voted for Republican congressional candidates; 69 percent of white men with some college education, and 67 percent who are college graduates, supported the Republicans.

In many individual races, the votes by white males provided the crucial margins of victory. In California, for example, 60 percent of all males and about two-thirds of all white males voted for the Republican candidate for governor, incumbent Pete Wilson, who campaigned on a reactionary platform embracing Proposition 187 (which outlawed governmental services and health programs for undocumented immigrants). By contrast, 75 percent of all black voters, 69 percent of all Latinos, and 51 percent of all people regardless of race earning less than $15,000 per year voted for Wilson's Democratic opponent, Kathleen Brown. In Michigan, 61 percent of all males and more than two-thirds of all white men supported Republican senatorial candidate Spencer Abraham, a former aide to Vice President Dan Quayle. Conversely, 91 percent of all African-Americans voted for Abraham's Democratic opponent, Congressman Bob Carr.

And in New York state, Democratic gubernatorial incumbent Mario Cuomo received his strongest support from African-Americans (86 percent), Latinos (78 percent), Jews (61 percent), people without a high school diploma (58 percent), and members of union households (51 percent)—in short, racial and ethnic minorities, low-income and poor people, and blue-collar workers. Republican victor George Pataki, by contrast, won the votes of people earning more than $100,000 annually (55 percent), of white Protestants (62 percent), of all white voters regardless of gender and income (58 percent), and of nearly two-thirds of all white men. In New York state and across America, the bedrock of Republican victories rested on white backlash, a political reaction against the social and economic reforms since Lyndon Johnson's Great Society. This was the third of a series of conservative movements undercutting the struggles for black equality and democratic rights.

To understand the full significance of the 1994 Republican congressional victories, we must place recent events within an historical and a political context. The 1994 congressional campaign, the vitriolic rhetoric of Republican leader Newt Gingrich and company, and the media controversy surrounding *The Bell Curve*, the pseudoscientific text that asserts black intellectual inferiority, are all part of a broad political and ideological assault against black people. What we are witnessing is the logical culmination of a process that actually began a generation ago.

After the political defeat of Jim Crow racial segregation across the South, highlighted by the 1964 Civil Rights Act and the 1965 Voting Rights Act, a white political backlash began to erupt. Led by Alabama Governor George Wallace, white racists and conservatives mobilized behind the banner of "states' rights." "Dixiecrats" who had belonged to the Democratic Party moved to the Republican Party, including South Carolina Senator Strom Thurmond and North Carolina Senator Jesse Helms. By the late 1960s, Richard Nixon successfully appealed to these reactionaries by advancing what became known as the "southern strategy." Nixon opposed court-ordered busing for school desegregation, attempted to elevate southern conservatives to the Supreme Court, and made direct appeals to Wallace voters. This "first wave" of political reaction produced Nixon's massive electoral landslide against liberal Democrat George McGovern in 1972. The political scandal of Watergate, combined with the major economic recession of 1974, led to the collapse of the southern strategy. Nixon was forced to resign in disgrace, and the Democrats by a narrow margin were able to recapture the White House in 1976.

The "second wave" of white reaction came with the election of Ronald Reagan in 1980. Reaganism made direct appeals to white ethnic voters who had previously been a central component of the New Deal coalition of the 1930s and 1940s. Millions of white ethnics had supported the Democrats because of political reforms such as Social Security and programs like the GI Bill. In the postwar years, many of these white ethnic voters became homeowners, moved from the cities to the suburbs, and moved up to the middle class. As they climbed the socioeconomic ladder, their material and political interests began to be reflected more by the Republicans.

As president, Reagan manipulated race in order to consolidate the Republicans' base within the white ethnic electorate. He aggressively attacked affirmative action and gutted the Civil Rights Commission, and he implemented policies that increased poverty and homelessness. Ideologically, Reagan stood for extreme anti-communism, the massive expansion of military expenditures at the expense of social programs, and the elimination of regulations and restrictions on the corporations at the expense of the public welfare. But like Nixon before him, Reagan fell victim to his own scandal, the Iran-Contra affair. The 1986 congressional elections returned the Senate to Democratic control, and Reaganism was on the defensive.

The "third wave" of white reaction was built on the political foundations of both Nixon and Reagan, but has reached a stage of development that is far more sophisticated and institutionalized than either of these earlier movements. One can identify at least four central components of the "third wave" of white reaction: electoral politics, mass mobilization, media and the new technology, and ideology. In electoral politics, the far Right has seized control of a number of Republican state party organizations and has aggressively promoted its candidates against more "moderate" Republicans. It has established mass membership organizations like the Christian Coalition, reaching millions of white, middle-class voters. It utilizes the media and new technologies to promote its ideas. Conservative intellectuals such as William Bennett and Bill Kristol are critical in setting the theoretical and ideological agenda. This mass conservative movement has think tanks, presses, television and talk radio programs reaching millions, and broadly based nonpartisan but highly political organizations reflecting a wide range of constituencies.

Neither Clinton nor the Democrats are prepared or willing to fight aggressively against this dangerous, anti-democratic "third wave" of reaction. Clinton mistakenly believes that moving his administration in a somewhat more "conservative" direction will appeal to elements of white, middle-class America now firmly under the electoral domination of the Republicans. This strategy can only produce disaster. The only way to defeat this "third wave" is to offer a coherent public policy alternative built around a progressive set of economic and social programs. This means transcending the old "liberalism" of the Great Society, and creating something truly visionary and progressive, something appropriate to our own times. If we fail to do so, the Right will continue to win electoral victories, and we will have only ourselves to blame.

BREAKING THE TWO-PARTY SYSTEM

Speculation that retired General Colin Powell might be a presidential candidate—speculation rampant a year before the 1996 election—once again highlighted the inherent weaknesses of our two-party system. In head-to-head competition in public opinion polls, Powell was much more popular than either President Bill Clinton or Senate Majority Leader Bob Dole, the men then thought to be the most likely nominees of the two major parties. But Powell was "too liberal" to win the Republican nomination through the primaries, although there were strong indications that Dole might tap him for the vice presidential spot. And Powell had said privately that any independent campaign like that of billionaire Ross Perot had little likelihood of success.

Rarely had conditions been more favorable for a third party that would provide a genuine alternative within our political system, plagued as it is by deep disenchantment with government and the absence of accountability by elected officials.

The two major parties have a stranglehold on the legislative process, utilizing the government to control and reallocate resources to their clients and constituents. This sorry fact of public life is true regardless of the ideological affiliations of the politicians in either party. The *Wall Street Journal* noted in late 1995 that, despite their anti-government rhetoric, congressional Republican leaders have become "cozy controlling the levers of power."

For example, Republicans promised to eliminate or radically restructure the Department of Housing and Urban Development (HUD). But once in power, New York Republican Congressman Rick Lazio, who had just become Chairman of the House Banking Subcommittee that supervises HUD, fought a rear-guard action to maintain the federal housing bureaucracy. Lazio recognized that "doing away with HUD could shrink his brand new congressional fief," the *Journal* noted. Pennsylvania Republican Bud Shuster, Chairman of the House Transportation Committee, bragged openly about his control of highway construction funds, declaring, "There's no such thing as a Republican or Democrat on bridges."

In 1993, Republican Senator Larry Pressler of South Dakota was one of the leading critics of corporate and special interest political action committees (PACs), which flood millions of dollars into the political system. Pressler even introduced legislation that would have outlawed PACs. But when the Republicans seized control of the U.S. Senate a year later, Pressler was catapulted from obscurity to the chairmanship of the powerful Senate Commerce Committee. Because this committee controls new legislation on the telecommunications industry, Pressler immediately became the principal recipient of PAC donations from cable television, telephone, and broadcasting companies. Within months of assuming leadership of the Commerce Committee, Pressler received thousands of dollars in donations from the corporate PACs of AT&T, NYNEX, U.S. West, Walt Disney Company, Sprint, GTE, and the Home Shopping Network.

Before the November 1994 election, the Chicago-based Ameritech Corporation gave 56 percent of its PAC funds to Democrats. Since then, its PAC has been overwhelmingly pro-Republican. Pressler alone received $6,500 from Ameritech's PAC from January through April of 1995. The South Dakota senator expected to raise $3 million toward his 1996 reelection campaign. Although Pressler's committee was considering, in 1995, a bill described as "strongly favorable" toward the telecommunications industry's interests, the senator stoutly denied that their PAC contributions had any influence on this legislation.

Instead of focusing on Colin Powell, who has no intention of building a third party or responding to our needs, we must consider what it will take to develop a genuine alternative in American politics. One place to begin would be to support more liberal election laws, permitting smaller parties to gain access to the ballot. The winner-take-all electoral system must be challenged in the courts and eventually replaced by a more democratic proportional representation process, in which voters could rank candidates according to their order of preference. A proportional representation system allows minorities to concentrate their votes, lowering the threshold for election to below 50 percent in multimember districts. Black, Latino, labor, and progressive candidates would find it much easier to be elected, giving us a more effective voice in government.

To end the corporate stranglehold on U.S. politics, we need to break up the two-party system. The Congressional Black Caucus may represent a "liberal alternative" within government, but its agenda will never win the acceptance of the mainstream of the Democratic Party. Our next step must be strategies for progressive independent politics.

BOTTOM-UP DEMOCRACY

In the land of "free enterprise" and consumerism, citizens can freely express themselves in every avenue except politics. We can choose among a dozen different brands of toilet tissue at the supermarket, but we are stuck with two varieties of Brand X when we enter the voting booth. As the collapse of the Ross Perot campaign in 1992 illustrated, efforts to challenge the system from the outside are difficult to organize. Yet can we really claim to be a "democracy" when an entrenched political class is able to reelect itself by means of special interest contributions, and when the alternative views of millions of people are suppressed by archaic, oppressive election laws?

We have to be willing to reform the electoral rules if we want to increase our political alternatives. And the best method of increasing our alternatives is through "proportional representation." In this country, we usually have "winner-take-all" elections, in which the person who receives 51 percent of the vote takes the electoral seat. But what about the 49 percent of the voters whose views aren't being addressed or even heard?

In a proportional representation election, voters could rank the candidates according to their order of preference (one, two, three, and so on) and the top candidates would be elected. We could consolidate congressional districts into multimember districts, which would greatly increase the probability of electing more women and people of color. Politically divisive runoff elections would be avoided under the proportional representation system. And countries that use such a system have much higher voter turnout rates.

The chief impact of adopting proportional representation would be to promote the rise of new third parties, challenging the Democrats and Republicans. The key reason is that the threshold of victory in a three-member district would be much less than half of the total vote. Lowering the threshold for election would mean that progressives and the minority communities that have become disillusioned by the two-party system would have a much easier time getting their candidates elected to Congress.

Proportional representation is sometimes criticized as too time consuming to tally and too complicated for the average voter to comprehend. But optical scanning equipment, like that used to check prices in supermarkets, could quickly record the votes. And proportional representation would create powerful incentives for millions of new voters to turn out for the first time.

In 1992, the most outstanding African-American example of independent politics was provided by Ron Daniels of Ohio. In his "Project for a New Tomorrow," Daniels brought together a wide range of black and progressive formations dedicated to the goal of constructing "an independent third force in American politics utilizing an independent presidential campaign in '92 as a major catalyst." Daniels campaigned for president on a progressive platform to challenge the reactionary politics of Bush-Quayle and the conservative politics of Clinton-Gore.

By traveling across the nation, speaking at hundreds of community centers, churches, and schools, Daniels reminded us that politics can be energized, bringing thousands of new voters into the process with a sense of empowerment. Although largely ignored in the national media, Daniels's progressive effort was important for maintaining the social justice perspective that was the heart of

Jesse Jackson's presidential campaigns of 1984 and 1988. Daniels and others showed us that political action can contribute to the struggle for "bottom-up democracy."

PRESIDENTIAL POLITICS, RACE, AND THE 1996 ELECTION: BEYOND LIBERALISM

The 1996 electoral campaign which reelected both incumbent president Bill Clinton and the Republican-controlled Congress was, by all estimates, the most boring contest in recent memory. Millions of voters stayed home on election day. Public opinion polls indicated a deep distrust of both Clinton and Dole, and a strong desire for a real alternative in politics. Television ratings for the two presidential debates were the lowest ever recorded.

Clinton's reelection was greatly assisted by a relatively strong domestic economy. Since January 1993, 10.7 million new jobs were created in the United States—although millions of them were located in the service sector or at low to minimum wages. Corporate profits and the stock market soared under Clinton, so business was not dissatisfied with the political stalemate between a Democratic president and a Republican Congress.

The failure of the Democrats to win majorities in the Senate and House was also not surprising. In most of the major presidential landslides since World War II, the winning candidate's party has achieved modest legislative gains, if at all.

The major reason that the Republicans performed below expectations was the reality of the gender and racial gap between the two major parties. White males generally split their votes evenly between Dole and Clinton. White women, by contrast, voted for Clinton by at least a 15 percent margin. Dole's rejection of reproductive rights, family leave, affirmative action, and other liberal policies alienated millions of working women. African-Americans in record numbers also rejected the Dole-Kemp ticket. At the beginning of the campaign, Republican officials believed that they might win at least 15 percent of the total black vote. Colin Powell remains a popular figure among many African-Americans, and his decision to become a Republican was viewed as a hopeful sign. Jack Kemp's selection as the vice presidential candidate was also widely praised by African-Americans, due to his reputation as a defender of affirmative action and his advocacy of a more racially inclusive Republican Party. Back in 1992, even George Bush was able to take 10 percent of the national black vote; there seemed nowhere to go but up.

There were several problems with the GOP's black strategy. First, Dole and Kemp opportunistically repudiated their own moderate records on civil rights and affirmative action. The Republicans' "Contract with America," the ultra-right blueprint of congressional conservatives led by Newt Gingrich, was widely opposed by African-Americans, Latinos, labor, and other liberal constituencies. The Dole-Gingrich philosophy of smaller government, reductions in education and health care, and no support for urban policy and employment initiatives directly contradicted blacks' interests. Although Kemp scheduled public appearances in Harlem and other black communities, the Republican ticket placed virtually no advertisements in black media such as Black Entertainment Television.

Conversely, Clinton was able to emphasize his close and cordial relationships with African-American voters. His roots in Arkansas were readily apparent whenever he visited a black church or addressed the Congressional Black Caucus. Clinton understands the language and culture of African-Americans, and he appears personally comfortable around black people. Despite their disappointment with many of his policies and political decisions, African-Americans made the realistic judgment that Clinton and the Democrats were clearly the best of the available alternatives.

Finally, Clinton won the overwhelming support of the black economic and political establishment: the Congressional Black Caucus, NAACP, black elected officials, executives and public administrators, and the growing African-American professional and managerial class. Ideologically, much of this group interpreted Clinton's policies as being in harmony with its own moderately liberal agenda of working for reforms within the political system, liberalizing capitalism by increasing black business sub-contracts and by expanding the percentages of blacks in management, and cultural integration into the mainstream of white America.

The essential contradiction for the black elite is that neither Clinton nor the Republicans really favor a change in the racial status quo. Under Clinton's administration, blacks will undoubtedly have representatives at the table. But on a range of substantive issues affecting the lives of millions of working-class and impoverished African-Americans—on welfare, health care, urban renewal, etc.—Clinton's victory changes little to nothing.

*   *   *

Clinton and Dole are essentially representatives of two corporate political organizations that have little direct relevancy to the real concerns and interests of most American people. Clinton's basic political strategy is essentially "Liberal Republicanism"—modest implementation of social welfare programs, reliance on the private sector to generate jobs, and moderate to liberal policies on the environment, gender issues, education, and other social policy questions. Dole's strategy was reactionary Republicanism, the logical consequence of 12 years of Reaganism in the White House and the ideological bankruptcy of the "Contract with America" promoted by Newt Gingrich and company. Reaganism shifted the public discourse to the right, and discredited and nearly destroyed traditional liberalism.

Like a scratched CD, Dole's repetitious refrain was that "Clinton is a liberal." How liberal is Bill Clinton? Consider that Clinton capitulated to the Right by signing the welfare bill, a reactionary piece of social policy that demonizes women receiving Aid to Families with Dependent Children, and that will throw one million children into poverty. Ask labor if Clinton is a liberal, when he campaigned for the ratification of NAFTA and GATT. How liberal was Clinton, when he signed the 1994 crime bill, that undermined civil liberties and greatly expanded the categories of criminal offenses for which the death penalty is required? Ask gays and lesbians if Clinton's "don't ask, don't tell" policy in the military was excessively liberal. Ask Americans who are friends of the people of Cuba, who vigorously oppose our immoral 36-year embargo against that island nation, if Clinton's signing of the Helms-Burton bill this year was "too liberal."

In the federal courts, Clinton has kept his promise to appoint significant numbers of women and racial minorities; however, the ideological orientation of many of these new judges is more centrist than liberal. Indeed, if one surveys Clinton's entire public record as president—from his uncertain support for affirmative action to his failure to pursue meaningful employment initiatives for the central cities and his complete retreat on a single-payer health care system—in many critical areas this "New Democrat" is slightly to the right of Richard Nixon. What Clinton really is saying to African-Americans, Latinos, gays and lesbians, feminists, labor, civil libertarians, and progressives in the religious community is that *you have no where else to go.*

Why did so many progressives, therefore, vote for Clinton? Almost none of the reasons related to Clinton's personal abilities or strengths, his character, or his political vision of democracy. In fact, most progressives concluded that Clinton's reelection was necessary from the vantage point of practical politics, a series of decisions which are unfortunate but unavoidable. For example, a Dole-Kemp victory would have placed more reactionaries on the Supreme Court and federal courts, consolidating the conservative majority already placed there by Reagan and Bush. With the Republican control of both houses of Congress, plus the presidency, all major branches of government would have been dominated by the Right. Here, many progressives relied on what I term the "political space" argument: that in order to ensure the survival of liberal ideas and policy objectives, we need a shift in the balance of public power and discourse from the far Right back to the ideological center.

Finally, there was the cultural and ideological argument favoring Clinton. The ideological offensive of the far Right manipulates racism and bigotry as a cynical tool to divide Americans along racial and ethnic boundaries. Over the years, we've seen this repeatedly in the attacks against affirmative action; books like Dinesh D'Souza's *The End of Racism* which deny the fundamental human equality and intelligence of black people; the legal dismantling of minority economic set-aside programs and the criticism against them as inefficient, corrupt, and unfair; and the recent court decisions outlawing minority scholarship programs and measures to enhance the number of racial minorities in colleges. The view here was that Clinton's election will not necessarily halt this ideological, cultural, and legal assault against black people and other minorities, but his victory will affect the context for this struggle, changing the ideological contours of the debates about basic reforms such as affirmative action and reproductive rights.

The debate over whether we should have voted for Clinton or not is, in the long run, less important than what progressive activists—in the civil rights community, in feminist politics, in gay and lesbian politics, inside trade unions, in community-based organizations—actually do collectively to transform society. That activist agenda begins with constructing a broad-based, new resistance movement for radical democracy and progressive change.

Bill Clinton was not nervously pacing along the political sidelines, worrying about whether he would win the support of the Left. Does Clinton really care if he obtains the endorsement of *The Nation* or the *Progressive*? Clinton's victory was not a fundamental victory for the Left; it was not a fundamental victory for black people's interests; it was not a fundamental victory for feminists. It was, however, a defeat for the politics and politicians of the Right. It was not the coming to power of the politics of what we are for, but the defeat of the politics we oppose.

Liberalism is in disarray, and it cannot sustain an oppositional dialogue with the forces of conservative reaction. Historically, liberals have been forced to look to the Left for their critical ideas and policy initiatives. The challenge is for us to build a democratic, progressive alternative to both

Clinton and the Republicans, beyond the old liberalism of the New Deal and Great Society, toward the construction of democratic movements for fundamental change in our country.

RACE AND REVOLUTION— TRANSNATIONAL PERSPECTIVES

APARTHEID IN TRANSITION

As the 1990s began, the system of racial oppression known as "apartheid" had brought South Africa to unprecedented crisis. International sanctions against the apartheid regime and domestic protests by Africans had disrupted the nation's economy throughout the 1980s. Thousands of white professionals and workers lost their jobs as European and American firms scaled back or eliminated their investments in the country. The crisis had hit rural areas as well, as the worst drought in a century severely reduced agricultural production. The many privileges and comforts long taken for granted by the majority of South African whites began to disappear.

In early 1991, South African President F.W. de Klerk announced the repeal of the basic laws of apartheid, the racist regulations that permitted black oppression. Repealed laws included the Land Acts of 1913 and 1936, which allocated 87 percent of the country to the white minority. The Separate Amenities Act was also gone, ending the legal basis of segregation in public accommodations. The Population Registration Act of 1950, which divided South Africans into four major racial groups at birth, was eliminated.

And white South Africans voted in March 1991—by a margin of more than two to one—to negotiate an end to white minority rule. In an unprecedented turnout exceeding 80 percent, the white electorate agreed to share power with Nelson Mandela's African National Congress (ANC) and other nonwhite political forces. The referendum was a victory for de Klerk and his ruling National Party. "Today we have closed the book on apartheid," de Klerk declared, "and that chapter is finally closed."

President de Klerk's strategy was to persuade whites, fearful and frustrated by the economic and social crisis, that their interests could be protected under a multiracial democracy based on capitalism. During the referendum debate, de Klerk insisted that extending voting rights to blacks would not mean the termination of white authority. A new constitution would provide checks and balances limiting the majority power of the black electorate. A devolution of the central government's authority to regional authorities would also serve to safeguard whites' rights. In effect, de Klerk called for the government's economic enterprises to be transferred into the private hands of white capitalists, while permitting blacks to gain votes within a weakened political system. White power would remain—but without legal apartheid.

Whites also voted "yes" because they saw that disastrous consequences awaited if the referendum failed. The Johannesburg financial newspaper *Business Day* warned that "a right-wing victory" by the referendum's opponents "will stop investment and economic growth and bring a crime wave no government could handle." The South African Council of Churches declared that a "no" vote would lead "to civil war."

Mandela and the ANC recognized that de Klerk's scheme would maintain white authority without a formal apartheid system, but their options against him were severely limited. There was no choice but to support de Klerk's referendum against those white reactionaries who opposed *any* negotiations with blacks. "If whites make a mistake and vote for repression," Mandela warned, "the country is in for a hard time."

Despite approval of the referendum, white opposition to a nonwhite majority government remained substantial. To the right of de Klerk was the Conservative Party, which deplored the referendum for "selling whites out." The party called for a return to apartheid and the establishment of a "white homeland."

Even further to the right was the openly fascist Afrikaner Resistance Movement, a paramilitary terrorist group. Movement leader Eugene TerreBlanche called for total racial warfare against blacks. As TerreBlanche declared, "If we have to deal with them, then it will be over the barrel of a gun." Many white police and military officers were sympathetic to the conservatives and the Afrikaner Resistance Movement.

The bitter irony for South African blacks was that all of de Klerk's promises and reforms did nothing to alleviate their economic and social oppression. More than seven million blacks still lived in shanty towns, in houses without running water, heat, or electricity. Blacks' schools were overcrowded and inferior to whites' schools. Blacks' incomes were only a tiny fraction of whites' salaries. Real democracy is empowerment, and de Klerk was bitterly opposed to fundamental changes that would actually transform the inferior status of black people.

Mandela understood: "Ending apartheid is not just announcing the results of a referendum," he said right after the vote. "It means there should be enough houses, more medical facilities, and better pensions for blacks. We are still far from this."

But President de Klerk was widely applauded as an "enlightened" liberal. The United States, Japan, and the Western European nations happily abandoned their sanctions against the apartheid regime. But mounting evidence suggested that white South Africans hadn't relinquished their long-term goal of domination. Despite the rhetoric and the reformist legislation, the system of racism hadn't disappeared—it only became more sophisticated and complex.

The white minority government still rejected the fundamental principle of democracy—one person, one vote. The apartheid Minister of Constitutional Government Gerrit Viljoen claimed that extending to blacks the right to vote must await the ratification of an entirely new constitution, and electoral rights could not be negotiated "in a piecemeal, interim, transitional way." Planning and Provincial Affairs Minister Herus Kriel condemned what he termed the "so-called affirmative action" program adopted in western countries as efforts to redress historic patterns of racial discrimination in employment. Kriel also declared that there were "no plans under way" to give any compensation to Africans for the seizure of thousands of acres of rich farmland by the white government. There were no plans to build racially integrated housing projects in all-white neighborhoods. Kriel explained that housing segregation would have to be broken down very gradually by "market forces," not by government initiatives.

White domination was also preserved by an extensive network of violence, surveillance, and terror. The infamous Internal Security Act, which permitted state security personnel to imprison or hold suspects for an unlimited period of time without trial, had not been abolished. For years, the apartheid government subsidized an elaborate secret network of black and white collaborators, including journalists, professors, businesspeople, and community leaders. These individuals were formed into "joint management committees" by the state security force, which used them to spread propaganda and attack liberal critics and opponents of the white minority regime.

The South African government and western media continued to spread the myth of "black-on-black violence," in which "tribal conflicts" between the African National Congress and the Zulu Inkatha organization were supposedly responsible for the deaths of thousands of blacks. But many of these murders and assaults were actually the work of state-sponsored terrorists. Many black gangs were instructed by police in the methods of violence or murder. ANC leaders and sympathizers in the black townships became victims of political assassinations. Many poor black people were so afraid that they even refused to wear the ANC's T-shirts.

But the greatest force for terrorism inside South Africa was represented by the Conservative Party, which sought to reverse the racial reforms and return to a rigid form of apartheid and the total denial of human rights for blacks. Instead of opposing these reactionaries, though, de Klerk repeatedly compromised with them. Meanwhile, thousands of white South African neo-Nazis joined gun clubs, preparing themselves for the final racial confrontation.

The new look of South Africa seemed kinder and gentler to George Bush, but white domination, white power, and white privilege still existed across that nation. The fight for genuine democracy and human freedom was far from finished.

By early 1993, the political situation seemed close to collapse. The country had averaged 8.5 politically motivated deaths per day in the preceding year. In April, Chris Hani, the leader of the South African Communist Party and a popular spokesperson for the African National Congress, was murdered by a white racist outside his Johannesburg home. Despite his militant reputation as former chief of staff of Umkhonto we Sizwe, the ANC's military wing, Hani had been in the forefront of a national campaign calling for peace and nonviolence.

Hani's murder was followed by the untimely death of another prominent ANC leader, Oliver R. Tambo, reinforcing the climate of crisis. Upon learning of Hani's death, ANC President Mandela warned that "our whole nation now teeters on the brink of disaster...We must not let the men who worship war, and who lust after blood, precipitate actions that will plunge our country into another Angola."

But despite the growing danger of political terrorism by the neo-Nazi Afrikaner Resistance Movement, progress toward a postapartheid society was maintained over the next several months. The number of political assassinations and killings declined by half nationwide by mid-summer. In January, the ANC and the ruling National Party reached an agreement permitting minority parties with at least 5 percent of the national vote to share in governing the country. ANC General Secretary Cyril Ramaphosa denied that this was a "power-sharing" agreement, because the majority party within the parliament would get its way on the lion's share of the issues.

Nevertheless, this historic compromise meant that the National Party, the major architect of the hated apartheid system, would retain junior governmental status for the rest of the century.

In June, the ANC and the National Party agreed to hold South Africa's first democratic election in mid-April of 1994. Voters from that nation's black population of 30 million would cast ballots, and no one doubted that Mandela would become South Africa's first democratic president.

As the ANC and the National Party moved closer to the elections, many of the old parameters of debate shifted, creating unlikely political bedfellows. For example, for many years the ANC was critical of apartheid-style authoritarian capitalism and favored the democratic nationalization of large corporations and businesses. But, fearful that its socialist politics might frighten away American and European investors, the ANC moved its economic program decisively to the right. ANC Foreign Relations Director Thabo Mbeki emphasized the ANC's new support for private market economics: "The issue of investor confidence is important. You can't threaten to nationalize property and expect people to invest. Economic growth is urgently required and it will necessitate massive foreign investment." By contrast, the South African trade union federation COSATU opposed any compromise that undermined the living standards and wages of black workers.

This delicate balance between accommodation and militancy could be heard in the political language of Mandela, who continued to appeal to all currents within the ANC's broad and often conflicting national constituency. Mandela cooperated with de Klerk on constitutional matters and increasingly on the economy, aware that the ANC would soon have to assume responsibility for the government. Yet Mandela continued to promote activism—especially to his more militant supporters, who had followed Hani as their hero. At a New York anti-apartheid meeting, Mandela noted critically: "If we ever forgot our source of power, which is the masses of the people, both inside and outside of the country, then we would be committing suicide."

Elements among South Africa's growing body of nonwhite elites had a clear interest in backing constitutional reforms and compromises with the white ruling class. It seemed highly possible that South Africa would become another Zimbabwe, in which nonwhites are permitted to assume control of the government while the real instruments of power in the economy and corporate sector remain under white domination.

The new developments within South Africa generated a growing debate among the veterans of the anti-apartheid movement inside the United States. Some activists favored the ANC's emphasis on compromise and cooperation with the capitalists. In 1992, for example, the prominent African-American lobbying group Transafrica staged an ANC-sponsored tour of black businesspeople to South Africa to promote investment possibilities. The real question was whether political freedom would also bring economic and social justice to the masses of African people. Only then would apartheid's oppressive legacy be ended. The 1994 electoral victory of Mandela and the African National Congress was widely celebrated as a triumph for democracy.

Despite the killing of 21 people and the wounding of scores more in the Johannesburg area alone during the week of the election, and despite evidence of vote tampering by the conservative Inkatha Freedom Party in Zulu areas, most of the voting across the country was judged to be free and fair.

In the aftermath of euphoria surrounding Mandela's election as the country's first black president, though, an honest and critical assessment of what actually happened in South Africa showed several things. First, it is clear that in no way had the decisive power of that nation's corporate and capitalist class been transferred to the black majority. The vast majority of businesses, the land, and the great economic wealth of South Africa remained in white hands.

Within the national government, the effect was a partnership between the ANC and the former masters of the apartheid dictatorship, the National Party of former President de Klerk. The state's bureaucrats and managers reflected the racist hiring policies of the past. Among the top 3,000 employees within the government, about 95 percent were white and hardly any were women. Most of the two million state employees were white Afrikaners. And, in the first few months of black rule, some were insubordinate to the point of outright rebellion against their new black supervisors. Several African administrators moved into government offices completely stripped of computers, furniture, and files. At the state-controlled South African Broadcasting Corporation, the phone number of the new chief executive was altered so that he could dial out, but no one could phone him.

The liberation struggle did not prepare the ANC to actually run the government bureaucracy. The best and most educated ANC leaders and blacks from the labor unions were largely elected to seats in the parliament or the provincial legislatures, leaving relatively few experienced activists to take over jobs within the civil service.

An even greater obstacle to democratic development inside South Africa was—and is—a massive class division within the African community itself, which threatened to erupt into unanticipated political disputes and debates. About one-fifth of the black population consists of Africans representing a relatively privileged social group. This class includes civil servants, small entrepreneurs, factory workers and skilled laborers, clerks, teachers, and administrators. As a group, their salaries rose dramatically compared to whites' wages during the 1970s and 1980s, even under apartheid, and they were in a position to become the chief beneficiaries of the new ANC government.

But the other four-fifths of the black population is incredibly oppressed and marginalized. This group includes unskilled and illiterate workers, farm laborers, domestic workers, and millions of alienated young people. About half of the black labor force is either unemployed or works within the "informal" or "underground" economy. About one black family in five is a squatter or lives in a shack without running water, a toilet, or electricity. Two-thirds of all blacks' homes are without electricity and 70 percent lack running water. Experts state that South Africa would need 300,000 housing units per year just to meet the current needs of the poor black population; the government has been building barely one-tenth that number.

It was clear soon after the election that the most oppressed blacks would not be patient with Mandela and the ANC government; they expected solutions to their problems immediately. In Soweto township near Johannesburg, about 20 percent of the impoverished residents had refused to pay their utility bills for at least two years. Thousands of households had initiated rent strikes. Black families who had defaulted on their loans refused to leave their homes and forcibly stopped local police from seizing their personal property.

Mandela was careful not to alienate whites who had benefited from and supported apartheid for decades. He declared, "We have to be very careful and not create the fear that the [black] majority is going to be used for the purpose of coercing minorities."

No one imagined that the task of transforming South Africa from a racist authoritarian state to a multicultural democracy would be easy or quick. Less than three months after the electoral triumph of Mandela and the African National Congress, there were already disturbing yet unmistakable signs that a golden opportunity to dismantle the system of white power, privilege, and property might be rapidly passing. The ANC was not adequately addressing the long-standing grievances of the masses of black South Africans.

Mandela's personal commitment to ensure a peaceful transition from white minority rule to multicultural democracy was part of the problem. Despite his imprisonment by the apartheid state for half a lifetime, Mandela has emphasized themes of reconciliation and reassurance to the white population. He was reluctant to fire police officers accused of atrocities against blacks and other opponents of the former government. He uttered no public criticism when his own defense minister tried to suppress the release of documents proving the South African military had engaged in surveillance and disruption of the liberation movement.

In the general election campaign of 1994, the ANC attacked the white minority National Party government for maintaining high salaries and posh living standards for bureaucrats in the midst of the nation's poverty and hunger. But once the ANC took over the parliament, annual salaries of members were raised to $55,000. Some of the ANC's closest supporters in the black working class became deeply concerned that the new government was becoming alienated from those who had been chiefly responsible for its election. The Congress of South African Trade Unions, for example, declared that the ANC had succumbed to "the gravy train mentality which had permeated apartheid governments." The power and privileges that were once only the right of white political elites were now extended to non-whites.

In another disappointing move, the economic agenda of the new government was a mirror image of the old apartheid regimes' pro-business policies. Mandela's first budget submitted to the parliament delayed the initiation of massive social programs such as education and housing for the poor, and froze taxes except for a one-time 5 percent income tax to pay for the costs of the national election. The all-white city councils across the country were to be replaced within six months by democratically elected, multiracial councils, but the ANC decided to postpone this necessary reform of local governments for a year, due to fierce opposition by white racists. Meanwhile, Mbeki, the ANC's first vice president, started conducting negotiations with white separatists on the possibility of creating an Afrikaner homeland. No basic territorial or economic redistribution from the privileged white minority to blacks was even being explored.

The breaking point for many of the ANC's staunchest supporters came in mid-June of 1994, when the government refused to declare a national holiday marking the anniversary of the 1976 Soweto uprising. The Soweto upsurgence of black rebellion against white oppression was a central event leading to the destruction of apartheid. But the holiday was opposed by many whites, especially corporate leaders. In response, black newspapers published stories critical of the ANC, with headlines such as "How Quickly They Betray the People."

It is always difficult to criticize one's friends, especially if they have experienced hardships and tragedies. No one more than Mandela merits our political understanding and solidarity. Yet friendship is meaningless without constructive criticism and thoughtful commentary. The friends of the anti-apartheid movement in the United States, Canada, and throughout the world also sacrificed for the ideal of multicultural democracy in South Africa. We understand that the current "government of national unity" that created a coalition between the ANC and the National Party will remain in place until new elections in 1999. But we also understand that the ANC is in danger of losing its base of popular support among the masses of African people, unless a more progressive public policy agenda is adopted. It is not enough just to have blacks in the parliament and official bureaucracy, and to declare apartheid's demise. Dismantling apartheid is only the beginning in the struggle to achieve genuine multicultural democracy.

FARRAKHAN'S WORLD TOUR—
THE ISSUE OF NIGERIA

Nation of Islam leader Louis Farrakhan managed to outrage and anger white America again, just a few months after the Million Man March he spearheaded in Washington, DC in October 1995. On a highly publicized 20-nation "world friendship tour" in early 1996, Farrakhan caucused with many African and Asian heads of state. This new level of political prestige and international recognition for Farrakhan was largely due to the dramatic success of the march.

The stated purpose of Farrakhan's tour, according to the Reverend Benjamin Chavis, was "to spread the uplifting spirit of the Million Man March abroad, particularly where issues of atonement, fratricide, reconciliation, and peace are of paramount concern." Farrakhan's itinerary and his controversial statements abroad, however, provoked widespread criticism in the U.S. media.

In Iran, Farrakhan was reported to have joined the celebration of the 17th anniversary of the overthrow of the Shah. The Iranian press quoted him as saying: "God will destroy America by the hands of Muslims. God will not give Japan or Europe the honor of bringing down the United States; this is an honor God will bestow upon Muslims."

In Iraq, Farrakhan expressed solidarity with dictator Saddam Hussein and suggested that United Nations economic sanctions against that country created a situation parallel to that of the Jews in Nazi death camps.

In Libya, according to the Libyan press agency, Muammar el-Gadhafi, that nation's leader, offered $1 billion to Farrakhan to finance his political activities inside the United States. Gadhafi declared after his meeting with Farrakhan: "Our confrontation with America used to be like confronting a fortress from the outside. Today we have found a loophole to enter the fortress from within."

It was not surprising that these statements and actions abroad provoked harsh condemnations from the government and the media. The State Department accused Farrakhan of "cavorting with dictators." The Departments of

Treasury and Justice demanded information on Farrakhan's negotiations with Gadhafi and other foreign leaders. Even Kweisi Mfume, the new President of the NAACP, declared that Farrakhan's visit to such countries did "not help" efforts to establish "conformity with international law." But frankly, many of these criticisms will not influence the opinions of most African-Americans. The white political establishment has always criticized black American leaders who have addressed international issues or traveled abroad—including Paul Robeson, Martin Luther King, Jr., and Malcolm X.

While I am skeptical of some of the establishment's criticisms, I feel compelled to challenge Farrakhan's political judgment on Nigeria. During his visit to the most populous nation of Africa, Farrakhan, in effect, gave his personal approval to the military regime that only three months before had hanged noted writer/playwright Ken Saro-Wiwa and eight other human rights activists.

The background to the execution of Saro-Wiwa is a mixture of corporate greed, environmental racism, and the brutality of a military dictatorship. Saro-Wiwa was the leader of a political movement among Nigeria's Ogoni people calling for greater democratic rights and environmental protection measures to check oil pollution in the region. Shell Oil Company produces about half of Nigeria's oil and has vast petroleum holdings in the Ogoni area. In the Ogoni ancestral land of 400 square miles, there are 96 oil wells and 5 pumping stations, where vast amounts of natural gas are burned off, 24 hours a day, every day. Frequent oil spills have polluted water supplies and destroyed crops.

Virtually no profits from Shell's oil production go to the Ogoni people. When protests developed, Shell authorized the Nigerian government to send mobile police to suppress dissent. Shell paid for the transportation and salary bonuses of troops, known as the "kill-and-go mob," who terrorized the local population.

In 1995, Saro-Wiwa was arrested on false charges and tried before a mixed military-civilian court with no right of judicial appeal. Two witnesses for the prosecution later retracted their testimony, admitting that the government had bribed them. Nevertheless, Saro-Wiwa was executed. Nineteen more Ogoni are now awaiting trial. Human rights groups throughout the world were outraged by this example of despotism.

But Farrakhan chatted amicably with Saro-Wiwa's murderers. He even criticized western governments for their condemnations of the Nigerian dictatorship. Farrakhan was reported to have said: "They say that you hanged one man. So what? Ask them, too, 'How many did you hang?'"

Randall Robinson, President of Transafrica, expressed "extreme disappointment" with Farrakhan's visit to Nigeria's military dictatorship: "His statements and the things that were said appear to make Minister Farrakhan an apologist for an authoritarian, corrupt, and repressive regime."

Farrakhan's actions in Nigeria illustrate the reactionary character of his entire political agenda. His right to travel and to engage in international dialogues must be defended. But on the issue of Nigeria, as far as black people's interests are concerned, he has much explaining to do.

RACE AND REVOLUTION IN CUBA

In late 1995, President Clinton announced major changes in the laws regulating U.S. relations with Cuba. Contacts among U.S. humanitarian, cultural, and educational groups and their Cuban counterparts were expanded. But Clinton refused to lift the 35-year-old economic blockade against Cuba, which prohibits direct U.S. investment and makes it illegal for most Americans to visit the island.

As Clinton made his announcement, I was in Cuba as the invited guest of that country's Center of American Studies, along with Leith Mullings, professor of anthropology at the City University of New York. We met with a range of Cuban intellectuals, government officials, and leaders from women's and cultural associations. Our objective was to understand the new developments within Cuba's economic system, its politics and race relations, and Cuban society as a whole. What emerged was a portrait of a lively, dynamic nation, in the midst of a series of fundamental changes.

The basic economic challenge behind Cuba's current transformation is the collapse of the Soviet Union and the socialist countries of Eastern Europe. The Soviet bloc had accounted for 75 percent of Cuba's trade. From 1989 to 1993, as the Soviet Union disappeared, Cuba's gross domestic product decreased by more than 34 percent, as Cuba ran short of supplies of all kinds. Subsequently, the U.S. blockade against Cuba became the most comprehensive ever applied by the United States against any country except in wartime.

By 1990, Cuba was forced to cut its oil imports by half. Consumption of electricity was sharply curtailed, with lengthy blackouts or reductions in service soon becoming the norm. Because of the fuel crisis, public transportation became sporadic and unreliable. Bicycles became the chief means of transportation. Food supplies in state-owned stores began to dwindle, as the government implemented strict rationing procedures. There were sharp reductions in medical supplies and services. Milk, which had previously been freely provided to all children up to age 14, was now limited to children under 7. Soap, toothpaste, toilet supplies, and other personal care items virtually disappeared. This devastating economic situation was aggravated even more by new repressive restrictions in the U.S. embargo.

The Cuban government's response to the new realities of what was termed the "special period" has been a profound rethinking of virtually every aspect of production, ownership, and exchange within society. One of the principal architects of Cuba's new economic policies is Alfonso Casanova Montero, the Vice Minister of Economics and Planning. In discussions with Professor Mullings and me, Casanova characterized the situation as Cuba's "deepest crisis in many decades."

The first challenge was to put food and consumer items back on the shelves and restore confidence. The only effective way to proceed was to decentralize the economy, encouraging individual initiative and innovations in patterns of production and ownership. The possession of U.S. dollars was decriminalized, injecting a "financial resource of tens of millions of dollars" into the legal economy. Half of all state land was transferred to cooperatives, giving rural families greater freedom and motivation to produce for themselves. Farmers were now permitted to sell their agricultural produce and goods directly to consumers in open, public markets.

In industry, the government decided to move away from Soviet-style, large-scale enterprises, toward "smaller-scaled industries with greater efficiency and a better management of scarce resources." While rationing of basic commodities continued, state prices were increased sharply on cigarettes and alcoholic beverages. Individuals were now permitted to engage in entrepreneurial and commercial ventures on a private basis, in order to "increase employment opportunities," according to Casanova. By 1995, more than a quarter-million Cubans were self-employed.

None of these changes could be successful in the long run without a massive infusion of capital. Even before the special period, the Cuban government had put resources into development of a tourist industry. By the late 1980s, an infrastructure catering to foreign visitors and guests was in place: restaurants, gift shops, hotels, night clubs, and taxis. All these commercial enterprises operate on dollars or other hard currencies, not Cuban money. Cubans are unable to obtain consumer goods and food of the same quality provided for tourists.

Because prostitution is not illegal in Cuba, the tourist industry inevitably created the conditions for a renaissance of sex-for-hire. At my hotel, I noticed a number of young Cuban women, mostly aged 15 to 20, walking in front of the taxi stand on the street. White tourists, eager for the bodies of young brown and black women, have little difficulty finding what they want.

On this visit to Cuba, I met many government officials, intellectuals, and community leaders, who provided critical insights. One of the highlights, though, was a lengthy conversation with Assata Shakur, who had been a prominent black American activist in the 1970s. Unjustly imprisoned in the United States, Shakur escaped and managed to reach Cuba. Today, a lecturer and teacher, she is active in local affairs, and remains an astute judge of society and politics.

Shakur emphasized that while Castro's Cuba has its problems, some of his government's strongest supporters are Afro-Cubans. This is because the actual conditions of daily life for black people—incomes, educational opportunities, health care, and so on—have greatly improved. The old system of racial segregation imposed upon Cuban society by the United States has been dismantled for decades. The Castro government has more recently become supportive of black cultural and religious phenomena such as Santeria, which draw their orientations from African spiritual traditions. Many black Cubans who are proud of their African heritage and culture, Shakur said, also support the revolution.

Shakur's comments highlight the long and continuing relationship between African-Americans and Cuba. Black abolitionists, such as Frederick Douglass and Henry Highland Garnet, actively supported Cuba's struggle for independence from Spain more than a century ago. After the revolutionaries seized power in 1959, Castro made a powerful impression among African-Americans by staying in Harlem during his first visit to the United Nations. To the great consternation of the U.S. government, Castro's famous September 1960 meeting with Malcolm X reinforced the solidarity felt by progressive black Americans toward the revolutionary government. As one black newspaper, the *New York Citizen-Call*, defiantly described Malcolm's private session with the Cuban leader at the time: "To Harlem's oppressed ghetto dwellers, Castro was that bearded revolutionary who had thrown the nation's rascals out and who had told white America to go to hell."

Since the 1959 revolution, Cuba has developed a special relationship with black people throughout the world. Castro has personally and politically identified himself and his entire nation with the cultural heritage and legacy of Africa. Since Afro-Cubans had been at the bottom of the social and class hierarchy before the revolution, they have gained the most from the vast societal changes that have occurred. A quarter-century after the revolution, employment, infant mortality, and life expectancy rates were better for blacks in Cuba than for blacks anywhere else in the world—even in the United States. Nevertheless, when our Cuban comrades sometimes insist that racism has been completely uprooted and destroyed in their country, many African-Americans have expressed strong doubts. Any multiracial nation with many generations of slavery in its past will retain a powerful legacy of racial discrimination. Even in a revolutionary context, old habits and attitudes are difficult to uproot.

How is "race" manifested within Cuban society in the 1990s? One member of the Cuban Communist Party's research staff admitted to me that genuine advances for blacks "have mostly occurred in the public sphere" rather than in civil society. With the exception of some cultural reforms made in the first decade after the revolution, Cuban television today is still monochromatically white. There are virtually no black actors on television. Most Cuban playwrights and filmmakers don't want to address the contradictions of race within contemporary society, preferring instead to focus on the role of blacks in earlier historical periods. Some white Cubans still engage in a massive denial of the existence of prejudice, yet nevertheless perpetuate and tolerate unequal treatment across the boundaries of color. White police officers today still stop and interrogate Afro-Cubans much more frequently than whites.

I spent part of one day with a prominent Cuban anthropologist, who discussed her ethnographic research in one particular urban neighborhood of Havana. She explained that although formal racial discrimination has been outlawed for years, prejudice is still virulent. "White values and standards" that were the cultural background of the traditional Cuban upper class before the revolution continue to influence behavior. For example, no discrimination in employment is permitted, she observed, "but an employer can still manifest his prejudices by not hiring blacks." In many communities, blacks and whites live side by side, working and interacting closely. But many of these same whites, "don't want their daughters to marry black men."

The struggle to destroy racism still remains a central challenge in Cuba. But on balance, the Cubans are far more honest about their shortcomings and have achieved greater racial equality for blacks than we have in the United States.

THE NEW INTERNATIONAL RACISM

On a street corner in Paris in 1991, I witnessed a massive public demonstration against racism. Thousands of Arab, African, and Asian working people were in the streets, denouncing a blatantly racist statement by the city's mayor, Jacques Chirac. But the white Europeans I saw watching this anti-racist rally seemed indifferent—even hostile.

All across Europe, from England to the former Soviet Union, there is a growing tide of racial and ethnic hatred. In part, the new racism results directly from the collapse of communism. As the Stalinist system fell apart, older ethnic rivalries began reasserting themselves in Yugoslavia, Bulgaria, and elsewhere in what used to be the Eastern Bloc. Inside the Soviet Union, minorities in the Baltic states, Georgia, Ukraine, and other republics agitated for independence.

In Western Europe, other factors were at work; political parties blamed their nations' economic recession on recent immigrants from nonwhite countries. In France, the neofascist sentiments of the National Front seeped into the major capitalist parties. In the Netherlands, the Centrum Party was formed, advocating policies discriminating against nonwhites. In England, Margaret Thatcher's government warned it would not permit that island nation to be "swamped by people with a different culture." The western capitalist nations moved swiftly to implement policies checking the immigration of Arabs, Asians, Africans, and other non-Europeans.

In 1992, as thousands of fires inflamed Los Angeles, I visited England to speak in black communities in Manchester, Nottingham, and several parts of London. Blacks in England were fascinated with the struggles of African-American people and wanted to learn more about the urban uprisings here. But I soon learned that England's black community faces a whole range of problems and challenges of its own.

The nonwhite population there, nearly 4.5 million, is located disproportionately in the working-class neighborhoods of Liverpool, London, and other cities. The largest percentage of "blacks" are actually people of South Asian ethnic background. More than 1.5 million blacks trace their heritage to the Caribbean or Africa. Although half of all blacks in Britain were born there, virtually all are viewed as recent or temporary migrants. They experience discrimination in employment and are over-represented in prisons and the criminal justice system. Although several blacks have been elected to the British parliament, the level of their political influence is much smaller than their actual numbers within the society.

I talked with dozens of blacks across the country and heard several key topics of concern expressed repeatedly. First was the question of identity. "Are we black or are we British?" asked one teenaged girl at a community meeting in north London. "You can see the racism in their faces," she continued painfully. One Guayanese woman who worked in a department store explained that it was the store's unofficial policy to shadow all black customers, watching out for possible shoplifting. "Whites waiting to be served are even pushed out of the way," she observed, "in order to wait on black customers quickly, and thus remove them from the store!"

As in the United States, the white power system makes repeated attempts to divide Afro-Caribbean, Asian, and African people from each other. In Nottingham, at one intense encounter with the black community, an Asian social worker expressed her frustration with the bickering among nonwhites. "We are manipulated against each other," she declared. "I go into the Asian community and racism towards blacks makes me sick....Some Indians actually believe they are slightly better off economically," and therefore should align themselves with conservative whites.

Because of their ambiguity about their cultural and political identity, many black Britons engage in interracial relationships. About a third of all black men are married to or involved in a sexual liaison with white women, a much higher percentage than in the United States. There is also a growing population of "mixed race" children raised by white mothers who have, at best, a fragmented ethnic and racial identity. Many see themselves as basically British in language, culture, and values, and consider the nonwhite half of their ancestry as secondary.

But in response to interracial contacts, many blacks are reasserting their links to their Afro-Asian heritage and cultures. "Saturday schools" are being established by black parents in dozens of cities across Great Britain. Typically, these informal schools have an Afrocentric curriculum, providing young blacks with lessons from black history, music, literature, and politics.

Black parents explained to me that they were motivated by the examples of self-hatred and internalized racism they had found within their own children. One teacher described how some of her black elementary schoolchildren had drawn pictures of themselves "with straight blond hair" to "make themselves more beautiful." Black children "are constantly told that they are stupid." An articulate black attorney from Nottingham, who chaired my visit to that city, explained: "Black people are afraid of discovering the pain within themselves created by racism. We need a space for healing one another."

Speaking on the subject of Malcolm X in London's black community of Brixton, I encountered more than 600 black people, mostly young adults eager to learn about black protest. As one young man explained to me, the examples of both Malcolm and the revolt in Los Angeles are directly relevant to blacks in Britain. "We are also part of the worldwide struggle against racial and class oppression," he asserted. "Like our sisters and brothers in America, we're ready to 'fight the power.'"

Events in France the following year showed what that fight would be like. Late in 1993, I again stood on a street corner in Paris as darkening clouds rumbled above. Dampened by intermittent showers, I watched several hundred members of the French racist political party, the National Front, marching in crude military formation. Most of the party members wore casual work clothes, blue jeans, and worn leather jackets. The majority appeared to be in their 20s and 30s. All were shouting. And all were white.

I followed the motley procession as it made its way from the Boulevard Raspail through the business district of the narrow Rue de Rennes on the city's Left Bank. National Front members and their supporters were busy posting racist fliers on the walls of dozens of buildings and doorways. One attacked French participation in the General Agreement on Tariffs and Trade (GATT) negotiations, which were just being concluded in Geneva. Another condemned symbols of "American imperialism," which supposedly undermined French culture. These symbols included the Statue of Liberty—which had been made in France and given to America as a gift—the trademark of the McDonald's hamburger chain, and a gross depiction of an African-American basketball player with huge lips and grotesque eyes. The National Front's slogans were provocative: "France for the French!" "Immigrants Out of Europe!"

The demonstration blocked an intersection, trapping a small automobile. Evidently, the driver had made the mistake of showing his outrage at the fascists. National Front members surrounded the vehicle and pounded it furiously with their feet and fists. The motorist fled for safety as his car was smashed. As the panic in the streets escalated, I wondered aloud, "Where are the French police?"

Saturday afternoon shoppers who had come to the busy district for Christmas shopping now huddled anxiously against the walls of the brightly decorated buildings. One elderly woman with red hair, perhaps a survivor of the German occupation of France a half-century ago, was not intimidated. Stepping forward, she bitterly denounced the young thugs: "Fascists! Fascists!"

When the demonstrators reached a McDonald's restaurant, they began to shout in unison, pounding against the large glass windows and doors. Terrified patrons and employees fled. Then from the rear of the mob, about 20 "skinheads" covering their faces with red handkerchiefs sprinted forward. They smashed a large plate glass window in the front of the restaurant, as well as the front doors. Triumphant and cheering, the National Front members marched to the Tour Montparnasse, thrusting their rain-soaked racist banners into the dark sky. Once more, the police were nowhere to be found.

The neo-fascist National Front has tens of thousands of members and has garnered the support of several million French citizens. The Front appeals chiefly to the country's unemployed and working-class whites, who feel that they are losing their jobs to nonwhite immigrants. By purging Arabs, Africans, and others lacking French citizenship from the country, the Front declares, poor whites will advance economically.

Fascist, anti-Semitic, and racist movements are growing rapidly across Europe in the post-Cold War period. In the past three years, right-wing extremists in Germany have murdered 30 nonwhites and have burned the homes of Turkish and African workers. In Russia's parliamentary elections, the racist and ultra-nationalist party of Vladimir Zhirinovsky received significant support. In Italy, the granddaughter of fascist dictator Benito Mussolini, running on a reactionary program, was only narrowly defeated in her bid for mayor of the city of Naples.

The immediate political outlook in Europe is more dangerous today than at any time since the defeat of Hitler's fascism 50 years ago. As the real wages of white workers fall and unemployment grows, the foundations for scapegoat politics and ethnic chauvinism are strengthened. We must monitor closely the growth of parties like the National Front, and provide support whenever possible to progressive and anti-racist organizations throughout Europe. As Paul Robeson, W.E.B. Du Bois, and Malcolm X all observed, the struggle against racism must be waged internationally.

As I walked toward my hotel after the National Front's rally, I encountered one final poster, the most vicious of all. A white man was shown under violent assault, with two black hands covering his mouth from behind. The slogan beneath read simply: "Freedom of Expression for Whites!"

Nonwhites in Europe cannot watch disinterestedly as apartheid in South Africa is subtly transformed into a kinder, gentler variety of racism, as racism in the United States assumes distinctly new forms. Neither Jim Crow-style segregation nor apartheid will characterize the oppression black people will be forced to confront in the 21st century, and that oppression won't be confined to Africa or America. The black people of the world will require greater determination than ever to fight the coming struggle for justice and democracy.

SECTION SIX

THE NEW RACISM

WHAT IS "RACE"?

Our national cultural mythology of the melting pot has never prevented U.S. society from allocating power, privilege, and the ownership of wealth and property unequally. Those who benefit directly from these unequal institutional arrangements have historically been overwhelmingly white, upper-class, and male. Thus, to be "all-American" is generally *not* to be Asian-American, Pacific Island-American, Latino, Native-American, Arab-American, or African-American. To be identified as "white" is to have increased access over others within the systems of decisionmaking, private- and public-sector authority, and intellectual leadership.

Ironically, because of the centrality of "whiteness" within the dominant national identity of being "American," most of us make few distinctions between our "ethnicity" and our "race," and the two concepts are usually used interchangeably. "Black" and "white" are usually perceived as very fixed, specific categories that define millions of human beings and their behavior. Yet in reality, "ethnicity" refers to the values, traditions, rituals, languages, music, and family patterns created by human beings within all social groups. All of us have some kind of ethnic identity that has nothing to do with the color of our skin.

"Race" is something completely different. First, race should be understood not as a thing that exists in every human society, or as an entity based on certain biological or genetic differences between people. A race is actually an unequal relationship between social groups, reinforced by the intricate patterns of power, ownership, and privilege that may exist inside the social, economic, and political institutions of society.

"Race" only becomes "real" as a social force when individuals or groups behave toward each other in ways that either reflect or perpetuate the patterns of inequality in daily life. These are, in turn, justified and rationalized by assumed differences in our physical or biological characteristics, or in bogus theories about cultural deprivation or the intellectual inferiority of "nonwhites." Thus, far from being static or fixed, "race" as an oppressive concept in social relations is fluid and ever-changing. What is defined as an oppressed racial group changes over time, geographical space, and history. What those in power define as "black," "Hispanic," or "Oriental" continues to change from one country to another.

Although native-born African-Americans and dark-skinned immigrants from Trinidad, Haiti, Nigeria, and Brazil would all be given the racial designation "black" on the streets of New York City, they have remarkably little in common in terms of language, culture, ethnic traditions, religion, and history. Yet they are all "black" racially, in the sense that they share many of the pitfalls and prejudices built into the established system of American power.

Similarly, an even wider spectrum of divergent ethnic groups from the Asian continent and islands—among them, Japanese, Koreans, Pakistanis, Indians, Mongols, Tibetans, Thais, Chinese, Cambodians, Filipinos, Hawaiians, Indonesians, and even at times Arabs and other peoples from the western extreme of Asia—are defined by the dominant society under the single category of "Asians" or, even worse, "Orientals," as if their identity relied solely on their geographic relation to Europe. Yet these people have sharply divergent languages, cultural traditions, social patterns, and philosophies of life. The American tendency to categorize and segment human beings into neat little racial groups ignores and trivializes the unique and very meaningful cultural characteristics of millions of people.

The new Civil Rights Movement for the 21st century must begin by challenging our old concepts of race and constructing new traditions of unity among various ethnic groups. We must deconstruct or eliminate the entire ideology of whiteness, the system of white power, privilege, and elitism that remains heavily embedded within the dominant culture, the social institutions, and the economic arrangements of our society. To destroy "race" means to democratize the leadership of our country to reflect the full spectrum of our ethnic, gender, and class diversity. By going beyond race, we may begin to recognize the common humanity and creativity of all divergent ethnic groups within our country.

WHY THE CHURCHES BURN

Every year it seems that there is a national event involving black people that allows virtually all white Americans to "prove" they aren't racist. During the Clarence Thomas confirmation hearings in 1991, white reactionaries in Congress took great joy in the public defense of a black man, condemning liberals for committing a "high-tech lynching." In the presidential election year of 1992, white Republicans and Democrats alike deplored the racial uprising in Los Angeles, rarely examining the deeper reasons for the black community's rage. In 1995, when O.J. Simpson was acquitted by a predominantly black jury, or when a million African-American men marched on Washington, DC, nearly the entire white establishment accused black folks of "reverse racism."

Once again, in 1996, we have an issue that allows prominent and powerful whites to be sanctimonious on race: the epidemic of racist burnings of African-American churches.

In the last six years, there have been 216 fires and desecrations in churches throughout the United States, half of them since January 1995. And nearly three-fourths of these recent ones have victimized African-American churches in the South. For months, few outside the black community listened or cared about this escalating crisis of vigilantism. Finally, as the pace of burnings increased, officials used the opportunity to take a public stand against intolerance and bigotry.

Republican presidential candidate Robert Dole attempted to win a few black votes by calling upon the Justice Department and police agencies to identify "the cowards responsible for these vicious acts of hate." Republican Senator Lauch Faircloth of North Carolina cosponsored a bill with liberal Democrat Ted Kennedy that would permit the Department of Housing and Urban Development to guarantee private loans to repair and rebuild African-American churches.

President Clinton finally denounced the burnings and established a joint task force of the Departments of Treasury and Justice that involved more than 200 investigators. Although Clinton rejected the argument that the church burnings were part of a "conspiracy," he declared that they "tear at the very heart of what it means to be an American. ...I think this is a place where nearly 100 percent of Americans are in accord." Similar expressions of outrage were made by conservative Republican Governor George Allen of Virginia. "Thirty and 40 years ago, people were making excuses for this behavior," Allen declared. "Now everyone, 100 percent of people who are speaking out, are condemning this."

But the most astute political gesture was made by Ralph Reed, Director of the Christian Coalition. Meeting with African-American ministers in Atlanta, Reed pledged to raise $1 million to help rebuild the churches. This was part of a strategy of "racial reconciliation." As Reed admitted: "I would not deny that there was a time in our nation's history when the white evangelical church was not only on the sidelines, but on the wrong side of the most central struggle for social justice in this century. I think that was wrong; I think we paid a price for that."

Please excuse me, but I think it's time for a reality check. Perhaps these politicians and the leader of the Christian Coalition mean what they say. Maybe there's finally a faint connection between rhetoric and reality on race. But would someone please answer these two questions for me?

First, if 100 percent of all Americans oppose this racist terrorism, then *who is burning the churches*? As columnist Bob Herbert observed, this is certainly not a case of "spontaneous combustion. The fuel for these fires can be traced to a carefully crafted environment of bigotry and hatred that was developed over the past quarter-century."

Second, if racial oppression is the context for these burnings and desecrations, then who or what is responsible for creating this climate of prejudice—the fear and loathing of African-Americans and other people of color? Where is Bob Dole on the issue of affirmative action? Where is the Republican Congress on the importance of job programs and social services for the urban poor? Where is the Christian Coalition on the issue of majority-people-of-color legislative districts and the defense of the Voting Rights Act? Ralph Reed apologizes for the past, but remains silent about the present. Racism is a real and powerful force in American politics and society, both yesterday and today.

The "conspiracy" Clinton refuses to recognize is the convergence of high unemployment; budget cuts; the assault on affirmative action, minority economic set-asides, and majority-black legislative districts; and the demonization of both welfare mothers and young black men. If a political, social, and economic environment of hatred is constructed by deliberate policy decisions, we should not be surprised when this hatred manifests itself in the burning of our houses of worship. We cannot end the burnings of our churches unless we uproot the cause of the violence: the burden of inequality and oppression of black America. What's needed are not more pious and pompous polemics denouncing bigotry, but more decisive action to create a just and more democratic society.

THE ETIQUETTE OF RACIAL PREJUDICE

Almost no white American today wants to be called a "racist." Yet millions of African-Americans are convinced that many whites live a racial double life. Because of affirmative action and civil rights reforms, nearly all whites follow a hypocritical racial etiquette in the presence of blacks, which disappears whenever they are among themselves. This is the basic premise of the film *True Identity*, in which a black man who dons white makeup discovers that whites act differently with each other.

There's abundant evidence supporting this thesis. A study by the American Bar Association, published in the *Harvard Law Review* in 1991, indicates that car dealers charge African-Americans and women higher prices than white males. Male and female researchers, black and white, presented themselves as "middle-class car shoppers" at 90 car dealerships in metropolitan Chicago. They used identical negotiating styles and bartered for an automobile with a list price of $11,000. The car dealers' offer to the consumers followed a pattern of gender and racial inequity. White males received an average final price offer of $11,352; white women, $11,504; black men, $11,783; and black women, $12,237.

In the workplace, most white males behave publicly in a manner that is race-neutral. Virtually no one openly calls African-American employees or supervisors "niggers." But millions of whites harbor deep resentment against black and Latino co-workers, who they believe have been unfairly advanced and receive excessively high wages due to affirmative action and equal opportunity programs. In one recent survey of several thousand white male corporate employees, only 10 percent expressed the opinion that "women were getting too much help" through affirmative action policies. But 50 percent said blacks and Hispanics unfairly gained "too much" of an advantage by affirmative action. Conversely, 55 percent of all Latino and black employees polled said "too little was being done for them" through corporate affirmative action efforts. Many whites perceive the presence of people of color in their workplace as a "zero-sum game"; the additional appointment of any single black person means that the potential job pool for whites has decreased.

Affirmative action programs have forced police departments to hire and promote thousands of minorities and women, partially in an attempt to respond to the changing urban demographics of race. But many whites have never reconciled themselves to these policy changes, which they perceive as an erosion of "standards" and professionalism.

Their anger and alienation are projected onto black and Latino citizens, who are generally assumed to be guilty rather than innocent in any confrontation situation. For example, a public commission reviewing the Los Angeles Police Department reported in 1991 that it found more than 700 racist, homophobic, and sexist remarks typed by officers into the department's car-communications system over the previous 18 months. Typical statements included: "Sounds like monkey-slapping time" and "I would love to drive down Slauson [a street in a black neighborhood] with a flame-thrower. We would have a barbecue." When challenged with these examples of police bigotry, Los Angeles Chief Daryl F. Gates suggested that black and Latino officers, "instead of white officers," sent many of the racist messages.

But the best evidence the typical black working-class woman or man perceives about the pervasiveness of white privilege is found in daily life. When inner-city blacks and Latinos return from work in the downtown district, they see the striking difference in the commuter buses and trains assigned to shuttle upper-class whites in comfort to their suburban enclaves. They feel the actual worthlessness with which the white establishment perceives them, as they wait for their graffiti-scarred, filthy trains in urine-stenched stations. They feel the anger they must hold in check when they see crack-cocaine merchants at their street corners, while police cars casually drive by, doing nothing. Everything in daily life tells them that, to those with power and wealth within the system, African-American life, property, beliefs, and aspirations mean nothing.

WHY INTEGRATION HAS FAILED

When George Bush nominated black conservative Clarence Thomas to replace liberal jurist Thurgood Marshall on the Supreme Court, most African-American leaders vigorously opposed the nomination. Most members of the Congressional Black Caucus quickly recognized that Thomas was an uncompromising opponent of affirmative action and civil rights. At the moment of decision, however, the NAACP flinched. Its refusal to take an immediate stand against a longtime Reaganite illustrated the limitations of its ideology and strategy for black advancement.

For half a century, the NAACP's basic orientation has been for racial "integration." Integrationism has usually meant the elimination of all structural barriers prohibiting blacks from fully participating in the mainstream of American life. Culturally, the goal was the achievement of a "color-blind society," which in the words of Martin Luther King, Jr. would mean that blacks "will not be judged by the color of their skin but by the content of their character."

The integrationists held an implicit faith in democracy American-style. The system could be made to work, they believed, if only people of color and others victimized by discrimination and poverty were brought to the table as full partners. This could be realized by expanding the number of African-Americans, Latinos, women, low-income people, and others holding positions of authority within the existing power structures in business, labor, government, and the media. When one encountered resistance, the integrationist strategy relied heavily on the intervention of a "benevolent" federal judiciary, which could be counted on to defend civil rights and civil liberties. Internationally, integrationists sympathized with the anti-apartheid struggle, but they failed to grasp the fundamental link between the battle against racism abroad and their own situation in the United States.

Integrationists placed great faith in the power of the political system. After the passage of the Voting Rights Act of 1965, they believed that all members of society now had equal access to the process of democratic decisionmaking. The central flaw of this political reasoning was the fact that democracy is only really possible when all participants have roughly equal resources as they enter the electoral field of competition. But, in fact, both major political parties had a vested interest in "managing" if not eliminating the electoral participation of blacks, the unemployed, low-income workers, and others.

In national politics, the Republicans had become by the 1980s an upper- and middle-class white united front, for all practical purposes. Two-thirds of all whites, and three-fourths of all upper-class whites, voted for Ronald Reagan in 1984. The Republicans saw few advantages in encouraging the electoral participation of constituencies that were highly inclined to vote Democratic.

But the Democrats also had problems with blacks and low-income voters, and for several reasons. Increased black electoral clout would be translated into organizational influence within the Democratic Party's structure, which would shift the ideological axis of the party to the left. Most white Democratic officials were convinced that the Democrats had to move to the right, incorporating elements of the Reagan agenda into their own programs. Consequently, throughout the 1980s, the actual influence of African-Americans as a group declined within the mainstream of both parties.

But the major short-sightedness of the integrationists is their widespread belief that the elevation of more blacks to positions of power will increase the clout of African-Americans as a group. From this perspective, they claim that it would be preferable to have a black, Latino, or woman conservative, rather than a white affluent male with the same political views. This sort of "symbolic politics," in effect, permits the white corporate and political establishment to select its own "minority leaders," such as Linda Chavez, Thomas Sowell, Shelby Steele, and Thomas, who have virtually no constituencies among people of color, and who vigorously reject affirmative action and civil rights.

Since the vast majority of African-American community-based leaders have little or no access to the media, little dialogue really exists between working-class and inner-city black communities and representatives of the white elite. Of course, no dialogue is really being sought by the latter; the object is to "manage" the volatile urban masses of blacks, Latinos, and unemployed by elevating small numbers of nonwhites to positions of authority.

These flaws in the integrationist philosophy have led the African-American community to an impasse in its pursuit of political freedom. A new approach to politics and empowerment must be initiated to challenge the system more effectively. The policies that succeeded in ending legal segregation a generation ago are not applicable to our current conditions.

TWO KINDS OF BLACKNESS

One of the most perplexing political events in recent African-American history was the controversy between Anita Hill and Clarence Thomas. Most blacks recognized that Thomas's civil rights record was nonexistent, that he had performed a dishonorable role in the Reagan administration. Hill's testimony of sexual harassment by Thomas was also persuasive to many. Nevertheless, most African-Americans gritted their teeth, swallowed their political pride, and embraced Thomas for elevation to the Supreme Court. Why?

My own impression is that most African-Americans rationalized their support for the black conservative in racial terms: "He may be an apologist for Reaganism, but at least he's black." If Bush was going to replace the liberal jurist Thurgood Marshall with a conservative, shouldn't he be "one of us"? This was the reason that Jesse Jackson, who expresses himself on practically every political issue, was virtually silent on Thomas. The problem with this argument is that there are two very different types of blackness, and Thomas was the beneficiary of African-American confusion on this issue.

"Race" is essentially a group identity that is imposed on individuals by others. During Jim Crow segregation, a person's color told much about his or her background, kinships, social behavior, culture, and politics. We were isolated as a group from the mainstream of American society by the walls of legal racism.

But in the post-civil-rights era, this is no longer true. "Blackness" in purely racial terms just means belonging to a group whose members have in common a certain skin color and other physical features. In this limited sense, both Thomas and I are "black." But this racial identity today doesn't tell us anything about a person's political beliefs, voting behavior, or cultural values.

"Blackness" or African-American identity, however, is much more than "race." It is also the traditions, rituals, values, and belief systems of African-American people. It is our culture, history, music, art, and literature. Blackness is our sense of ethnic consciousness and pride in our heritage of resistance against racism. This African-American identity is not something that our oppressors forced upon us. It is a cultural and ethnic awareness that we collectively have constructed for ourselves over hundreds of years. This identity is a cultural umbilical cord connecting us with Mother Africa.

When African-Americans think about blackness, we usually are referring to both definitions simultaneously—"racial identity," a category Europeans created and deliberately imposed on us for the purpose of domination, and "cultural identity," which we constantly reinvent and construct for ourselves. But according to white Americans, blackness is basically one definition only—racial identity. They have little awareness or comprehension of African-American history, politics, religion, or culture. Blackness to them is skin color and a person's physical features, period.

Today, there's an entire generation of African-Americans who were born after the struggles of the Civil Rights Movement. They never witnessed the sit-ins, freedom rides, or desegregation boycotts. They never took part in Black Power demonstrations. Many of these African-Americans, particularly in the upper-middle class, grew up in the white suburbs, attended white schools, and now are employed in predominantly white businesses. They typically don't attend black churches or belong to black social organizations. They have little personal contact or experience with the harsh problems of the inner-city. One can argue that these individuals are certainly black in racial terms, as defined by white society. But as far as cultural connections are concerned, their blackness is limited.

The great danger is that the white political and corporate establishment can manipulate racial images to the detriment of the black community. Black professionals have been elevated to positions of influence within the system, and we are told that this represents an advancement for all African-Americans as a group. But how true is this? Is the appointment of a red-haired white male to the Supreme Court an example of empowerment for all Americans with red hair? If a black person is only *racially* black and has few cultural or political connections with the actual struggles of other African-Americans, he or she will feel no shred of accountability to other blacks. The best example of this is, of course, Clarence Thomas. Despite his skin color, his appointment to the Supreme Court—and subsequent service there—has been no victory for black people as a group.

THE COLOR OF PREJUDICE

In November 1993, Khalid Abdul Muhammad, national spokesman for the Nation of Islam, delivered a speech at Kean College in New Jersey. Over a three-hour period, he presented an analysis that was blatantly anti-Semitic and filled with hatred.

Muhammad declared that Jews are "the bloodsuckers of the black nation," that they "have our entertainers in their hip pocket" and "our athletes in the palm of their hand." Muhammad stated that Jews "call yourself Mr. Reubenstein, Mr. Goldstein, [and] Mr. Silverstein because you [have] been stealing rubies and gold and silver all over the earth." He even revived the controversial statement Louis Farrakhan made a decade ago: that Adolf Hitler was "wickedly great." The Holocaust was attributed to the role of the Jews, who had "undermined the very fabric of [German] society."

As the text of the speech was circulated, largely by the Anti-Defamation League of B'nai B'rith, conservative Jewish leaders and journalists used the issue to condemn not only Louis Farrakhan and the Nation of Islam, but also the vast majority of African-American leaders and officials who had any relationship with the Muslim community. A.M. Rosenthal of the *New York Times* pompously and falsely asserted that "with few exceptions, black political and intellectual leadership has kept silent about . . . the surge of anti-Semitism and anti-Semitic propaganda among blacks, particularly among young and more educated blacks." Rosenthal attacked Benjamin Chavis, then leader of the NAACP, the Congressional Black Caucus, and Jesse Jackson for establishing dialogue with Farrakhan, insisting that black mainstream leaders "are willing to ally themselves with the salesmen for a new Holocaust." In the weeks that followed, virtually every African-American national figure criticized or denounced the anti-Semitic slurs and sentiments represented by Muhammad's talk. But the political impasse between large segments of the Jewish community and African-Americans, characterized previously by differences over affirmative action and Israel's relationship with the former apartheid government of South Africa, grew even worse.

Let us separate the key issues in this growing political controversy. As much as I reject and oppose the political perspective of Muhammad, he had a right to speak at Kean College or at any other public institution. If Patrick Buchanan, Newt Gingrich, and David Duke have a legal right to spew their respective political poisons and to advance an unconditional program of oppression for black people, Muhammad must be permitted that same freedom. To extend the right to speak only to those with whom we agree is a dangerous doctrine. "Freedom" is always and only for those who think differently.

We must be honest about the root factors in the debate about Muhammad, Farrakhan, and the charges of anti-Semitism in the black community. There *is* anti-Semitism among some African-Americans, as well as racism and prejudice toward black people among some Jews. But anti-Semitism has *never* been a mass movement among African-Americans, and no national black leader is calling for anything that approaches "a new Holocaust."

To be sure, there are real tensions and disagreements separating key elements of the Jewish community and African-Americans. The intolerance and discrimination that Jews have experienced in this country never equaled the fierce oppression African-American people have suffered—and continue to suffer. There are parallels between the bigotry of anti-Semitism and the exploitation of racism, but the two dynamics of discrimination are not identical. Jews as a group are middle and upper class, while an ever-growing number of African-Americans are trapped in a cycle of poverty, unemployment, drugs, and violence. To say simplistically that the two groups have identical interests is simply not true. But it is equally false to assert that Jews are "turning against" black interests. Consistently, even in the 1993 mayoral election in New York City, Jewish voters have been among the strongest white supporters of black candidates and issues.

Nothing can ever justify the articulation of hatred. Color prejudice transcends the barriers of black and white. The great strength of the black freedom movement—from Frederick Douglass to Martin Luther King, Jr.—has been the realization that our struggle for equality is not just for ourselves, but for all humanity. When we surrender this moral and ethical principle, we sacrifice our greatest weapon in the battle for democracy for all people who experience discrimination.

THE CHASM OF RACE

Even Martin Luther King, Jr. would be perplexed by the growing pessimism that pervades American race relations. Despite the passage of civil rights legislation and the elimination of legal barriers to equality, the differences between African-Americans and most whites seem greater today than during the segregationist era of George Wallace. Ironically, the greatest racial divisions seem to be among young people below the age of 25.

In October 1991, Peter D. Hart Research Associates conducted a nationwide poll of youths aged 15 to 24 concerning their racial beliefs and perceptions. As the profile that emerged illustrates, many young Americans live in two virtually separate racial universes. When asked whether colleges should give "special considerations" to recruiting and admitting students of color, 51 percent of the young whites were opposed. Two-thirds of all young whites expressed opposition to businesses that "gave special consideration to minority job applicants." White opposition climbed to 78 percent on the question of whether employers should extend "special preference" in evaluating minority job applicants.

The figures indicate that millions of young white Americans think that white racism no longer exists and that the chief victims of discrimination are whites. For example, when asked whether "discrimination was more likely to hurt a white or minority person seeking scholarships, jobs, or promotions," 49 percent of the whites declared that they "were more likely to lose out." In contrast, 68 percent of young African-Americans, 52 percent of the Latinos, but only 34 percent of the whites believed that "minorities were more likely to lose." About half of all young Americans polled characterized race relations as "generally bad."

The striking differences in racial perceptions can be attributed partially to the reactionary rhetoric and repressive policies of the Reagan and Bush administrations. Reagan's open embrace of apartheid in South Africa, and his hatred of civil rights and affirmative action regulations, have influenced the racial outlook of many young whites. Instead of approaching racial problems with honesty and objectivity, many whites would prefer to live in a world of lies, myths, and illusions. Like Reagan, Bush, and Buchanan, it is easy to twist reality to conform to one's own self-serving interests.

Many white students believe the myth that less qualified minorities are displacing more qualified whites as faculty and administrators. But the truth, according to a Carnegie Commission educational report, is that when the level of educational attainment and scholarly productivity are equal, African-Americans still receive tenure and promotion at lower rates than whites. Whites hold about 87 percent of all tenure-track faculty positions at American universities.

White students frequently complain that affirmative action policies elevate "unqualified" students of color into their colleges. Yet few discuss the policy of "legacies," the practice at many colleges of admitting the sons, daughters, and grandchildren of alumni even when their academic records are less than competitive. At Harvard College, for example, the general admission rate for legacies is 44 percent.

There is a myth that hundreds of thousands of Latino, Native-American, and African-American students are taking opportunities away from whites. But the reality is that during the 1980s, the percentage of minority high school graduates who went on to college actually declined. In 1975, about 36 percent of all Latino high school graduates aged 18 to 26 were enrolled in college. By 1988, only 26.8 percent of all Latinos in this age group were in college. The same retreat from educational equality occurred for black students. In 1975, 32 percent of all black high school graduates in this age group were attending college; 13 years later, the percentage had fallen to 28.1 percent. Meanwhile, the enrollment of white students in these years actually increased, from 32.4 percent in 1975 to 38.1 percent in 1988.

At the heart of the fractured soul of America is the frightening chasm of race. So long as many whites prefer to live in a world of dangerous illusions, while cynical politicians peddle the poison of "reverse discrimination," no genuine interracial dialogue is possible. Fighting for full equality, strongly enforcing affirmative action, and challenging the myths about race are the only ways to achieve real understanding across the color line.

BLACK RACIAL FUNDAMENTALISM

It was nearly 1:00 am, and I was sitting in an over-crowded bar amidst several hundred Cornell University students. I'd been invited to the Ithaca, New York campus to give a talk sponsored by the African-American Student Association. The semester was nearly at an end and most white students were in the mood for celebration. But the young black women and men who had escorted me to the bar were serious, determined—and angry.

"White people are basically untrustworthy and inherently evil," one young black man insisted passionately. "Coalitions with them are impossible. They have always been against us, and our only hope is to build up our own system separate from theirs."

Other black Cornell undergraduates agreed, extending the young man's thesis to campus relations. One black female student condemned the efforts by white feminists to engage in a dialogue with women of color. "What do we have in common besides gender? Nothing!" declared the young woman. When I pointed out that this was not the position of black women's rights activists and intellectuals such as Angela Davis, bell hooks, Julianne Malveaux, and Patricia Hill Collins, the students expressed little knowledge of their works. I observed that any analysis of the oppression of black people had to begin with institutional racism, but that it could not end there. We also had to explore the connections linking the exploitation of people of color across the globe, and examine the class, gender, and political divisions that cut across narrowly defined racial lines. With emphasis, I added that great black nationalists, such as Marcus Garvey, and Pan-Africanists, such as Ghanaian leader Kwame Nkrumah, never employed a simplistic racial analysis.

"That was Garvey's problem and the principal reason for his downfall," one black student responded immediately. When Garvey, Nkrumah, and even Malcolm X are dismissed as being "not black enough," and when young black women uncritically defend pugilist Mike Tyson as a "victim" of both the criminal justice system and of rape victim Desiree Washington, then something is deeply wrong within the black community.

There is a spiraling sentiment of "racial fundamentalism" among many young African-Americans across the country today. The dominant characteristic of this fundamentalism is a fixation and preoccupation with "difference." Instead of being clear and confident in one's history, culture, and heritage, focusing on our potential and possibilities, we become preoccupied with the actions and attitudes of others who do not share our racial identities. Instead of articulating our own interests and objectives in the context of affirming our unique culture and humanity, we seek to negate and destroy any and all links that bind us to a larger network of communities. The new black fundamentalism wants to stand *against* something, rather than *for* ourselves.

Part of the reason for the new black fundamentalism is the deteriorating social environment experienced by younger African-Americans. The Centers for Disease Control recently reported that African-American males are shot to death five times more often than white males, and that the leading cause of death for black males aged 10 to 34 is "bullets." But even more important is the recognition that whites and blacks perceive the state of race relations radically differently. In a recent *U.S.A. Today* national poll, for instance, far more whites than blacks—74 versus 48 percent—state that the police "do a good or excellent job in their cities." Blacks conversely are more than twice as likely—67 versus 31 percent—to state that racism against African-Americans is a "serious problem where they live."

This deep sense of racial division extends directly to college campuses, where affirmative action programs and multicultural reforms are under increased assault by white conservatives. In 1993, the American Council on Education reported that only 23.6 percent of all 18- to 24-year-old African-Americans were currently enrolled in college, compared to over 34 percent of whites in this age group. Higher tuition and fees, the financial aid shift from grants to loans, and in some quarters the reaction against affirmative action have all combined to erode the status of thousands of young black people in higher education. In this context of racial reaction, it is scarcely surprising that a spirit of pessimism and racial isolationism has taken root.

Our response to "racial fundamentalism" on college campuses and throughout every black community must be based on a clear vision of empowerment and collective pride, that does not become sidetracked in the dangerous traps of alienation and chauvinism against others. As black feminist bell hooks tells us, "We can bear witness for our own cause, for what we believe in, without denigrating others." To believe that literally all whites are our enemies is just as dangerous and erroneous as the argument that all blacks have the best interests of the African-American community at heart. Clarence Thomas, for one, may be racially "black," but politically and culturally he is one of the "whitest" men in America. If we are clear about who we are as a people and what is in our own interests, we should be able to work with anyone for our empowerment.

AN AMERICAN DILEMMA

In the spring of 1994, the Morehouse Research Institute of Morehouse College in Atlanta sponsored a major conference on the state of American race relations. The year marked the 50th anniversary of the publication of the most influential study of racial inequality—Gunnar Myrdal's *An American Dilemma*. Scholars and researchers came to Atlanta to explore the importance of this work and the history of sociological studies on the black community.

The burden of race has always been at the heart of America's greatest dilemma—whether this nation can create avenues of opportunity, representation, mobility, and empowerment for its increasingly multicultural, non-European population. Part of the difficulty resides in the ever-changing definition of what race is, whether it is biologically derived or historically constructed, and whether it is a permanent feature in the social interaction of human societies. Can "race" be overcome and, if so, how?

In the early 1900s, many social scientists argued that African-Americans were genetically or biologically inferior to whites. Research selectively taken from African cultures was used to "prove" that blacks as a group were retarded and primitive. In Europe, Hitler's Institute of Racial Biology provided pseudoscientific "evidence" that Jews and Africans were backward and subhuman. Studies of head sizes and the weight of human brains were used to illustrate black people's lack of mental capacity. IQ tests were used by social scientists in a similar manner, seeking to prove beyond doubt that blacks were racially inferior to whites.

Against this tradition of racist research, first and foremost, was W.E.B. Du Bois, the major black scholar of the early 20th century. With the publication of *The Philadelphia Negro* in 1899, Du Bois established the field of black sociology. His Atlanta University research conferences in the early 1900s produced important studies on the black experience in America. Continuing this tradition of anti-racist research were other scholars, such as Fisk University sociologist Charles S. Johnson and E. Franklin Frazier, author of many important studies on the black church, the black family, and the black middle class.

During World War II, Swedish scholar Gunnar Myrdal utilized the research of black scholars to prepare a comprehensive analysis of the state of U.S. race relations. Myrdal believed that racism in the United States was essentially a matter of "caste." People who belonged to the black caste received a second-class education, lacked democratic voting rights, and had inferior health care and higher rates of unemployment. For Myrdal, the American caste system was rigid and static.

Myrdal cited social psychology as a principal factor in the perpetuation of this system—the belief among the majority of whites in their inherent superiority over blacks. Some of whites' fear was translated into distinctly sexual terms. For example, Myrdal's researchers asked southern whites the question, "What is the motive for racial segregation?" Whites responded to the question in this order: first, segregation was essential to halt interracial sex; second, to stop social equality between the races; third, to maintain segregation in schools and colleges; fourth, to halt black political power and voting rights; fifth, to maintain discrimination in the courts and legal system; and sixth, to halt blacks' economic progress—land, credit, capital, and jobs. When blacks were asked the question, "What do you want?," they gave an identical list of priorities, *but in reverse order.* For African-Americans, freedom first and foremost meant economic equality, jobs, and legal and political rights—not interracial sex.

Myrdal believed that the essence of the American dilemma was moral and ethical: how long would white America continue to ignore the claims to democracy and equality by those held within the inferior caste, chained by the political shackles of Jim Crow segregation? With the perspective of history, we can criticize many of Myrdal's assumptions. He was incorrect to ignore the fact that racism did not benefit all whites equally. Poor whites' wages and living conditions were also repressed when blacks were paid less. Myrdal's use of "caste" also ignored the actual historical evolution and changing pattern of race relations since slavery, and underestimated the importance of black activism and struggle to change society. Nevertheless, *An American Dilemma* was an important study challenging the burdensome concept of racial inequality that continues to undermine American society.

SECTION SEVEN

BLACK EMPOWERMENT

BLACK HERITAGE AND RESISTANCE

When I was 20 years old, a simple event took place that I will never forget. I was a student at the University of Nairobi in Kenya, in East Africa. At the time, the university was run largely by Europeans and British-educated African scholars, so it retained much of the atmosphere of an English college despite its African student population. Examinations were used to judge student progress in particular courses, and grades were often posted outside a faculty member's door or in the hallway outside the department secretary's office. A student couldn't hide behind the nameless reference of a Social Security number posted along with his or her grade; it was public knowledge how well an individual did on a test.

With some fear, I went along with a classmate to check my grade in a particular class. In the best Swahili I could muster, I remarked that she had done very well for herself. She smiled. Then, shaking her head, she replied: "*Hapana, ndugu* [No, friend]. I didn't do well. My people did well, and my village did well."

And so I learned an invaluable lesson in black history and individual excellence, which I have carried forward to this day: whatever successes, victories, or merits we attain in life, whatever awards or accomplishments we receive, we're never the sole product of our individual activities. They are also due to the collective sacrifices and the sweat, the pain, and the hopes of many others who permitted us to aspire to a better life.

As my grandmother might say, "If you don't know where you are going, any road will take you there." This means at least two things—that the road we travel had a beginning telling us much about who we are and how we got to our current point of development, and that the road goes past our own personal horizon, into the distance. If we don't know where we have been, how can we possibly know where destiny is taking us? And if we don't understand the origins of the road we travel, how can we know where we are going in the future? Our history and cultural heritage connect all of us to people who struggled in the past to build the foundations of our current success. And we have a special obligation to do the same for the children of the world who are yet to be born.

More than 160 years ago, Nat Turner, an African-American minister in Virginia, organized one of the most important slave uprisings in American history. More than 60 whites were killed over several days. Hundreds of African-Americans were slaughtered in retaliation by white militia and armed slave holders. When Nat Turner was finally captured, a white newspaper reporter named T.R. Gray was assigned to interrogate him. The record of that interview was published as the "Confessions of Nat Turner."

Gray could not comprehend why a black man as intelligent as Turner had engaged in such an obviously futile endeavor. There was absolutely no possibility of success against the armed power of white authorities; the slaves were unarmed and unorganized, and some among them were so dominated by their masters that they were likely to reveal the plot in all its details in order to curry favor with whites. Gray demanded to know why Turner had acted as he did.

Turner replied: "Was Christ not crucified?" Christ was a revolutionary in faith, Turner was saying. As he was prepared to die for his belief, Turner could do no less for his own people suffering the oppression of enslavement.

Turner's courage and vision speak to the condition of African-American people throughout history and today. A sense of heritage and commitment means that one is linked to the ordeals of the past and the promise of the future. Today's freedoms that are the result of the Civil Rights Movement—the freedoms of African-Americans to vote, purchase homes in all-white neighborhoods, stay in formerly all-white hotels, and attend previously all-white schools—are only the beginning. To envision a world without racial discrimination, poverty, illiteracy, and black-on-black violence is to travel further down that freedom road first charted by our black foremothers and forefathers.

REMEMBERING MARTIN

Every year during Black History Month, we honor those women and men of African descent who made special contributions to the struggle for black freedom in America. We often fail to understand that the only history oppressed people have is collective memory—the experiences that give us a sense of identity, tradition, and purpose. As we rethink the past, we begin to appreciate the personalities and struggles that make the heritage of African-American people unique.

More than 30 years ago, when I was a teenager, Martin Luther King, Jr. was invited to speak at Wilberforce University, the African-American college near my hometown of Dayton, Ohio. My parents decided that it was an excellent opportunity for the entire family to hear the preeminent advocate of the struggle for Negro equality. I remember the days leading up to the event, nervously anticipating the chance to hear the leading voice in the Civil Rights Movement.

But when we arrived at the small campus for the speech, we encountered several thousand automobiles parked tightly along the edges of the narrow, two-lane road. Hundreds more seemed to surround the building where the Reverend King was scheduled to speak. Masses of black people were packed inside and around the building. Others seemed to be everywhere, sitting on the lawn, watching the whirl of television cameras and newspaper reporters. We managed to hear much of the formal program, including King's address, as we stood beneath the open windows of the building.

When the program finally ended and the gospel choir sang, King and his small entourage were quickly ushered offstage. The members of the audience rushed toward the building's main entrance, eagerly awaiting the chance to embrace and to touch the single individual who best personified their own political hopes and dreams of freedom. The newspaper reporters and photographers scrambled into position.

Something told me it was quite unlikely that King would venture through the main entrance. No one could possibly navigate through the sea of admirers and media representatives. I squirreled my way around several overweight men in tight suits, crawling low along the brick wall on all fours. Eventually, I twisted my way through the maze of people, reaching the rear of the building near a cluster of tall trees.

Beneath the trees was parked a very impressive, freshly polished black automobile, with four black men sitting inside. In the back seat on the left side sat Dr. Martin Luther King, Jr., talking quietly with the other men. Slowly, gathering every ounce of courage I had, I walked toward King. Reverend King turned his head slightly and, noticing me, began to smile warmly. "Hello, young man," he said softly.

There was silence. "Hello," I replied, and ventured to the car. King leaned toward the door, grasped my outstretched hand, and embraced it.

Stammering slightly, I asked if I could have Dr. King's autograph. A man in the driver's seat responded that I couldn't be given the autograph because hundreds of other people would want King's signature as well. I was disappointed, but I was pleased that I had had the rare opportunity to meet my hero, one-on-one.

Several years later, only weeks before I was scheduled to graduate from high school, I heard over the radio that Dr. King had been assassinated in Memphis. The local black newspaper, the *Dayton Express*, agreed to send me as a reporter to write a commentary on Martin's funeral in Atlanta. My mother drove me to the airport in Dayton, and I flew for the first time in my life, arriving in Atlanta on the night before the funeral. The next morning at 6:30 am, I arrived at the front door of Ebenezer Baptist Church. With my pad and pencil in hand, I was a witness to the entire funeral that day, walking with thousands of others through Atlanta's streets in honor of King's life and ideals. But thousands of other African-Americans in more than 130 cities, from Washington, DC to Chicago, lashed out in anger and outrage. Before the fires burned out, 34 African-Americans and 5 whites lay dead in the rioting. Property damage exceeded $130 million. The dream of nonviolence had come to an end, and Black Power was now on the agenda.

King's continuing significance to African-American people is that he and others—Malcolm X, Fannie Lou Hamer, Paul Robeson—represented the very best within ourselves. Young African-American girls and boys can take special pride in the memory of Martin, because through study and commitment to the continuing fight for equality, they will become "new Martins and Malcolms."

BLACK LIBERATION— WHERE DO WE GO FROM HERE!

Once again, in the presidential election year of 1996, African-Americans were confronted with a series of candidates who could not or would not address our interests. And so, once again, we need to evaluate what has happened to the black community—politically, economically, and socially—over the past few years and map a strategy that will lead to greater empowerment. Black liberation will not be achieved by some pleasant-sounding phrases of white politicians, either Democrats or Republicans. Black liberation must instead be based on a critical analysis of the social forces that have divided our people and what political steps can bring us together.

Many of our current political dilemmas can be traced back to the collapse of Jesse Jackson's Rainbow Coalition as a national, mass political force after the 1988 presidential election. As extreme conservatives seized power in the

1994 elections, millions of African-Americans felt that their interests were unrepresented and unheard. Conditions in U.S. central cities, particularly for blacks and Latinos, reached a critical state. As corporations relocated jobs and capital investment from urban centers, unemployment became widespread. Social services, health delivery systems, public housing, and public transportation all experienced sharp cutbacks. The quality of urban education seriously declined. Increasingly, the criminal justice system and prisons became the chief means for warehousing unemployed black and Latino young people. By 1995, 30 percent of all black males in their 20s nationwide were either in prison or jail, on probation or parole, or awaiting trial.

The Los Angeles social uprising of April-May 1992 symbolized black collective outrage against the brutality of the police and the racism of the legal system, with the festering grievances of inferior schools, poor housing, second-class health care, and widespread unemployment. As racial polarization and reaction increased throughout white political society, African-Americans were forced to sharply reevaluate their strategies for political and social change. In 1993, the position of NAACP National Secretary was narrowly won by Benjamin Chavis over Jesse Jackson. Chavis pursued a complex agenda: advocating liberal and progressive public policies and social programs; building strong black institutions and coalitions; establishing cooperative dialogues among all representatives of the black community, including Louis Farrakhan and the Nation of Islam; and encouraging productive contacts with the alienated hip-hop generation, urban black gangs, and young people inside the criminal justice system. Chavis's approach briefly won remarkable support from a broad spectrum of black activists, from nationalists like Maulana Karenga and Haki Madhubuti, to black socialists such as Angela Davis, Cornel West, and Charlene Mitchell.

But within one year, a campaign to oust Chavis was orchestrated in the media, supported quietly by more moderate, old-style civil rights leaders and many "post-black" elected officials. The political space that remained was quickly seized by Farrakhan and the Nation of Islam, advocating a socially conservative agenda markedly to the right of both Jackson and Chavis.

As Martin Luther King, Jr. once asked, "Where do we go from here?" We must recognize that there is an alternative to Farrakhan's black nationalism. It is the politics of "democratic transformation": challenging the real structures of inequality and power, restricting the power of corporate capital, expanding social programs to ensure greater opportunities for human development, and building multicultural, multiclass resistance movements.

The politics of "democratic transformation" must be grounded in the real struggles for empowerment by African-Americans around day-to-day issues. A political culture of resistance must be constructed around practical concerns: health care, the environment, reproductive rights, housing, and education. As the practice of coalition-building occurs in communities, different groups of people may learn to overcome their stereotypes and fears of each other. Part of this process must certainly occur within electoral politics, both through the support of progressive Democrats who are committed to this agenda, and more decisively, by the development of independent politics represented by the New Party, the Labor Party Advocates, the Green parties, the Campaign for a New Tomorrow led by activist Ron Daniels, and other organizations. But the next decisive struggle will be waged at the community level, in thousands of neighborhoods, through efforts to transform the consciousness and political practices of those who are most oppressed by the system.

Black Americans throughout their history have always been challenged by the harsh and often brutal reality of institutional racism. As a system of unequal power, political racism led to the disfranchisement of African-Americans after the Reconstruction era's brief experiment in democracy. Within America's cultural institutions, the representations of blackness were frequently racial stereotypes and crude distortions. And within the economy, generations of African-Americans found themselves excluded from the best jobs, the last hired and the first fired. This structure of racial domination and unequal power created the context and necessity for the development of black political and intellectual leadership.

Three basic models of leadership have informed the development of political struggles for black liberation within U.S. society during the past century. The first strategy to emerge after the Civil War and the demise of Radical Reconstruction can be termed "accommodation." With the codification and social consolidation of Jim Crow segregation in the 1890s, with the rise of lynchings and the political disfranchisement of blacks throughout the South, the possibilities for advancing civil rights became extremely limited. It was this repressive context that produced conservative black educator and political leader Booker T. Washington. Washington publicly counseled blacks to accept disfranchisement and segregation, and to establish coalitions with conservative white elites in business and the Republican Party. Accommodationist politics favored "black capitalism," the establishment of black-owned businesses that produced goods and services solely for the African-American community. It opposed coalitions with labor unions and poor whites.

Instead of relying on the government to provide resources or to guarantee civil rights, blacks were urged to "help themselves." Washington's political organization, the "Tuskegee Machine," used its influence with Republican administrations to place some middle-class blacks in the federal bureaucracy. Washington mobilized black public opinion for his conservative policies through his control of major African-American newspapers. In the rapidly growing black urban ghettos of the North, accommodationist politics was reflected in the increased cooperation of black middle-class elites with conservative white bosses and political machines, which were frequently aligned with the Democratic Party.

Although Washington died in 1915, his basic approach to the achievement of black empowerment had a profound impact upon the political culture of black America. In the 1960s, black capitalism, self-segregation, and coalition-building with white Republicans were central to the "Black Power" programs of Floyd McKissick, Roy Innis, and many other conservative black nationalists. (Indeed, it is largely forgotten that the only presidential candidate in 1968 who openly endorsed "Black Power" was Richard Nixon.) Today, Washington's tradition of accommodation is expressed, in part, by black conservative intellectuals such as Shelby Steele, Glen Loury, Walter Williams, and Thomas Sowell, and by black apologists for reactionary policies and Reaganite economics like Tony Brown. Even Louis Farrakhan's program of self-help, social conservatism, and separatism has more in common with Washington than with Malcolm X. Unlike Malcolm, neither Washington nor Farrakhan actually put forward a strategy that directly challenged white capitalism or institutional racism.

The second strategy for achieving black liberation can be called "reform-from-above" politics. Its social foundations came largely from the black middle class and professionals, black elected officials connected with the Democratic Party, and moderates within the Civil Rights Movement. In a nutshell, their strategy favors: the complete integration of blacks into U.S. society, the passage of civil rights and equal-opportunity legislation, and increasing the number of blacks in influential positions in government and the private sector. The federal government is viewed as the principal vehicle for addressing the black community's social problems and human needs, such as health care, housing, and education. Implicitly, reform-from-above is based on a pragmatic partnership between black middle-class and political elites and white liberal groups in foundations, education, organized labor, and the Democratic Party.

The limitations of reform-from-above as a strategy for black liberation have been obvious to many black working-class and poor people for decades. The chief beneficiaries of reform-from-above politics have been, and continue to be, the black middle class. The basic thesis of this class can be described by the concept of "symbolic representation": increasing the actual number of blacks in positions of authority within every institution of society will directly empower African-Americans as a group. Fundamental social progress would occur only in cooperation with white liberal institutions and organizations. Loyalty to the national Democratic Party is central to this approach for gradual change. Thus the insurgent presidential candidacy of Jackson in both 1984 and 1988 did not challenge the two-party system, but operated solely within the confines of the Democratic Party primaries. Although Jackson frequently criticizes the Clinton administration's policies, he is not prepared or willing to launch a truly independent political movement for blacks and other oppressed groups.

An alternative third political vision has also been represented within African-American leadership: the radical politics of "reform-from-below." With their massive migration from the rural South to the northern ghettos, African-Americans soon became the most urbanized population in the United States. With the expansion of the black industrial working class and the subsequent growth of urban poverty and unemployment, political protest began to assume a more militant character. As early as the Great Depression, black street radicals in Harlem initiated rent strikes, boycotts, and "don't buy where you can't work" campaigns. Thousands of African-Americans joined the Communist Party and other radical organizations; thousands more participated in trade union struggles. In the Cold War, the more radical wing of the black freedom movement, led by W.E.B. Du Bois and Paul Robeson, challenged McCarthyism and domestic political repression. In the 1960s, a similar spirit of radical internationalism, Third World solidarity, and peace was advocated by Martin Luther King, Jr. in the months before his assassination. And as the movement for desegregation was supplanted by the demand for Black Power, new models of black militancy and radicalism emerged, such as the Black Panthers and the League of Revolutionary Black Workers.

What each of these African-American leaders and protest groups had in common was a radical rejection of the existing power structure of the larger society. They were convinced that the traditional methods of political engagement, working solely through the system, would not produce meaningful changes. African-Americans had to pressure the political and corporate establishment from below, by active participation in protests of all kinds: mass demonstrations, renters' strikes, labor unrest, economic boycotts, sit-ins, civil disobedience, and even armed struggle. This perspective fostered a type of activist-oriented leadership that saw itself as part of a broad social movement for black empowerment and the radical redefinition of American democracy. In an international context, reformers-from-below embraced the parallel struggles of African, Asian, and Latin American people against colonialism and economic domination by the West. Black Americans' problems were an integral part of a much larger human dilemma, the inequality and oppression of non-European people along a global boundary of race, nationality, and class.

"Accommodation," "reform-from-above," and "reform-from-below" represent distinct strategies and approaches to the problematic of black empowerment. If we're really serious about fundamental change for African-Americans, we must recognize that the transformation of this system will occur *not from the top down, but from the bottom up.*

THE VISION OF HAROLD WASHINGTON

Historians of black America will one day mark three significant protests launched against the conservatism of the 1980s—the Rainbow Coalition presidential campaigns of the Reverend Jesse Jackson, bringing millions of multiracial voters to the polls around a progressive agenda; the anti-apartheid demonstrations of 1984-1986, which fractured President Ronald Reagan's "constructive-engagement policy" toward South Africa and contributed to the freedom of Nelson Mandela; and the mass electoral mobilization in the city of Chicago in 1983, which brought U.S. Representative Harold Washington to power as mayor. All three of these political events must be understood as linked, because all were part of a broad, collective struggle for black empowerment and democratic representation at the municipal, national, and international levels.

The critical elements behind the Washington mayoral triumph of 1983 have been documented by many political scientists and scholars. For a half-century, Chicago's African-American community was dominated by Cook County's Democratic Party machine. Patronage was used to overcome class and neighborhood loyalties and bind elected officials to the interests of the machine. Under Richard J. Daley's control from 1955 to 1976, white neighborhoods reaped a disproportionately large share of resources and jobs. Black and Latino communities suffered under higher rates of unemployment, and City Hall frequently shortchanged their basic needs, such as garbage collection and street sanitation. Hundreds of incidents of police brutality and harassment were ignored.

It was in this oppressive environment, in the 1970s and early 1980s, that groups such as Jackson's People United to Serve Humanity (PUSH), Chicago Black United Communities (CBUC), elements of the black religious community, and the 16 community-based organizations that had created People Organized for Welfare and Employment Rights (POWER) coalesced behind a drive for fundamental democratic change. In 1982, more than 160,000 new voters were registered, including about 127,000 blacks from the 17 predominantly African-American wards. This mobilization found a very reluctant Washington to be its champion in challenging the machine. Washington had run a largely symbolic independent campaign for mayor in 1977, receiving barely 10 percent of the vote against Michael Bilandic.

Washington loved his job in Congress and didn't want to leave the capital. Yet he also realized that a political strategy of community-based empowerment, social reform, and an anti-corruption platform could rally significant sectors of the white, Latino, and African-American electorates. More specifically, in the Democratic primary's three-way race, which matched Washington against incumbent Mayor Jane Byrne and State's Attorney Richard M. Daley (the son of Richard J. Daley), the numbers actually favored a black victory. As black leader Renault Robinson put it, victory was possible with an "80-80 strategy." If 80 percent of the African-American population registered and 80 percent voted, Washington could win.

On primary day in February 1983, Washington won by 33,000 votes, with 85 percent of the African-American vote being cast for Washington and with over 90 percent of blacks voting in many precincts. Recognizing their error in political judgment, most of the city's racists, power brokers, and machine hacks clustered around Republican mayoral candidate Bernard Epton as their "great white hope." Epton shamelessly exploited the city's volatile racial tensions, running on the slogan, "Epton, Before It's Too Late." But in the general election, these vulgar race-baiting tactics failed. Washington defeated Epton by 46,000 votes out of almost 1.3 million ballots cast. Citywide, Washington received nearly unanimous support from African-Americans. Yet the campaign had clearly forged the basis of a progressive rainbow coalition. Washington also won crucial votes among white workers, Northside liberal whites, Latinos, and gays and lesbians. Of Washington's total votes cast in the general election, 53.5 percent came from blacks, 10 percent from Hispanics, and 36.4 percent from whites.

Since Washington's tragic death in November 1987, shortly after his reelection as mayor, the process of political reform in Chicago has been sharply reversed. Richard M. Daley occupies the mayor's office as firmly and as determinedly as his father once did. Black progressives and moderates have become divided, as key Latino and white liberal leaders have defected to Daley and the Democratic Party organization. The optimism, energy, and political courage that made Washington a folk hero to thousands of black people has largely disappeared. Yet in retrospect, the Washington electoral movements of 1983 and 1987 provide the keys for the construction of a progressive vision of democratic empowerment and multicultural coalition-building in contemporary urban America.

MIKE TYSON VERSUS
THE MORALS OF OUR MOVEMENT

One of the central tenets of the struggle for freedom in African-American history is the idea that what is politically necessary also must be morally uplifting. From Frederick

Douglass to Malcolm X, the ends have never justified the means. Ethical behavior toward each other is an important feature of the African-American community. The violence of black-versus-black crime and the peddling of drugs to innocent children have been denounced as socially destructive behaviors that have to be expelled if the black community is to survive.

During the 1992 rape trial of former heavyweight champion Mike Tyson, however, disturbing trends developed within the national African-American community. Some compared Tyson's prosecution unfavorably to the acquittal of William Kennedy Smith's controversial rape trial of the year before. Others complained that the behavior and motives of Tyson's victim were "highly questionable." Why would Desiree Washington, an intelligent woman who had been crudely propositioned by Tyson earlier in the day, willingly go back to his hotel room in the middle of the night? Black Baptist ministers clustered and prayed for the black pugilist in his hour of need.

With Tyson's conviction, some of these sentiments assumed ugly dimensions. A black student newspaper in New York City declared that the young woman raped by Tyson "willingly went to his hotel room to win her fame and fortune, but realized that a one-night stand would not have been enough." Tyson's conviction was "a grave injustice to the whole black community" because the loss of another black role model means the imprisonment and death of many of our black youth.

At some black radio stations, telephone calls ran at least five-to-one in favor of Tyson and against the woman he had raped. Many of the callers supporting Tyson were black women. Some argued that the woman's decision to enter a man's bedroom voided any right she had to claim she had been sexually violated. The same attitude could be observed on the streets. In Los Angeles several days after the jury returned a guilty verdict, I witnessed several black young adults—male and female alike—wearing sweatshirts that protested the Tyson conviction in bold letters. In vulgar, sexist language, the shirts proclaimed: "The bitch set me up!"

Enough is enough. On this issue, we must draw a line. To stand with Tyson is to stand for everything the black freedom struggle has been against.

No man has a right to rape any woman, no matter what the situation or context. When people argue that the woman shouldn't have gone to his hotel room, our response must be, "So what?" Do people who use poor judgment deserve to be raped? There are no excuses for criminal behavior, and the evidence indicates that Tyson was indeed guilty of rape.

Within the African-American community, we need to discuss the social destructiveness the black male faces in our society. The popular culture bombards our young men with values and images of violence, vulgarity, and self-hatred. In rap music, black women are routinely described as "bitches" and "ho's." On NWA albums, there are titles such as "Findum, Fuckum, and Flee." Given this social conditioning and sexism, is it surprising that too many young males make a connection between violence and sexuality?

We must challenge the glamorization of male brutality, the concept that males with status, money, and power, of whatever race, can act in ways that are destructive to women. By placing Tyson on a pedestal, by ignoring the evidence and accepting his brutality against one of our sisters, we embrace that same violence against our daughters, mothers, and ourselves. Instead of projecting a vision of humanity that enriches the spirit, we devalue and degrade ourselves.

No doubt, black men suffer disproportionately from the violence and discrimination of the political and criminal justice system. Racism is alive and well, limiting black males' economic opportunities. But the pain of oppression doesn't justify violence against another person. Tyson was guilty and, for the sake of our own humanity, we must draw the line.

JUSTICE FOR MUMIA ABU-JAMAL

The U.S. criminal justice system is, in part, an institution designed to perpetuate black oppression. It is no accident, for example, that nearly one-fourth of all young black men between the ages of 18 and 29 in the United States are either in prison, on probation or parole, or awaiting trial. It is no accident that African-Americans and Latinos convicted of crimes routinely receive much longer prison sentences than whites who commit the same crimes.

But the outstanding element of coercion within the system of legal punishment remains the death penalty. As criminal justice scholar David Baldus observed several years ago, any black person is 4.3 times more likely to be given the death penalty than any white person under the same circumstances. Since 1900, thousands of African-Americans have been executed by prison officials, police, or white lynch-mobs, all in the defense of white supremacy. In the past century, *fewer than five* white Americans have been executed for either the murder of a black person or the rape of a black woman.

It is in this repressive context that we must consider the case of Mumia Abu-Jamal. An outstanding African-American radio journalist and political commentator, Abu-Jamal established a strong following in Philadelphia in the early 1980s. Abu-Jamal's reports documenting widespread police brutality and political repression in that city were broadcast on National Public Radio and other networks. In 1981, Abu-Jamal was arrested and charged with the killing of a police officer, Daniel Faulkner. Abu-Jamal had been shot by the police at the scene and then was beaten into critical condition.

The prosecution's case against Abu-Jamal was weak. Four eyewitnesses described a person fleeing the murder scene: Abu-Jamal had been so severely injured that physically he could not have run. Ballistics experts failed to match Abu-Jamal's legally registered gun to any bullets at the scene or in the officer's body. One eyewitness at the trial could not identify Abu-Jamal as the shooter and was ordered by the prosecution not to talk with the defense.

One trial witness was so harassed and hounded by the police and prosecutors that he left Philadelphia prior to the trial; he had reported that Abu-Jamal was not involved in the crime and that the real shooter had actually fled the scene.

None of the evidence meant anything to the Commonwealth of Pennsylvania. All that mattered was that a police officer was dead and that a black man had to be executed for the crime, whether he was innocent or guilty. During the jury selection process, Abu-Jamal was assigned an incompetent public defender. The prosecution challenged and removed 11 black jurors without cause. As a result, all but two jurors were white. Supervising the trial was Judge Albert Sabo, who had sentenced more people to death than any other judge in the United States. Of the 31 individuals sentenced to execution by Judge Sabo, all but two were people of color. The prosecution was even permitted to interrogate Abu-Jamal about his teenage membership in the Black Panther Party. Predictably, the jury convicted Abu-Jamal, and Judge Sabo ordered him to die.

In his years on death row in Pennsylvania, Abu-Jamal has refused to be silenced. His political analysis and commentaries have been published in a book, *Live From Death Row*. But on June 2, 1995, the governor of Pennsylvania signed Abu-Jamal's death warrant. The growing opposition to the execution forced authorities to delay the implementation of Sabo's decision. Nevertheless, the threat of capital punishment still exists for this political prisoner.

Intellectuals, public officials, journalists, and hundreds of prominent public leaders nationally and internationally have rallied in support of Mumia Abu-Jamal. In the struggle to stop the execution, we are doing more than just saving the life of an innocent man. We strike a blow for freedom against a criminal justice system pervasive with racism. We take a stand for justice against a legal system that punishes thousands of black and Latino young men for crimes while white men are permitted to go free. By fighting to save the life of Mumia Abu-Jamal, we struggle for a truly just and democratic society.

RACIAL STEREOTYPES OF BLACK CULTURE

I've witnessed this scene many times. As young blacks or Latinos walk into a store, private security guards nervously shadow them. As they walk toward the cash register and the checkout line, white matrons tightly hold their purses. With video cameras recording every step, the teenagers finally leave the store.

Millions of white Americans refuse to talk honestly about their racial anxieties and prejudices, or the not-too-subtle changes in their behavior when confronted by a person of color. Much of what white, middle-class America knows about black America is what it sees on television and in films. For generations, African-Americans have been depicted negatively: as overly sexed maniacs and crack-smoking criminals, as dumb athletes and Aunt Jemimas, as lazy, shiftless, ignorant, and hopeless. But in recent years, television has added a new degree of popular pathology to the general image of blackness in the white mind.

Only a tiny fraction of all African-American inner-city residents are drug dealers or criminals. Most black people have little tolerance for crime and violence because we understand all too well that we are its principal victims. Yet the majority of recent television programs and films released by major studios focus on that tiny minority of the African-American community that engages in drugs and violence.

As black comedian/director Robert Townsend explained to the *New York Times* in 1993, "As long as it's in the ghetto and people are carrying guns and even the dogs speak in four-letter words, they'll give it four thumbs up and nine stars." White film executives say, "Give us the ugliest side of the world." Charles S. Dutton, the star of the Fox television series *Roc*, explained: "If the kids who made *Menace II Society* had gone to a studio and said that they wanted to make a movie called *Contributors II Society* about black kids going to college, it would never have been made."

The vast majority of African-Americans work for a living. The majority of people in the United States who are on welfare, Aid to Families with Dependent Children, are white, not black. The majority of Americans who consume cocaine and other illegal narcotics are white, not black or Latino. Millions of black people struggling to keep their households together and raising their children with love and attention are responsible and hard-working people. Yet that is not the image we so often see in the popular culture, particularly not on television.

When the reality of blackness contradicts the stereotypes of racism, television producers, directors, and corporate executives demand that "reality," as portrayed in their products, conform to their prejudices. When black film director Kevin Hooks shot a park scene in Harlem, the white executives demanded that more trash, filth, and litter be dumped onto the set. Harlem was simply too "clean" for white folks to believe.

How deeply rooted are racial stereotypes? In 1993, a national survey of more than 2,200 American adults, funded by the National Science Foundation, was designed to measure contemporary racial attitudes. The study's directors, including Stanford University political scientist Paul Sniderman and University of California, Berkeley professors Philip Fetlock and Anthony Tyler, stated that "the most striking result" of the survey "is the sheer frequency with which negative characterizations of blacks are quite openly expressed throughout the white general population." Not surprisingly, white conservatives had little reluctance in expressing their prejudices about African-Americans. But what surprised researchers was the deep racial hostility expressed by white liberals.

According to Sniderman, for example, 51 percent of the white conservatives, but also 45 percent of the white liberals, agreed with the statement that "blacks are aggressive or violent"; 34 percent of the conservatives and 19 percent of the liberals agreed that "blacks are lazy"; and 21 percent of the conservatives and 17 percent of the liberals concurred that African-Americans are "irresponsible." The researchers found that those white liberal Democrats with intolerant views of blacks differed little in their policy pref-

erences from Republicans. This explains why it is so difficult to pass meaningful legislation addressing the inequality and discrimination black people face every day: white
liberals basically dislike blacks almost as much as white
conservatives do.

Racial stereotypes mask the central dynamics of what
racism is and why it exists. Racism is nothing more or less
than white privilege, white power, and white violence. And
unless white Americans are seriously forced to confront
their stereotypes about people of color, there will be no racial dialogue or peace in this country.

THE POLITICS OF BLACK AWARENESS

In 1995, I attended a statewide conference sponsored by
the Kentucky Association of Blacks in Higher Education.
The three-day conference was held at Kentucky State University, an historically black institution. The conference
theme was significant: "Multiculturalism: Myth or Reality?"

In a series of workshops and plenary sessions, the conference examined issues of diversity within higher education. It explored ways to introduce African-American
culture, history, and perspectives on social themes into the
curriculum. I delivered the keynote address at the conference, but what was most striking to me was the manner in
which African-American people have incorporated a vision
and cultural sensibility that can be described as *both* multicultural and Afrocentric. In a real sense, what is occur-
ring all over the country is a renaissance of black
nationalism, collective pride, and awareness.

This is happening for several reasons. Politicians in
Washington, especially the Republicans, have clearly
turned against our interests. Affirmative action is under
withering attack. Racial stereotypes are manipulated on
the nightly news to boost ratings and justify assaults on
welfare and the poor. In this environment of political reac-

tion, most African-Americans have concluded that our political system is hopelessly antagonistic toward our community's interests, or even its survival.

Another reason for the rebirth of black awareness is the failure of mainstream civil rights organizations and traditional integrationist-oriented leadership to effectively represent the black community. The sad and sorry debacle concerning the struggle over leadership of the NAACP, which marred 1994, only illustrated to many blacks that we do not have the power to select and confirm our own leaders. The electoral arena has not produced the kind of fundamental changes in the social and economic status of black people that we had hoped for at the end of the segregation era.

Whenever there is a crisis of confidence in middle-class black leadership, and whenever this occurs at a time when white political and corporate power turns aggressively against black folk, the conditions are ripe for an upsurge of black nationalism and black awareness. This social eruption is cultural, educational, political, economic, and ideological. It involves tens of thousands of educators, administrators, artists, performers, cultural workers, journalists, and entrepreneurs. Some have joined the Nation of Islam, seeking an organizational base for greater effectiveness in reaching out to larger numbers of people. Others express their black awareness through programs within sororities and fraternities, community associations, and educational institutions. There is a new hunger for knowledge that reaffirms the heritage, spirituality, and cultural dignity of black people. It is reflected in a massive cottage industry of Afrocentric books, records, clothing, and even television videos.

Jawanza Kunjufu, noted public speaker and writer on the crisis of black youth, is only one example of this trend toward greater black awareness. Na'im Akbar, professor of psychology at Florida State University, gives hundreds of public lectures and workshops on black male/female relations and on cultural issues related to black development. Maulana Karenga created the Afrocentric celebration of Kwanzaa, which, in only three decades, has become one of black America's most important cultural events. The chief

theoretician of the Afrocentric movement in universities is
Molefi Asante, who chairs the Black Studies Department at
Temple University.

Frequently in the media, there is a tendency to create
conflict and dissension within the ranks of the advocates of
black awareness. It is true that scholars such as Asante
and I may disagree on specific issues related to the incor-
poration of diversity within the curriculum, but both of us
favor Pan-Africanism, and both of us strongly defend the
need to build all-black institutions for the empowerment of
the community. Outside of the major media centers, in
hundreds of small towns and neighborhoods where black
people live and work, any distinctions between "Afrocentrism" and "radical multiculturalism" are frequently
blurred and are always secondary to the search for strategies to improve the quality of life for black children. We
should never fall into the trap of disagreeing with ourselves
to the point where we simply foster divisions that only
benefit our oppressors.

Black awareness is the essential beginning step in creating a framework for understanding and accomplishing the
educational and political work that values our humanity.
Real empowerment begins by learning the lessons of our
own heritage and by knowing something about ourselves.
But we must also begin to join hands with others of different racial and ethnic backgrounds, divergent classes and
social groups, to build bridges and challenge structures of
inequality and oppression.

WILKINS VERSUS STEELE—
BLACK INTELLECTUALS IN CONFLICT

In African-American history, the classic political debate
that defined the parameters of the Civil Rights Movement
occurred nearly a century ago, in the struggle between
Booker T. Washington and W.E.B. Du Bois. Washington
was the cautiously conservative Negro educator, founder of

Tuskegee Institute, and leader of the National Negro Business League; Du Bois was the liberal socialist, civil rights advocate, and founder of the National Association for the Advancement of Colored People. Washington suggested that the keys to black progress were to be found by working within the capitalist system, cooperating with the white power structure, and employing self-initiative to address blacks' problems. Du Bois countered that black empowerment demanded institutional changes within the system, the abolition of racial segregation, and challenging white racism within America's culture and ideology.

In late 1992, in the pages of *Mother Jones* magazine, a replay of this classical debate was waged between neo-conservative ideologue Shelby Steele and liberal progressive Roger Wilkins over the current state of American race relations. Like many white conservatives who love to blame the victims of oppression, Steele argued that blacks as individuals should take the chief responsibility for their own uplift and advancement. Steele, who evidently believes that liberalism is the African-American community's chief enemy, declared: "The biggest problem poor blacks have today is neither the government nor white America, but people like Roger Wilkins," whom he accuses of displaying "a kind of black *noblesse oblige* that I find a little repulsive." Taking the Du Boisian position, Wilkins declared that white racism in America has deep cultural and historical roots that have never been overcome, despite the passage of civil rights laws. The idea of "black inferiority" is reinforced within the economic and political arrangements of society, Wilkins asserts, and until whites recognize that racism remains "a terrible virus," no social peace between the races is possible.

It's obvious that mainstream, middle-class white America would find Steele's thesis comforting to its ancient and contemporary prejudices, just as it would perceive Wilkins's analysis to be subversive of the pristine pillars of white corporate (overwhelmingly male) power. But let's take the debate a step further, out of the pages of history and into the political future.

What is really being debated is the nature of the relationship between people and government in the context of the goal of social equality. What do human beings who experience discrimination or oppression (whether because of race, gender, sexual orientation, class, disability, or whatever) have a right to expect from their government in fostering an environment nurturing equality of human conditions?

Steele's analysis focuses myopically on the activities and actions of individual citizens, rather than on the profound social, economic, and cultural forces that prefigure and limit opportunities for virtually all individuals within any social system. No matter how hard individuals who have been oppressed may labor for themselves, the oppressed as a group find themselves distanced from the levers of power and limited by lack of access to capital. Steele ignores the reality that power is wielded not by individuals, but by classes and social groups. By placing the blame for black poverty, teen pregnancy, and homelessness on the victims of our unequal system, he deliberately obscures the institutional nature of discrimination in our society.

Whether one is considered "disadvantaged" or "advantaged" within any society is relative. A person may have certain rights or privileges in some respects—such as the right to vote—and not in others. In America, our democracy now permits formal, legalistic equality as in one person, one vote. But equality of conditions is another matter: the human right not to starve, the right to employment, the right to decent shelter for all—these are not recognized. Even conceiving of such a democracy goes far beyond Steele's feeble ability because it sharply contradicts his own deeply rooted elitist bias and pro-corporate ideology. Roger Wilkins correctly suggests that racial integration by itself did not alter the basic situation for most working-class and poor blacks, because they were still disadvantaged in relation to middle-income whites in the suburbs.

To end the cycle of poverty, hunger, and violence in our central cities, we must build protest movements to train the next generation of people of color to demand policies that actually create the "equality of conditions," not just racial integration or civil rights alone. It's time to move beyond Booker T. Washington.

SHOULD FARRAKHAN BE ALLOWED TO SPEAK?

For more than a decade, the anti-Semitic speeches of Louis Farrakhan have been fostering divisions between the Jewish and African-American communities. In early 1994, for example, Farrakhan declared in a two-hour speech in Harlem that Jews were deliberately exploiting the statements of his controversial lieutenant, Muslim Minister Khalid Abdul Muhammad. Farrakhan declared: "They're trying to use my brother Khalid's words against me to divide the house.... They don't want Farrakhan to do what he's doing. They're plotting as we speak."

These remarks were vigorously condemned by Benjamin Chavis, then the new leader of the NAACP, and by Jesse Jackson, who characterized Farrakhan's address as "racist, anti-Semitic, divisive, untrue, and chilling."

But another controversy involving Farrakhan erupted a few months later, when the NAACP extended an invitation to the Muslim leader to participate in a national black leadership conference. Liberal Jews were outraged that Chavis had agreed to permit Farrakhan to join the discussions, which were held in Baltimore. Michael Lerner, the editor of the liberal Jewish magazine *Tikkun*, called for a public protest at the NAACP's national headquarters. Lerner explained that the picket was not "a protest against the NAACP. What we are asking is that the black leadership publicly condemn anti-Semitism in the black community and dissociate themselves from Farrakhan and others who preach anti-Semitism." Several prominent blacks, including philosopher Cornel West and Michael Meyers, the leader of the New York Civil Rights Coalition, endorsed the protest.

Although I agree with Lerner's commitment to fight against anti-Semitism, the strategy of picketing the NAACP for permitting Farrakhan to speak and to engage in dialogue with other African-American leaders has to be vigorously opposed.

The black freedom struggle in the United States, at its best, has always joined together a political demand for equality with a moral and ethical critique of all forms of social injustice and bigotry. We should have no reservations in condemning anti-Semitism. Statistically, anti-Jewish harassment and violence is on the increase throughout the United States. The Anti-Defamation League of B'nai B'rith reported more than 1,800 anti-Semitic acts in 1993, the second-most in a 15-year survey.

But the question that must be asked is why hundreds of thousands of African-Americans support Farrakhan, why hundreds gather to attend lectures by Muhammad? Denouncing Farrakhan does not explain the fact that he does have "legitimacy" within a section of the African-American community, which the NAACP's invitation acknowledged.

There are three basic reasons that African-Americans in large numbers listen to Farrakhan. First, since the demise of the Black Power movement, radical black voices have been largely silenced within the African-American community. The Black Panther Party was destroyed, in part, by the FBI's counter-intelligence program, COINTELPRO. Black socialists, nationalists, and community activists who favored fundamental social and political change were often isolated, harassed, and/or imprisoned. The destruction of the black Left created a leadership vacuum within the ghetto that no single leader or protest organization has managed to fill in the past two decades. The decline of black radical alternatives created the social space for the emergence of "black racial fundamentalism."

Second, Farrakhan is popular because traditional black middle-class leadership, both within the civil rights establishment and within electoral politics, has failed to articulate the rage and anger of the hip-hop generation, the unemployed, and marginalized black workers. Third, some of Farrakhan's primary arguments—black self-sufficiency, vigorous opposition to drugs and black-against-black violence, and the promotion of black business ownership—are generally viewed as constructive and positive by the vast majority of African-Americans. Most African-Americans do not favor or condone the anti-Semitism of Farrakhan and the Nation of Islam. But the social and economic crisis of our inner-cities is so severe that many people are now willing to listen to any argument that promises some degree of relief and community development.

We must make a critical distinction between black "militancy" and "radicalism." Farrakhan and the Nation of Islam are indeed "militant" and uncompromisingly "anti-white," but they are hardly "radical." In fact, Farrakhan is essentially a "militant conservative," a leader who strongly favors economic solutions within the framework of American capitalism, just like Booker T. Washington a century ago. Farrakhan supports sexism and homophobia. In fact, if Louis Farrakhan did not exist, the American government and media would have to invent him. Nothing in his entire program would radically transform the real power relationships between blacks and those who control the American corporate and political system.

And this is exactly why Farrakhan must be invited into dialogue with other African-American leaders. If we refuse to speak to Farrakhan, we are saying that we do not value the opinions or perspectives of those thousands of black people who support him or the millions who reject his anti-Semitism, but agree with part of his program. If Israelis can have dialogue with Yassir Arafat and the Palestine Liberation Organization, certainly African-Americans can have dialogue with each other, despite the very real differences on ideology and ethics that may divide us. Farrakhan must be allowed to speak, and black progressives must be ready to critique his program and to reject his anti-Semitism. Opposition to *all* forms of prejudice and discrimination must be central to the African-American freedom struggle, and we are able to advance this perspective most effectively when we confront Farrakhan face to face.

And so the African-American Leadership Summit was held as planned in Baltimore. And, predictably, the media coverage focused largely on the attendance of Farrakhan. The three-day national summit brought together leaders from a wide variety of organizations, with the black separatist perspective of the Nation of Islam representing only one distinct voice among many. Yet if one watched the news programs of the national networks, it was possible to come away with the distinct impression that everything revolved around the controversial presence of Farrakhan.

A group of largely white protesters associated with *Tikkun* magazine organized a picket line near the NAACP's headquarters about a half-hour before the summit was scheduled to begin. I had personally talked with *Tikkun* editor Lerner several days before the summit, suggesting that a protest of this type would be counterproductive, and would only create a greater degree of solidarity and support among most African-Americans who were participating in the conference. But Lerner refused to reconsider his position, declaring that any dialogue with Farrakhan was a compromise with anti-Semitism.

Eventually, about 40 to 50 people took part in the demonstration. The small crowd chanted slogans, including, "Don't embrace the racist; Farrakhan is a racist." A few African-Americans who encountered the demonstration expressed sympathy and support, while maintaining that black leaders need to engage in critical and constructive encounters with each other. Professor Cornel West, then of Princeton University, told protesters that while he "deplored" Farrakhan's anti-Semitism, there was "a need to include him in a dialogue." Julian Bond was more critical of the NAACP. In a public statement circulated several days before the summit, Bond declared: "If actions speak louder than words, the NAACP's invitation to Minister Farrakhan may condemn its noble history to a shameful oblivion."

Also agreeing with Lerner's rejectionist position was Michael Meyers of the New York Civil Rights Coalition. "The NAACP is an organization that is supposed to be open to all people," Meyers told the demonstrators. "It is tearing up its charter to invite Louis Farrakhan. He is not a legitimate voice. His is extremist, radical." Meyers later announced that he was leading a campaign to oust Chavis as NAACP leader.

Sadly, what occurred was as predictable as the media coverage. The protest at the NAACP headquarters, followed by an anti-Farrakhan evening rally in Baltimore featuring Rabbi Avi Weiss, the President of the Coalition for Jewish Concerns, only polarized the vast majority of black leadership. Veteran Chicago journalist Vernon Jarrett expressed the leaders' sentiments in a query to Lerner: "Don't you feel a little awkward telling black people what they should have on their agenda?"

NAACP national Chairman William F. Gibson vigorously defended Farrakhan's participation, describing the summit as an effort "not to create a new organization, but to form an alliance, a coalition, to address the problems" of the black community. Chavis was even more explicit than Gibson. "Those who try to drive a wedge between me and Minister Farrakhan," Chavis said, are really worried that African-Americans will "gain control of our communities."

Even among many African-American elected officials and civil rights leaders who had been privately critical of Chavis for inviting Farrakhan and who had not come to the summit themselves, there was a surprising degree of support for the NAACP's position. Congresswoman Cynthia A. McKinney, a Democrat from Georgia, explained that some of her fellow Congressional Black Caucus members had backed away from Farrakhan because "some weak-kneed politicians can't stand up to some heat." McKinney justified the invitation extended to Farrakhan on the grounds that the Nation of Islam minister "can draw more people in 15 minutes than 40 members of the Black Caucus." Representative Earl F. Hilliard, Democrat from Alabama, urged the Black Caucus to adopt a "neutral position" toward Farrakhan. "Farrakhan has his interests and agenda to protect," Hilliard explained. "Similarly, the Jews have their interests and agenda to protect. We can't let either one of them leverage their friendship with the Caucus against the interests and the agenda of the other one."

As a participant in the Baltimore summit, I do not exaggerate in saying the avalanche of negative media publicity and the public protests against the Nation of Islam's leader only served to reduce our internal criticisms of each other. With equal candor, I can also state my unqualified opposition to all forms of bigotry, including anti-Semitism. But we desperately need to engage in an honest dialogue with our Jewish and other liberal friends if we are ever to rebuild a multiracial, progressive political relationship rooted in equality.

White liberals need to understand that the NAACP cannot "convey legitimacy" on Farrakhan. Farrakhan's current popularity, especially among young African-Americans, has less to do with his odious anti-Semitism and ideology of racial separatism than with the fact that he actually articulates the rage of the most oppressed sectors of our community. No one within the Black Caucus, for example, is as effective as Farrakhan in denouncing black-on-black violence, drugs, and the destruction of our families. Farrakhan's expressions of black solidarity, economic development, and cultural pride explain why African-Americans might reject his statements of social intolerance while nevertheless attending the Nation of Islam's public rallies. Moreover, the repetitive demand to "repudiate Farrakhan" strikes African-American leaders as disingenuous at best. Black representatives and opinion makers, by contrast, have rarely gone to other ethnic groups demanding that they isolate and denounce one of their significant leaders and that if they fail to do so, all meaningful communications between their groups would cease.

Make no mistake: the Nation of Islam's anti-Semitism in no way advances African-American interests, and we must clearly articulate where our views on public policy issues converge with Farrakhan and where we disagree. But black folk of all ideologies and political persuasions resent being told that we cannot talk with controversial leaders inside our own community. The time is long past when white politicians, corporate leaders, and the media can play "kingmaker" by selecting "acceptable" black leaders for us.

ENVIRONMENTAL JUSTICE

In the 1960s, concerns about the general quality of life—
the condition of our air, water, and physical environment—
usually were expressed by middle- to upper-class whites,
who had the leisure to worry about such matters. Organizations like the Sierra Club and the Audubon Society drew
members from the privileged elite, who seemed to care
more about maintaining wetlands off the coast than about
saving the lives of Latino, black, and poor white children
threatened by poverty, hunger, and toxic wastes in their
communities.

With the initiation of Earth Day in 1970, interest in environmental issues soared. As a college student that year, I
recall spending most of Earth Day picking up trash and
nonbiodegradable items from the periphery of a state highway in Richmond, Indiana. Despite feeling good about my
own modest contribution to the environment that day, I experienced some degree of alienation and isolation from my
white fellow students, who had busily picked up garbage
and refuse all day long without a single word of complaint.

In my own mind, I wondered, "What does any of this
have to do with *racism?*" The whole issue of the survival of
the human species and the planet appealed to my holistic
sense of politics, the necessity to create a vision of society
that was mutually beneficial to societies of divergent cultures and conditions. But I was also aware that, at least for
most African-Americans, the issue of environmentalism
would appear to be, at best, abstract—and at worst, irrelevant—to the practical conditions of their daily lives.

Somehow, the environmental movement had to make the
conceptual and political leap from demanding biodegrad-
able paper products in the local supermarket to a passionate commitment to improve the quality of the air, water,
and physical environment in the cities, where the vast majority of people of color in the United States live. The struggles for social justice in the ghettos and barrios of our
country had to link up with the problems articulated by
"elitist" and affluent whites from the suburbs and fashion-
able urban townhouses of America.

The odds of this kind of political dialogue, much less an effective, permanent coalition, seemed less than hopeful. Back in 1970, at the Earth Day mobilization at San Jose City College in California, white environmentalists purchased a new Cadillac and then buried it, symbolizing their opposition to the culture of conspicuous consumption and the rampant materialism of the Nixon years. African-American students, by contrast, were outraged by this display of white, middle-class protest. They argued that the thousands of dollars used to pay for the posh automobile should have been put to better use. Even in the aftermath of Three Mile Island in 1979, when the East Coast came close to experiencing a nuclear meltdown, and even after the nuclear tragedy of Chernobyl, in which millions of Russian and Ukrainian people were contaminated with radioactive materials, it appeared that environmentalism would remain a "white issue."

Two black political leaders were largely responsible for transforming the environmental issue into a dynamic one in which people of color could become engaged: Jesse Jackson and Benjamin Chavis.

In his first presidential campaign, in 1984, Jackson repeatedly raised environmental issues, from the toxic wastes dumped in working-class and minority neighborhoods, to the connections between poverty, institutional violence, and the physical quality of life experienced by minorities and the poor. After listening to Jackson speak out against acid rain in New Hampshire, for example, David Brower, founder of the environmental lobby Friends of the Earth, characterized the candidate's remarks as "the best environmental statement that any presidential candidate has ever made."

Three years later, under Chavis's leadership, the United Church of Christ Commission on Racial Justice produced a major report, *Toxic Wastes and Race in the United States*. This crucial study deepened awareness of the links between institutional racism, corporate greed, and the environmental problems of the poor. The study found that three out of five African-Americans lived in communities with abandoned toxic waste sites, and that the populations of urban areas with the highest number of toxic waste sites were disproportionately black. Although African-Americans comprise less than 12.5 percent of the total U.S. population, for example, they account for 43 percent of the population of Memphis, which has 173 uncontrolled toxic waste sites; 28 percent of St. Louis's, with 160 sites; 24 percent of Houston's, with 152 sites; and 37 percent of Chicago's, with 103 sites. In Alabama, heavily black Sumter County alone accounts for nearly one-fourth of the nation's total capacity for commercial hazardous waste disposal. Chavis and Jackson successfully made the crucial connections between institutional racism and the environment.

In June 1993, I walked the picket line in the struggle against environmental racism. Dozens of community activists in conjunction with the Los Angeles Labor/Community Strategy Center protested at the headquarters of the South Coast Air Quality Management District (AQMD), the regulatory agency responsible for controlling toxic emissions from stationary sources of air pollution in metropolitan Los Angeles. With an annual operating budget of $110 million, the AQMD monitors a population of 13 million people, the second largest urban area in the United States.

This public confrontation concerned the ongoing battle over L.A.'s "lethal air," whether large corporations would continue to spew thousands of tons of dangerous, life-threatening chemicals, such as benzene, lead, formaldehyde, methylene chloride, and chromium, into the environment. The L.A. basin is one of the nation's most polluted environments. Erick Mann, Director of the Labor/Community Strategy Center, reported that "smog-forming hydrocarbons released in the air each month equal the amount released by the *Exxon Valdez* oil spill." During the summer months, for southern California residents of Riverside and San Bernadino, "breathing the air is the equivalent of smoking one pack of cigarettes per day."

The economic and social costs of Los Angeles's polluted environment are enormous. According to the AQMD, smog and particle pollution costs $9.4 billion per year for human health care alone. Pollution obviously hurts all people who have respiratory problems such as asthma, but it also targets many other potential victims: people with AIDS, whose immune systems are weakened; the elderly, whose health problems can range from bronchitis to emphysema and cancer; and children, whose lungs are developing and who take in up to three times as much air per unit of body weight as their parents. In Los Angeles, about 140,000 pregnant women are affected each year by high levels of toxic air emissions.

The immediate issue being debated at the AQMD hearing concerned new definitions for "acceptable" levels of toxic emissions. On one side of the debate stood a regiment of lawyers representing L.A.'s largest corporations. They argued against tighter safeguards on pollution, asserting that higher costs to businesses reduce profits and cost jobs. They asked for rules that, in effect, would permit them to become self-regulated.

Health risks to the general public are small, they claimed, even though millions of pounds of airborne toxins were being emitted every year. Tall smokestacks can spread emissions high into the air, they said, distributing the toxic wastes to hundreds of thousands of people in small amounts. Thus, according to the corporate polluters, the actual health risks to what is termed the "maximum-exposed individual" are reasonable.

Community activists and researchers from the Labor/Community Strategy Center challenged these claims at the AQMD governing board meeting. Standards for toxic polluters, they argued, should take into account the total quantity of toxic chemicals emitted, as well as the total number of people exposed. As the issue was debated, many board members casually stood up and walked out of the hearings, when black, Latino, and working-class people were testifying. But when the corporate lawyers in thousand-dollar suits walked to the podium, all AQMD board members scrambled back to their seats. The board decided to delay its final vote for a month to consider the new evidence. Many board members seemed all too eager to defend corporate polluters rather than the public health standards.

American industries overall are responsible for pumping 2.4 billion pounds of toxic chemicals into the air each year. And, all too often, the people most tragically affected by toxic pollution are African-Americans, other people of color, and the poor. In Houston, for example, until the late 1970s, all the city's landfills and six of its eight garbage incinerators were located within the black community. As Robert Bullard, editor of the groundbreaking book *Confronting Environmental Racism*, noted, the result was "lower property values, accelerated physical deterioration, and disinvestment." Our neighborhoods, in effect, became "dumping grounds."

The consequences of environmental racism are most clearly manifested in health care statistics. In Chicano farm communities, where pesticides are abundantly used, childhood cancer rates are several times the national average. Because of urban air pollution, young African-American men are dying of asthma at three times the rate of young white men.

Charles Lee, the principal author of the 1987 study *Toxic Wastes and Race in the United States*, highlighted these devastating statistics:

- the predominantly African-American and Latino South Side of Chicago had the greatest single concentration of hazardous waste sites in the nation.

- African-American children in one West Dallas neighborhood had suffered irreversible brain damage due to exposure to lead.

- Puerto Rico is one of the world's most heavily polluted places, poisoned for decades by massive wastes from pharmaceutical companies, oil refineries, and petrochemical plants.

The environmental movement within white middle-class America must confront the reality that the state of the environment is inextricably connected with the existence of social justice, the possibility that all members of society share the decisionmaking, the resources, and the power within the social order. Environmental racism is a symptom of the inequality of power relations between people of color, working people, and the poor and those who have power, resources, and privilege. Unless we are prepared to link political relations to more substantive socioeconomic relations, we will never get at the roots of the problem.

African-Americans and other people of color have a major stake in the continuing struggle for a safe, clean environment. Blacks and Latinos are over-represented in jobs that rely on dangerous chemicals, such as custodial work, dry cleaning, textile manufacturing, and the furniture industry, for example. Is it surprising, then, that the average African-American male dies before he can even collect Social Security? The fight for strict environmental standards to safeguard workers on the job and ensure clean air—and for the right to shut down major corporate polluters—must be at the heart of our new movement for multicultural democracy.

WANTED—A NEW BLACK POWER MOVEMENT

Once the fires of Los Angeles had died down, the racial insurrection in the streets could be seen to highlight a fundamental problem squarely confronting black politics: the growing gap between many African-American politicians and civil rights leaders and the militant millions of young inner-city and working-class blacks fed up with the system.

The Rodney King case in 1992, as well as the national controversy surrounding the Anita Hill-Clarence Thomas hearing in 1991, indicated a breakdown of consensus among black America's political elite. Most African-American leaders still believe in the old political strategy of unquestioned loyalty to the Democratic Party and what can be called the tactics of "symbolic representation."

Blacks have been told for generations that if another African-American from the upper-middle class is appointed to a high position in the legal system, elected governor, or sent to Congress, then the entire race is empowered. "Symbolic representation" was a major factor in the debate about Clarence Thomas: because Thomas is black, this theory argues, he shares our common history of racial oppression; therefore, he'll look out for our interests once he's safely in office. The problem with this assumption is that it ignores a crucial fact about a politician's behavior: his or her class identity and ideological commitments frequently outweigh his or her racial identity. Why some leaders couldn't comprehend this speaks to their basic confusion about what kind of new political approach we need.

Blacks have the same problem in their relations with the Democratic Party. The majority of African-American people agree that our political process stinks and that the system rarely offers us real choices. Black voter turnout slipped down to 44 percent in the 1988 presidential contest due largely to widespread alienation. The truth is that neither the Democrats nor the Republicans, by themselves, will ever initiate a progressive agenda for domestic reconstruction, rebuilding the cities, establishing universal public health care, and attacking discrimination. We must explore new avenues to pressure the Democrats from outside the party's ranks. Conversely, black conservatives who argue that blacks should fall in line behind conservative white politicians are advising us to leap from the political frying pan into the fire.

The Los Angeles uprising showed us that most middle-class black leaders are totally out of touch with the hip-hop generation. Today's black youths are so alienated that they have been forced to resuscitate a black leader who died a quarter of a century ago—Malcolm X—because he symbolizes their militancy and rage far better than anyone alive and on the political scene today.

This is the central reason that reactionary black nationalism has emerged as a cultural and social force among our young people. When white society and our government become blind to the harsh realities of inner-city poverty, unemployment, and social chaos, young people turn their activism and militancy inward. Why advocate coalition politics or protest strategies such as Jackson's Rainbow Coalition when there are apparently no allies within the white population? The narrow, dogmatic, race-based separatism of a Khalid Abdul Muhammad parallels the reactionary black nationalism of a Mangosuthu Buthelezi in South Africa. But black progressives who were part of the Black Power movement of the late 1960s and early 1970s have failed to reach out to young people, failed to listen to their grievances and their pain, and failed to help them create a viable alternative to racial reaction.

Despite the legal and political gains African-Americans have achieved, and despite the growth of a black middle class, the reality is that the basic conditions for the vast majority of black people—and youth especially—have become strikingly worse in the past 15 years. If the black community is going to move forward into the next century, we must take aggressive steps, and quickly, to bridge this generation gap.

We must revive the tradition of black protest in America if we are to have any hope of influencing public policies and empowering the black community. This will require new strategies, new organizations, and a new philosophy of political power.

First, we need a new SNCC—a 1990s incarnation of the Student Nonviolent Coordinating Committee. At the high point of the southern desegregation movement 30 years ago, young people in SNCC led hundreds of sit-in demonstrations and registered thousands to vote for the first time. We need to inspire a new African-American youth protest movement that taps our youths' energy and directs it constructively. Our new youth movement could attack black-on-black violence, drugs, and social problems like poverty, unemployment, and the abuse of blacks within the criminal justice system.

Second, we need a new black political "think tank," a center for political strategy directly connected to the ongoing debates and struggles in our streets. In the early 1970s, the Institute of the Black World, based in Atlanta, brought together progressive black scholars who challenged the system. We need to build our own center for black political analysis, one oriented toward activism.

Third, we need to devise an electoral strategy both inside and outside the established two-party system. By supporting independent and third party challenges, and by permitting "cross-endorsements" in which progressives could run simultaneously on third party slates as well as on the Democratic ticket, we can maximize our political options.

We can revive the freedom struggle of African-American people, but only if we are willing to break with the failed policies and outlook of the past.

The NAACP's black leadership conference in Baltimore in 1994 highlighted the need for a new movement for black power in America. In the three decades since the passage of the 1965 Voting Rights Act, the number of African-American elected officials increased dramatically, from barely 100 to more than 8,000. The number of African-American mayors jumped from literally zero in 1965 to more than 400. We have been well represented in presidential cabinets, on school boards and city councils, and in state houses across America. But we have failed to make the leap from representation to empowerment.

Power, in the final analysis, is the ability or capacity to realize your specific, objective interests. Power is not a "thing," but a process that uses existing resources, personnel, and institutions for your own objectives. Before you can exercise "power," you must first clearly understand yourself and those whose interests you seek to empower. If our goal is to empower the African-American community, we must have a detailed understanding of who we are and what our people want. This requires an honest and detailed analysis of where we are as a people—our genuine social problems and contradictions, our strengths and weaknesses, our internal resources and potential elements of leadership. We must listen to what the masses of African-American people really want and how they truly perceive the world around them.

Programmatically, this means that the national black community needs a regular public opinion poll to assess the state of black America on a wide range of public issues. Instead of looking to the white media to learn what we think, we should draw on our own networks and resources to present our own collective views. We need to initiate leadership training seminars within black institutions in order to identify and educate the next generation of African-American leaders.

One achieves power by building a strategy or plan of action based on reality. We must articulate a concrete analysis of concrete conditions—not a romantic wish list of things as we would prefer them to be. We are a people of African descent, to be sure, but the vast majority of our people will live, work, and die right here in the United States. We need a plan of group development that is grounded fundamentally in the here and now, not in ancient Egypt. Our basic struggle for power is right here in America.

We must also search for common ground—the basic unity of interests that brings together people of different backgrounds, genders, sexual orientations, languages, and social classes to advance the ideals of democracy. Power comes from coalitions, not through isolation or alienation from others.

A commitment to a new black power movement means that we must have the courage to periodically revitalize our movement for freedom. In South Africa in the 1940s, the African National Congress was essentially an "inclusionist" organization—it sought reforms and the symbolic representation of black people that required new strategies and programs. New leadership arose, personified by Nelson Mandela and Walter Sisulu, who launched a new program of massive resistance calling for the democratic transformation of South African society.

We have a similar situation in black America today. The masses of our people recognize that most of the defining issues of the Civil Rights Movement *no longer exist*. We face an unprecedented crisis of poverty, violence, joblessness, and social despair, and the old approaches are no longer sufficient or viable. We must transform our situation, to extend the principles of political democracy to economic and social relations, and build the foundations of genuine opportunity for our people. We need a bold new leadership with a democratic vision of black empowerment and equality. As Frederick Douglass reminded us more than a century ago: "Without struggle, there can be no progress."

MULTICULTURAL AMERICA

WHY CONSERVATIVES FEAR MULTICULTURALISM

In recent years, a national debate has erupted among educators, politicians, and scholars over the controversial concept of "multiculturalism." White conservatives such as William Bennett, who was Secretary of Education in Ronald Reagan's cabinet, attack the term for undermining the centrality of traditional western culture and civilization within school textbooks. Conservatives claim that multiculturalism fragments and divides Americans by highlighting the diverse ethnic contributions of various cultures.

In 1992, Bennett and I appeared on the ABC News program *Nightline* to discuss whether schools should adopt new textbooks and teaching techniques that cover the full range of America's ethnic, racial, and gender diversity. I knew that Bennett would attempt to dismiss ethnic pluralism and an increased emphasis on nonwhite contributions to the larger society as irrelevant to quality education.

So, from the outset, I explained that "multiculturalism" really means two fundamental things. First, it is a recognition that American history and this nation's accomplishments are not reflected in the activities of only one race (white), one language group (English-speaking), one ethnicity (Anglo-Saxon), or one religion (Christianity). African-Americans, Latinos, Asian-Americans, Native-Americans, and others have also made central contributions to U.S. society. Second, multiculturalism is a recognition that beneath these differences lie some principles and values that bring Americans together, such as the ideals of human equality, democratic government, and individual liberty. Multiculturalism is an antidote to the poisons of racism and sexism, which can distort young minds in our classrooms. When multiculturalism is presented in this manner, even the arch-conservative Bennett cannot disagree.

Where Bennett and I did express sharp disagreement was on the issue of textbooks. Bennett argued that history books should report the "truth" and any deviation from the central facts in history is nothing less than propaganda. He also insisted that the "truths" of "Western Civilization" should be the basis of our educational system. Bennett was wrong on at least two counts. As a professor of history, I know that there is no singular "truth" in anyone's history or textbook. Our history books have always reflected the interests and perspectives of the people in power in America. That's why, until recently, Native-Americans, Latinos, and African-Americans were excluded from the textbooks, and our achievements ignored or stolen. When oppressed people struggle successfully for their democratic rights, the textbooks inevitably change.

Moreover, despite the achievements of Western Civilization, many of the greatest scientific, technological, and cultural advances in world history have come from Asia and Africa. To overcome the prejudices reinforced by their parents, many white students need to read the works of scholars of color.

Bennett is only one of many intellectuals who campaign against what they consider the specter of multiculturalism. Other conservative educators hostile to the politics of multiculturalism include civil rights critic Linda Chavez, writer Dinesh D'Souza, and the late University of Chicago professor Allan Bloom. Another thing these ideologues have in common is that they have all been richly subsidized by the conservative Olin Foundation, which is headed by William E. Simon, Treasury Secretary under Presidents Nixon and Ford. In 1991, according to the *Chronicle of Higher Education*, the Olin Foundation awarded a $175,000 fellowship to Bennett, $25,000 to Chavez, $98,400 to D'Souza, and $800,000 to Bloom's program at the University of Chicago. Unlike other foundations, Olin has clear partisan affiliations and an extremely reactionary agenda without so much as a shred of scholarly balance or objectivity.

Why are conservative intellectuals and foundations so frightened by multiculturalism? Behind their public rhetoric are several political realities. The one threat that once unified conservatives was communism. Now that the Soviet

Union has gone out of business, American reactionaries don't have a common "enemy." By attacking multicultural education and affirmative action, they are deliberately manipulating racial and gender symbols to mobilize their supporters.

Why is it so necessary to mobilize public support for white supremacy and patriarchy? Because conservatives recognize that pushing people of color out of the textbooks —and defeating all efforts toward affirmative action and expanded democracy—is only the precursor to pushing back political rights for those only technically enfranchised members of our society. With the on-going demographic shift in the United States from a majority white nation to an increasingly multicultural one, conservatives are feeling an urgency in their efforts to shore up the foundations of white supremacy and their personal power.

The Clinton-Gore campaign of 1992 offered a clear example of the application of conservatives' theories about curriculum to the real world of national power. Bill Clinton and Al Gore campaigned not as leaders ready for the new multicultural realities but as party hacks desperately employing a racist strategy of going after the "political center." What they meant by this "center" is the disaffected, upper-middle-class white electorate, which had long voted consistently for Republican presidential candidates. Since 1952, a majority of the white electorate had voted for a Democratic presidential candidate only once—for Lyndon Johnson in 1964. About 60 percent of all whites generally voted for Republican presidential candidates. About 70 percent of southern whites consistently voted Republican in general elections. The Democrats in 1992 reached this lost group by disavowing their traditional programs favoring economic redistribution and civil rights.

The problem with this Great White Hope political strategy is that it completely ignores the major demographic, ethnic, and class changes that have occurred in the United States during the past 20 years, and no one—neither the Democrats nor conservatives in general—will win elections by continuing to ignore them.

The theory of the political center holds that middle-class white voters, people whose incomes are expanding and who dwell in comfortable suburban homes, are pivotal in winning elections. Even setting aside the racist dismissal of significant portions of the population, this theory neglects millions of so-called middle-class whites, who have experienced a severe drop in their standard of living in recent years. In the 1980s, according to the Census Bureau, median income levels as adjusted for inflation shrank in 24 of the 50 states. Thirty-two million Americans are poor, and the majority of them aren't black or Hispanic—they are white. About one-fourth of all poor people are children. These people are not floating in the comfortable, affluent mainstream.

What about Americans who are physically challenged, regardless of their racial identities or income? The Census Bureau states that 16 million people aged 16 to 64 have impaired mobility or need assistance to perform basic personal tasks. About 10 million people over the age of 65 also suffer from limited physical mobility. Millions more suffer from physical disabilities or illnesses. Would this group favor or oppose new federal initiatives in health care and entitlement programs for the elderly?

The theory of the political "center" focuses on English-speaking, white, ethnically European people. But America is increasingly multicultural, not white. In the past 10 years, there has been a 40 percent increase in the number of Americans who speak foreign languages in their homes, and the number of foreign-born residents totals more than 20 million. In New York City, for instance, 41 percent of all residents speak a second language at home. In the year 2000, *one-third* of all Americans will be people of color. And by the year 2060, people of color will constitute the majority of the U.S. population.

Many of these newcomers are from Latin America, the Caribbean, and Asia. According to the 1990 census, 7.3 million American citizens were of Pacific Island or Asian descent. More than 22 million American citizens are of Latin American descent. The size of some ethnic groups has grown rapidly in recent years. In 1970, for example, the Korean population in America was barely 70,000. By 1990,

Korean-Americans numbered more than 800,000. About 33,000 new Korean immigrants are entering the United States each year.

People of color living in the United States encounter more social problems than other groups and have experienced the greatest declines in real incomes, with the accompanying dramatic increases in poverty rates. From 1973 to 1990, the incomes of families headed by a parent under 30 years of age declined 28 percent for Latino families and 48 percent for African-American families. The poverty rates for young families in the same years rose 44 percent for Hispanics and 58 percent for blacks. Along with cuts in federal support for housing, jobs, and public transportation, families of color are more marginalized than ever.

The myth of the middle-class center emphasizes the importance of white male upper-income earners. But the new reality of America is that about 60 percent of all mothers of preschool children and 75 percent of all mothers of school-aged children are in the labor force. The *Leave It to Beaver* household, with Mom at home and Dad going to work, is no longer the norm, Dan Quayle's rhetoric notwithstanding.

The real "center" of America isn't white, of European descent, and upper class. The vital center is black, Latino, and Asian; it is the physically challenged, working women, people with AIDS, the unemployed, and foreign-language speakers.

That is the multicultural America conservatives fear.

BUILDING LATINO-BLACK UNITY

Forging creative coalitions across ethnic lines is the major challenge facing all those who seek to revitalize the democratic movements for social justice for America's people of color. A major priority for African-Americans is the strengthening of our ties to the Latino community. Yet for various reasons since the late 1970s, the effort to build Latino-African-American unity has been largely unsuccessful.

There are at least four critical issues fostering tensions between Latino and African-American political leaders. First, after the 1990 census, scores of congressional districts were reapportioned to have Latino or African-American majorities or pluralities, guaranteeing greater minority representation in Congress. In cities and districts in which Latinos and blacks had shared control in previous years, but where Latinos were now in the majority, disagreements often led to fractious ethnic conflicts.

Latinos claimed correctly that they were grossly underrepresented within the political process. Many black middle-class leaders replied that Latinos actually represented four very different ethnic groups with little or no shared history or common culture—Mexican-Americans, concentrated overwhelmingly in the southwestern states; Hispanics from the Caribbean living in the Northeast and Midwest; Cuban-Americans, mostly middle- to upper-class exiles of Castro's Cuba who voted heavily Republican; and the most recent Spanish-speaking immigrants from Central and South America. Black leaders insisted that Cuban-Americans should not be considered an "underprivileged" minority and did not merit minority set-aside development programs, affirmative action, and equal opportunity programs.

Immigration issues were also at the center of Latino-black conflicts. The Latino population of the United States exceeds 24 million, and more than one-third is undocumented. Some middle-class black leaders took the politically conservative view that undocumented Latino workers deprive poor blacks of jobs in the lowest wage sectors of the economy. Third, bilingual education and efforts, such as "English-only" referenda, to impose language and cultural conformity on all sectors of society have divided many Latino and black voters. Finally, there is the factor of demography. Because of substantial immigration and birth rates that are relatively higher than those of the general population, Latinos will outnumber African-Americans as America's largest minority group by the year 2010. Many civil rights leaders and black elected officials are still accustomed to using simplistic "black-white" categories to discuss race relations. They become defensive when Latino perspectives and issues are placed on the political agenda.

The tragedy here is that too little is done by either African-American or Latino "mainstream leaders" to transcend their parochialism and redefine their agendas on common ground. Most Latinos and blacks can agree on an overwhelming list of issues, such as the inclusion of multicultural curricula in public schools, improvements in public health care, job training initiatives, the expansion of public transportation and housing for low- to moderate-income people, and greater fairness and legal rights within the criminal justice system.

There is also substantial evidence that in elementary, secondary, and higher education, Latinos continue to experience discrimination more severe in many respects than that experienced by African-Americans. For example, although high school graduation rates for the entire population have steadily improved, rates for Latinos have consistently declined since the mid-1980s. By 1992, the high school completion rate for Latino males had dropped to only 47.8 percent, the lowest figure ever recorded by the American Council on Education since it began compiling statistics 20 years ago. In colleges and universities, the pattern of Latino inequality was the same. In 1991, 34 percent of all whites and 24 percent of all African-Americans from the ages of 18 to 24 were enrolled in colleges. Latino enrollment was just 18 percent. As of 1992, about 22 percent of the non-Latino population held a four-year college degree. As of 1995, the college graduation rate for Latinos was only 10 percent.

Thus, on a major series of public issues—education, housing, health care, jobs, civil rights enforcement—Latinos and African-Americans share a core set of common interests. What is needed is creative, visionary leadership able to bridge the cultural, language, and ethnic divisions to begin a dialogue of mutual respect. Together, Latinos and African-Americans can win the fight for equality and social justice.

AMERICA IN SEARCH OF ITSELF

Social critic Harold Cruse once observed that "America is a nation that lies to itself about who and what it is. It is a nation of minorities ruled by a minority of one—it thinks and acts as if it were a nation of white Anglo-Saxon Protestants."

The standard of "whiteness" has always been closely associated with America's cultural identity. To be "all-American" is to be an English-speaking, middle- or upper-class white male.

But nationwide, one out of seven Americans considers English to be a second language. In New York City, 2.6 million residents were born in a foreign country. In the next 30 years, the number of American citizens of Asian and Pacific Island descent will triple, to more than 20 million. Increasingly and rapidly, America is becoming a "non-European" country.

Yet there are other forces at work, pulling apart the fabric of cultural consensus, racial identity, and social expectations that buttress the (Euro-)American Dream. For millions of young people of all cultures and racial backgrounds, there is a deep sense of social frustration and alienation. According to a *New York Times*/CBS News poll taken in 1994, American teenagers today are forced to wrestle with a host of problems, unprecedented at least in scale. A majority of teenagers polled said they are "under pressure at home" and expressed anxiety about their future. Nearly one-fifth of white teens and one-third of all black teens reported that "organized gangs are a problem" in their high schools. One-third of white teens and 70 percent of African-American teens said they personally "know someone who has been shot in the past five years." Even teenagers living in affluent neighborhoods expressed deep concern about the rising levels of violence and the fact that some students carry weapons into the classroom. More than one-third of white teens and 54 percent of black teens said they "worry about being the victim of a crime."

Another type of fear dividing Americans is the anxiety produced by the lack of health insurance. About 17.4 percent of all Americans under the age of 65 have no health insurance. Most of these are working-class families with low to moderate incomes. In addition to those with preexisting conditions or high-risk factors who are excluded from insurance because of corporate greed, many of the uninsured work for businesses that provide no health insurance or not enough of a contribution to its cost to make the insurance affordable to those employed in low-wage positions. About 14 percent of all whites are uninsured. By contrast, 23 percent of African-Americans and 35 percent of Latinos lack health care.

Republicans claim that the health care crisis has been greatly exaggerated and that the vast majority of Americans are happy with the quality of their privately owned health care systems. But the frequently recited figure of 37 million Americans who are not covered by health insurance represents only a small aspect of the overall crisis. During a typical 12-month period, 58 million people lack coverage at least temporarily. According to the research of economist Timothy D. McBride of the University of Missouri, three-fourths of uninsured Americans, approximately 29 million people, remain uncovered for one year, and more than one-half of them, about 21 million people, stay without insurance for at least two years.

The vast majority of Americans want health care to be a human right, not a privilege. Yet Congress and the president refuse to consider the alternative of a single-payer, Canadian-style health care system. Thus millions of American families will face the anxiety and fear fostered by illness.

America is a nation in search of itself, because millions of people are forced to live in fear, frustration, and desperation. When violence and poverty determine the daily existence of Americans of all ages, racial groups, and social classes, there is no sense of a moral or political center that can bind people together for the common good. When children are afraid to leave their homes or venture into playgrounds because of drive-by shootings, yet Congress repeatedly refuses to pass tough legislation restricting the availability of deadly weapons on our streets, our system has failed us. People hate politics and politicians because the problems of their daily lives seem so overwhelming.

America can only begin to find itself when its mission as a democracy is redefined to reflect the energies, talents, and skills of *all* its people. People of color are the future of this country. And the debates about health care, violence in our schools and streets, and other issues are reflections of the larger question of what should be central to the "new" American identity.

THE RETREAT FROM EQUALITY

For nearly 20 years, the legal standard for implementing affirmative action has been the *Bakke* decision. In 1978, the Supreme Court ruled that strict racial quotas guaranteeing access and opportunity to blacks, women, and other minorities were unconstitutional. Yet the high court also declared that race and ethnicity could be significant factors in selecting applicants for colleges and graduate and professional schools. At that time, many civil rights advocates felt that the *Bakke* decision was unfair precisely because it failed to adequately take into account either the history and reality of discrimination, or the constructive steps necessary to create greater equality between racial minorities and the white majority.

In early 1996, the U.S. Court of Appeals for the Fifth Circuit took a great leap backward from *Bakke* in the *Hopwood v. Texas* decision. The details of the case are fairly simple. Cheryl Hopwood and several other whites were refused admission to the University of Texas Law School. They sued, arguing that the school's policies unfairly favored African-Americans and Latinos through a process that permitted different admissions standards for different groups. The attorneys for Hopwood *et al.* said their clients had been grievously denied their right to "equal protection of the laws" guaranteed by the Fourteenth Amendment.

These arguments basically turned history on its head. For generations, the University of Texas Law School had refused to admit a single African-American, solely on racist grounds. Finally, after years of civil rights agitation and litigation, blacks and other minorities were allowed in. But even after affirmative action programs were implemented, people of color were still under-represented in the school. Texas's statewide population is currently 11.6 percent African-American and 25.6 percent Latino. By contrast, the law school's entering class of 1992 was only 8 percent black and 10.7 percent Latino. Whites as a group remained statistically over-represented.

The appellate court judges not only sided with Hopwood, they went much further. The court declared that any use of race or ethnicity was illegal, "even for the wholesome purpose of correcting perceived racial imbalances." Admissions decisions had to be based solely on merit, with color or race playing absolutely no role. Furthermore, whites who were denied admission had the right to claim monetary damages for "intentional discrimination."

In effect, this ruling says that universities have no business attempting to diversify their student body, faculty, or staff on gender, racial, or cultural grounds. Purely from an educational standpoint, that's nonsense. Educational excellence is achieved, in part, when people interact with others from different faiths and nationalities, from divergent cultures and racial identities. Pluralism and diversity should be at the heart of this country's academic institutions, preparing our students to function in an increasingly multicultural, global society.

Moreover, we need to have an honest appraisal of what constitutes "merit." Standardized tests, like the SAT and GRE, are one type of measurement to determine whether a person is "qualified" to be admitted to school. But there are also many other measurements of "merit": a person's individual efforts to overcome poverty and adversity; his or her ability to speak different languages and to function in divergent cultures; and his or her experiences in coping with racist and sexist discrimination, and gaining the courage to overcome such obstacles to the achievement of excellence.

If democracy is to function in a pluralistic society, our universities must reflect the full range of knowledge and abilities that our diverse communities have to offer.

The final ruling on *Hopwood v. Texas* will be made by the Supreme Court. But what this decision is really about is denying African-Americans and other minorities access to higher education. When the factor of "race" is ignored within a racist, class-stratified society, whites with money, power, and prestige will always benefit.

AFFIRMATIVE ACTION FOR WHITES!

Affirmative action programs were initiated two decades ago to address the legacy of racial discrimination permeating American society. But today, a growing number of critics question whether so-called preferential employment policies for African-Americans, Latinos, other minorities, and women are still necessary.

One explanation for this position focuses on economic evidence indicating a growing polarization of incomes within the black community, which affirmative action policies don't really address. On the one hand, the black upper-middle class grew rapidly during the Reagan administration. By 1989, one out of seven African-American families had incomes exceeding $50,000 annually, compared to less than $22,000 annually for the average black household. Black college-educated married couples currently earn 93 percent of the family income of comparable white couples. On the other hand, the general experience of black working-class, low-income people, and families on welfare—the overwhelming majority of African-Americans—is characterized by steady deterioration.

According to the report "African-Americans in the 1990s," published by the Population Reference Bureau early in the decade, the average annual income of the African-American is only 56 percent that of a white person's income, and significantly less than the 63 percent ratio between black and white in 1975. Black female-based house-holds average less than $9,600 annually. Compounding the problem of poverty is the continued increase in the prevalence of out-of-wedlock births, which multiplied from 38 percent in 1970 to nearly two-thirds of all black families by 1988. "Stark differences" in home ownership, income, and education, the report says, indicate that there are "two separate worlds inhabited by poor and middle-class black children." This strongly implies that "the African-American population will become more polarized as these children mature."

Many white liberals have taken these statistics to mean that the source of material and social inequities that separate the races—institutional racism—no longer exists. A shift in liberal governmental policy from race-based remedies to economistic, class-based programs is therefore required. From the vantage point of liberal Democrats, this would solve the perception problem among millions of white males that the party's social agenda is being held hostage to the interests of blacks. Class-based programs would eliminate the argument of "reverse discrimination" because, theoretically, all benefits would be distributed in a color-blind manner.

Stuart E. Eizenstat, President Carter's domestic policy adviser, defends this economistic thesis. More recently, Richard Cohen, liberal columnist for the *Washington Post*, embraced this argument as well: "If economic need, not race, became the basis for what we now call affirmative action, most Americans would not object. Whites, too, could be helped. . . . After all, poor is poor, although a disproportionate number of them are black."

But when African-American community leaders, organizers inside the trade unions, teachers, and professionals read these statements, most cannot help but feel a sense of outrage and repudiation. The overwhelming majority of federal government social programs were predicated not on race, but on income. Poor whites already share substantial benefits from the initiatives of the Great Society. More than one-third of all students enrolled in the Upward Bound program, designed to prepare low-income students for college, are white. One-third of the children who attend the preschool program Head Start are white. The majority of people living in public housing or receiving public assistance are white.

The basis of affirmative action programs is the recognition that systemic discrimination exists within the society, and that it is grounded in the concepts of race and gender. Despite the passage of the Civil Rights Act of 1964 outlawing discrimination in public accommodations, "race" as a social construction is a powerful factor in determining the actual conditions of life for any African-American or person of color, regardless of income and education. My daughter or son is much more likely to be harassed or arrested by the police, for example, than the children of my white colleagues at the university, solely because of their racial identity. Through practical experience, African-Americans of virtually every social class recognize this reality. To argue that a shift in affirmative action policies from race to class will benefit them seems, at best, a gross distortion of reality. At worst, it is perceived by blacks and other minorities that white liberals have turned their backs on us, and that both political parties have little commitment to ending racial discrimination.

American democracy is meaningless unless citizens are able to compete on a roughly equal playing field. Such equality for blacks, Latinos, women, and others simply doesn't exist. Given the fact that the average white household's net worth is *ten times* that of a black family's, and that the overwhelming majority of leaders in business, government, banking, and the media are upper-class white males, the argument that whites suffer "reverse discrimination" is absurd. Justice demands affirmative action based on race and gender to address continuing patterns of inequality in America.

FULL EMPLOYMENT AND AFFIRMATIVE ACTION

What has escalated white America's opposition to affirmative action programs and policies that attempt to redress past and present-day patterns of race- and gender-based discrimination? More than any other single factor, I would say that the politics of discrimination is set into motion by white male *fear.*

The recent affirmative action debate has occurred in a world where white working-class and middle-income people have been steadily losing ground economically. Although gains in disposable personal income, adjusted for inflation and taxes, increased at an annual rate of over 3 percent in 1994 and the beginning of 1995, that increase is only due to the fact that millions of two-career couples are now in the labor force. Real wages for the average household over the past decade have been stagnant—or fallen sharply. According to economist Stephen S. Roach, in the first 50 months of the current economic recovery, job growth was almost 40 percent less than the average rate of job growth in the two previous expansions. Globalized capitalism increasingly pits workers against each other internationally, forcing down wages and benefits, and creating nonunion workplaces.

By all opinion polls, a major reason why white males, as a group, are most strongly opposed to affirmative action is that they perceive themselves to be particularly vulnerable in the new world (and domestic) economic order. Their perspectives are to some degree accurate and to some degree self-fulfilling prophesy. Since the mid-1970s, the real median income for U.S. males has remained flat or declined, while women's incomes actually rose 18 percent above the rate of inflation. This is due in part to the apparent unwillingness of men to reeducate themselves to seek new employment opportunities. According to the Census Bureau, more than one million women over age 40 are currently enrolled in college, twice the number of men in post-secondary institutions. As women and minorities compete successfully for traditionally "white male jobs," white men are inclined to blame the erosion of their opportunities on affirmative action policies.

What's really at work here is the structural transformation of the U.S. economy over the past quarter-century. According to economists Barry Bluestone and Bennett Harrison, between 1969 and 1976 more than 22 million jobs disappeared due to factory, office, and store closings across the United States, and through the relocation of businesses from one state to another or abroad. Given the white male stranglehold on the majority of unionized and better-paying industrial jobs, it's not surprising that factory closings have hit white males disproportionately to the rest of the general population.The total number of jobs destroyed represented more than one-third of all jobs that had existed in 1969. In the mid-1960s, there were 2.5 unemployed persons for every vacant job; by the late 1970s, the ratio had grown to 5.0 unemployed persons for every vacant job.

In a city like New York today there are roughly seven jobless people for every available job vacancy. In Harlem, about 40 percent of the population is below the poverty line, and nearly half of all people above age 18 are unemployed, underemployed, and/or involuntarily outside the formal labor market. Competition is fierce even for low-wage service employment. In Harlem's fast-food industry, the ratio of job applicants to hires is about 14 to 1.

In the mid-1990s, about 7.5 million Americans are "officially" unemployed, according to the Bureau of Labor Statistics. Moreover, nearly five million part-time workers want full-time work but cannot find it. There are also another seven million "discouraged workers," whom the Bureau of Labor Statistics classifies as outside of the active job market. When 20 million people who desire full-time employment aren't able to get it, an environment of political scapegoating and social hostility is created. Blacks, Latinos, women, and others are blamed for declining real incomes, unemployment, and the loss of job advancement. Yet overturning affirmative action programs and policies will do little to reverse these economic trends for white male workers.

This is why the advocates of affirmative action must carefully link their struggle for social justice with efforts to achieve full employment. I say "carefully" for the precise reason that many "neo-liberals" and conservative Democrats want to sacrifice race-based reforms in favor of class-based programs that address economic disadvantage. Affirmative action is *not* an anti-poverty program, and it was never designed to create full employment.

But the interests of people who have traditionally experienced discrimination and the concerns of those who are fearful of losing their jobs *are connected.* Unless the total number of jobs is significantly increased for everybody, millions of white male workers will be inclined to perceive affirmative action as counter to their narrow, material interests. Left-of-center political initiatives like affirmative action are always more popular when the economic pie is expanding.

THE STRUGGLE FOR DEMOCRATIC TRANSFORMATION

A few years ago, when I was teaching at the University of Colorado, I helped to organize a symposium on the "Novel of the Americas." The celebrated and controversial novelist Salman Rushdie was invited to be a keynote speaker. Because of his novel *Satanic Verses*, Iran had issued a death warrant against Rushdie. For nearly four years, he had lived the hunted life of the fugitive. The prominent novelists and artists who attended the symposium, as well as thousands in the audience, praised Rushdie's courage and integrity and reiterated the necessity of fighting for the essential freedom of creativity and expression.

Americans like to think of their country as the bastion of the freedoms outlined in our Constitution—freedom of speech and artistic expression, freedom of the press and political ideas. Yet throughout our history, political minorities in our nation have routinely been denied such freedoms. Writers, novelists, playwrights, and college professors have been silenced at various times, usually on political grounds.

Fifty years ago, 21 states required teachers to take loyalty oaths. With the outbreak of the Cold War against communism in 1946, another 15 states passed loyalty legislation for teachers. Controversial intellectuals were barred from speaking at many universities, including J. Robert Oppenheimer, the inventor of the atomic bomb; W.E.B. Du Bois, the founder of the NAACP and the leading black American scholar; and noted artistic performer Paul Robeson. Books by suspect intellectuals were burned or removed from library shelves; artists and writers who had been members of the Communist Party or who held even liberal political sentiments were refused employment.

Teachers were particularly vulnerable. In 1949, the National Education Association, which then had 425,000 members, stated that individuals who had joined the Communist Party had absolutely no right to teach in any classroom. The American Federation of Teachers declared three years later that it would not defend any teacher "proven to be a Communist." Only the American Association of University Professors opposed efforts to destroy thousands of educators' lives by denying them employment solely because of their political beliefs.

A generation later, conservatives are waging a new, unprincipled war against multiculturalism, affirmative action, and innovative courses such as women's studies. Education is once again a battleground for the far Right, which seeks to silence the voices of cultural and political change, voices that promote an academic environment open to gender, racial, and class diversity. Conservatives would be the last to offer a faculty appointment to someone with the radical cultural politics of a Salman Rushdie.

The Rushdie case, and the legacy of political intolerance passed down by American conservatives, forces us to ask the question, "What is freedom?" Freedom is more than a set of legislative provisions and legalistic regulations designed to organize public activity along the principles of political democracy. It is *not*, as conservatives in America seem to believe, the absence of government or state authority, the unrestricted liberty of individuals to act in any way they desire without regard for the common good.

Freedom is first and foremost a public understanding among the members of a society to protect and defend any opinions that are unpopular or at odds with opinions held by those who actually exercise power and privilege. Freedom is the fragile flower that must constantly be protected—not from those at the bottom of the social order but from the whims and desires of those at the top.

Freedom means fighting for the right of minorities to express their views and opinions. As political activist Rosa Luxemburg once observed: "Freedom is always and exclusively freedom for the one who thinks differently." As we struggle for the genuine diversity of ideas and cultural expression on our campuses and in our public schools, we are taking a stand in favor of human freedom and creative expression. We take a stand with Rushdie in his fight for life and literary freedom. And as we stand against such censorship—whether by the government of Iran or by conservatives in the United States—we nurture that flower of hope and human aspiration.

FROM FREEDOM TO EQUALITY

Among our most outstanding and celebrated actors are Ossie Davis and Ruby Dee. Two generations of Americans have enjoyed their presence as powerful artists on the stage and screen. They also possess a deep commitment to social justice and to the struggles of black people.

I talked recently with Ossie Davis about the challenges and problems confronting the African-American community as we enter the 21st century. Davis feels that, in some ways, the Civil Rights Movement failed to achieve a fully democratic vision and strategy for fundamental social change.

"Every generation needs a moral assignment," Davis insists. "We have yet to define that moral assignment for ourselves and in our time."

African-American people were challenged 150 years ago by the harsh realities of slavery. The great moral and political question of that era was the abolition of human bondage. Black abolitionists, such as Frederick Douglass and Martin Delany, pursued a vision of freedom that mobilized the energies of the black community, North and South. Nearly a century later, the great moral challenge confronting black people was the oppressive reality of Jim Crow segregation. African-Americans were denied access to schools, hospitals, hotels, and many other public establishments. The Fifteenth Amendment was a dead letter for several generations. Martin Luther King, Jr. and the Civil Rights Movement represented the courageous struggle of a people who yearned to be free.

The struggle for freedom was like crossing a turbulent river. In the religious imagination of black folk, the river was frequently identified as the River Jordan. Like the ancient Hebrews who had escaped Egyptian bondage, black Americans bravely crossed their own River Jordan to seek and to claim the promised land of freedom.

Now we are in an uncertain time, filled with dangerous and destructive social forces: violence, drugs, unemployment, poverty, social alienation, and fear. Our leaders seem unsure of how to articulate a new agenda for progressive change. Voices within our community call us to turn inward, away from potential allies with whom we can work to achieve positive change. What is required is the definition of a new moral assignment, a new vision of human emancipation.

Davis says, "We must cross a second river, the river of equality. We must insist that the Constitution create the conditions for genuine equality. Equality is an economic function, first and foremost." Davis clearly distinguishes between the goals of freedom and the goals of equality. Freedom is about "rights"; equality is about social justice and the material realities of human fairness—health care, education, housing, and a job.

Our movement must cross that second river of equality. In doing so, we must wage principled struggles like those of the desegregation campaigns throughout the South: the same willingness to sacrifice, the same tears, the same tenacity in challenging unjust laws, and the same impatience with oppression must propel us toward a new politics. To revitalize black America, we must move beyond civil rights to the realization of human rights and genuine equality.

R

Race, 12, 194-195, 203-204
  in Cuban society, 175
  definition of, 185-187
  identity and, 97-98
  presidential elections and,
    119-121
"Race card," 119-121
Race relations, 198-200, 202,
  203-205, 231
Racial fundamentalism, 201-203,
  234
Racial status quo, 153
Racism, 22-23
  church burnings and, 187-189
  criminal justice system and,
    43-47, 214, 224-225
  in Cuba, 171-176
  environmental, 239-244
  etiquette of, 189-191
  far Right and, 142, 143-146
  in higher education, 83-84
  institutional, 12, 40-42, 215-216,
    241
  international, 161-163, 176-181
Radical politics, 218-219, 234
Rainbow Coalition, 4, 6, 130, 213,
  219, 245
Ramaphosa, Cyril, 163
Rape, condoning, 221-223
Reagan, Ronald, 4, 63, 120, 219
  policies of, 49, 136, 145-146
Reagan administration, 61, 118
  policies of, 37, 89, 136, 140, 199
Reaganomics, 136, 140
Reed, Ralph, 188, 189
"Reform-from-above," 217-218
"Reform-from-below," 218-219
Reno, Janet, 62
Republican party
  1992 presidential election,
    120-126, 129-132
  1994 congressional elections,
    143-146

1996 elections, 151-153
  black conservatives of, 6-7
  in congress, 147-148
  constituency, 193, 253
  extreme Right of, 142
Reverse discrimination, 35, 122,
  263, 264
  in higher education, 78, 80-81
Reverse racism, 22-23, 187
Reynolds, William Bradford, 61
Right, the
  opposition to, 5-6
  reaction of, 143-146
  violence and, 142
Roach, Stephen S., 265
Robertson, Pat, 125, 130
Robeson, Paul, 17, 65, 170, 180,
  213, 218, 271
Robinson, Randall, 171
Robinson, Renault, 220
Rockefeller, Nelson, 135
Rodney King case, 244
Roediger, David, 97
Roe v. Wade, 67
Roosevelt, Franklin D., 135
Rosenthal, A.M., 123, 197
Rowan, Carl, 60
Rudman, Warren, 126
Rupp, George, 101-102, 104
Rush, Bobby, 117
Rushdie, Salman, 271, 272

S

Sabo, Albert, 225
St. Louis, living wage, 33
St. Paul, living wage, 33
Saro-Wiwa, Ken, 170-171
Satanic Verses, 271
Scalia, Antonin, 35
Scapegoating, 266
Schiraldi, Vincent, 45
Schmoke, Kurt, 27-28
Scholarships, minority, 77-79
School systems

A NOTE TO OUR READERS

South End Press is a nonprofit, collectively run book publisher with over 180 titles in print. Since our founding in 1977, we have tried to give expression to a wide diversity of democratic social movements and to provide an alternative to the products of corporate publishing.

Through the Institute for Social and Cultural Change, South End Press works with other political media projects—*Z Magazine; Speak Out!*, a speakers' bureau; Alternative Radio; and the Publishers' Support Project—to expand access to information and critical analysis.

For a free catalog or information about our membership program, which offers two free books and a 40 percent discount on all titles, please write to South End Press, 116 Saint Botolph Street, Boston, MA 02115; call 1-800-533-8478; or visit our website at http://www.lbbs.org.

RELATED TITLES OF INTEREST

How Capitalism Underdeveloped Black America
  by Manning Marable

African-Americans at the Crossroads by Clarence Lusane

Breaking Bread: Insurgent Black Intellectual Life
  by bell hooks and Cornel West

Another America: The Politics of Race and Blame
  by Kofi Buenor Hadjor

From Civil Rights to Black Liberation: Malcolm X and the Organization of Afro-American Unity by William Sales

Chaos or Community? Seeking Solutions, Not Scapegoats, to Bad Economics by Holly Sklar

Eyes Right: Challenging the Right Wing Backlash
  edited by Chip Berlet